JAMES LUTHER MAYS

AMOS

JAMES LUTHER MAYS

AMOS

A Commentary

10595

SCM PRESS LTD

BLOOMSBURY STREET LONDON

SBN 334 00039 4
FIRST PUBLISHED 1969
© SCM PRESS LTD 1969
PRINTED IN GREAT BRITAIN BY
W & J MACKAY & CO LTD, CHATHAM, KENT

CONTENTS

PREFACE

FOR SEVERAL AND various reasons this commentary on Amos and the companion work on Hosea appear separately rather than as part of one volume covering the first six Minor Prophets. Whatever the reasons, there needs be no defence for thus distinguishing Amos and Hosea within the arrangement of a series on the Old Testament. These two eighth-century prophets stand in an imposing position at the beginning of the period of canonical prophecy and play a role whose importance is far from being measured by the few chapters of material preserved from their activity.

Because of his importance, Amos has always received a great deal of attention from Old Testament scholars. Anyone who undertakes the exegesis of his sayings enters into a rich heritage of valuable and perceptive work by his predecessors. The knowledgeable reader will detect on every page of this commentary its debt to that heritage. The commentaries and monographs of J. Wellhausen, Ernst Sellin, W. R. Harper, Artur Weiser, and Victor Maag must receive special mention. It is an interesting and perhaps somewhat surprising fact that the question of the right approach to the interpretation of Amos has broken out afresh in this decade. The difference between the positions of H. Reventlow, R. Smend, and H. W. Wolff in their works listed in the bibliography could hardly be greater. The controversy furnishes a stimulating environment in which to attempt a commentary on Amos. The author can only regret not having had the opportunity to see more than one fascicle of Wolff's commentary on Amos in the *Biblischer Kommentar*. What has thus far appeared makes it clear that most of the primary issues about the meaning of Amos's theology will depend upon the settlement of literary-critical and form-critical questions about the text of Amos. From the fragments which he has seen, the author can predict confidently that David Noel Freedman's work on Amos in the *Anchor Bible* will make a new contribution to the understanding of the text. He regrets that he did not have the benefit of its insights before concluding his own work.

Though he hopes that this volume will find some usefulness among a broad clientele, the author has had a specific audience in mind

vii

during its preparation—the minister and theological student as they work on the interpretation and understanding of Scripture. This orientation explains some things about the commentary. The comment has been written with the intention of putting the reader in touch with the intention of the text and clearing the way for him to consider its significance as language of faith. Other literature has been referred to only where the reader might profit from further material or where the author wants to indicate direct contact with the work of another. The bibliography is quite selective and is oriented primarily toward a usefulness in studying the message of Amos.

The author cannot conclude his work on the volume without expressing his gratitude to several who have played a significant role in the history of its preparation. He wishes with this volume particularly to greet Professor H. H. Rowley, whose skill and encouragement as a teacher introduced him to research in Amos studies. Apart from the initiation and confidence of his senior colleague in Old Testament, Professor John Bright, the project would never have been undertaken. And finally, it is a pleasure to acknowledge with appreciation the unflagging persistence and high competence of Mrs Franklin S. Clark, the editorial secretary of *Interpretation*, whose labours and enthusiasm have made a real contribution to the entire project.

Union Theological Seminary   JAMES LUTHER MAYS
Richmond, Virginia
December 1968

I

INTRODUCTION

THE MESSAGE OF Amos was: Next time the fire! Through him
Yahweh said, 'I will send my fire on Damascus, Gaza,
Rabbah, Moab – and Israel. The end has come for my people.'
In the last quarter of the eighth century the word became history.
The kingdom of Israel passed through four decades of crises, defeats,
and assassinations on the way to the abyss, and then was swallowed
up by the Assyrian Empire. Amos spoke true. That was one cardinal
reason why his sayings were collected and preserved. But that outcome alone does not explain the book. Amos' words were a compelling
witness to the God of Israel. His prophecy inaugurated a new epoch
of Yahweh's dealing with Israel, for Amos brought the first word of
the time of judgment upon the entire nation.

THE TIME

When Amos came to the northern kingdom of Israel to prophesy,
the king of Israel was Jeroboam ben Joash (i.e. Jeroboam II). Amos
announced the imminent fall of his dynasty, an insolence reported
forthwith to Jeroboam by the priest of Bethel (7.9–11). Since Jeroboam II reigned from 786 to 746 BC, Amos' prophetic activity must
be dated within those limits in the middle decades of the eighth
century. The title (1.1) adds the reign of Uzziah, king of Judah, as a
further specification of Amos' time. Uzziah died in 742; but because
he had become a leper, his son Jotham had been regent since about
750. If the composers of the title reckoned Jotham's assumption of
regency as the end of Uzziah's reign, it was their opinion that Amos

I

appeared in Israel before then. The title also specifies a precise year for Amos, 'two years before the earthquake'. The earthquake may have occurred about 760 (see the comment on 1.1), and if its suggested date is correct Amos is to be placed in the last years of the fourth decade of the eighth century. The reference to 'two years before' also suggests that Amos' period of activity was not longer than a year at most. References to international events in the sayings of Amos (see 1.3, 13) cast no light on the problem, because the only record of events to which they can be related points to a period before the reign of Jeroboam II. Most of the sayings collected in the book of Amos fit appropriately into the circumstances of his reign.

The record of Jeroboam II appears in II Kings 14.23–29. The account is typical of the Deuteronomistic historian's treatment of Israel's kings in its single-minded interest in doing no more than classifying Jeroboam as one of the long list of rulers who made Israel to sin. The historian does, however, observe that Jeroboam restored the northern and southern borders of Israel east of the Jordan, and even concedes that Yahweh saved Israel by Jeroboam. Behind the observation and concession lay a remarkable achievement; under Jeroboam II, Israel knew her best years of prosperity and peace. The international situation was auspicious. Assyria's power had waned under a succession of inept rulers who had all they could manage in defending themselves against the kingdom of Urartu. Until the accession of Tiglath-Pileser III (745), Syria-Palestine was free of danger from that quarter. The kingdom of Damascus had not yet fully recovered from her earlier defeats by Assyria and was locked in a crippling struggle with Hamath on the north. And at long last there was peace with Judah. Taking advantage of these favourable circumstances, Jeroboam had pursued a vigorous policy of expansion east of the Jordan with great success. Reflections of an ebullient confidence among Israelites appear in the speeches of Amos (6.1, 8, 13). Along with political success came a burgeoning prosperity for many in the nation. The older homogenous economic structure of Israel gave way to sharp distinctions of wealth and privilege. The excavations at Tirzah (Tell el-Farah) uncovered evidence of the social revolution that had occurred. While the city's houses in the tenth century had been of uniform size, in the eighth century by contrast there was a quarter of large, expensive houses, and one of small huddled structures.[a] The result was the stark contrast between the

[a] R. de Vaux, *Ancient Israel*, ET, 1961, pp. 72ff.

luxury of the rich and misery of the poor which Amos repeatedly indicts. The rich enjoyed an indolent, indulgent existence (4.1f.; 6.1–6) in winter and summer houses (3.13; 6.11). The poor were a tempting target for legal and economic exploitation (2.6–8; 4.1; 5.10–12; 8.4–6). Meanwhile religion flourished in the nation. The populace thronged the shrines at festival time (4.4f.; 5.5f.) to practise an elaborate sacrificial ritual (5.21–24). Yahweh was trusted and patronized with presumptuous arrogance (5.14, 18–20; 6.3). To such a nation, Amos was commissioned to announce the word of the Lord.

THE PROPHET

Amos himself is known only from the book in which his sayings were collected and preserved. The direct information which it supplies about him is precious little. The title (1.1) warns that the book was not designed to serve any historical quest for Amos. It rather presents 'the words of Amos'; the message was the important thing, not the messenger. The notices about his career in the narrative of his encounter with Amaziah (7.10–17) and in the vision-reports (7.1–9; 8.1–3; 9.1–4) are virtually incidental, for in their present form these narratives were formulated to authenticate the speeches, and not as biography. They too are about the message, rather than the man.

According to the tradition known to the composer of the book's title (1.1) Amos came from Tekoa, a town in the hill country of Judah, some ten miles to the south of Jerusalem. Amaziah's command to Amos to flee to the land of Judah to carry on his work (7.12) indirectly confirms the tradition.[a] Amos was a Judean who, so far as one can tell from his speeches, prophesied exclusively in the northern kingdom!

In his vehement claim that his prophetic mission was subject only to the authority of Yahweh, Amos asserts that before he became a prophet he was a shepherd; Yahweh took him for the office while he was following the flock (7.14f.) In 7.14 two terms, 'herdsman' and 'dresser of sycamores', identify his vocation; and in 1.1 a third, 'sheepbreeder', is used (see comment). Clearly he had followed an agricultural life, but he is not to be thought a simple, uncultured rustic. 'Sheepbreeder' probably means an owner in charge of other shepherds, a substantial and respected man of his community. In

[a] Cf. the classic description of Tekoa and its environment in G. A. Smith, *The Historical Geography of the Holy Land*, 1907, pp. 310ff.

style and quality his speech is that of a man gifted in the oral arts of his culture (see 'The Sayings'). In his oracles there are clues that he was well informed about historical matters (1.3–8, 13–2.3; 9.7), the society of Israel, and its religious traditions. He never lacked presence in the face of opposition; though this was supremely a matter of his vocation, his confidence seems also to be based in his own person and talents.

Where did Amos speak? The narrative of 7.10–17 locates him at the temple in Bethel. Many of his sayings would fit an audience gathered at Israel's most important religious centre for the autumn festival (2.8; 3.14; 4.4; 5.5f.; 5.21–27). There are others which could well have been delivered in the capital city of Samaria to women in the streets (4.1–3), officials before the palace (3.9–11, 12; 6.1–3), merchants in the market (8.4–8). If Amaziah's order of expulsion from Bethel was enforced, his activity must have ended there, and he may have already been in Samaria. But reconstructions of Amos' career must remain largely hypothetical. The Bethel and Samaria oracles are scattered through the book. This movement about the land does suggest that his activity must have lasted for several months. But the restriction to not more than one year required by 1.1 is probably correct. The oracles betray no evidence of historical changes such as are found in Hosea and Isaiah.

Little as we know about Amos, there is no question about what was the most crucial fact of his life. It was the experience of Yahweh's call (7.14) and the visions which revealed Yahweh's decision to change his way with Israel from forbearance to action (7.1–8; 8.1–3). That call and revelation wrenched him out of his normal life and put him in another country crying 'woe' to its society, religion, and government in the name of God. He became solely the messenger whose life was the vehicle of the message.

THE SAYINGS

Since the book is primarily a collection of speeches, it is from the forms and features of Amos' oral style that we learn the most about his culture and self-understanding. The fashion and art of his speech discloses the man. He appears, first of all, as a messenger, bringing the word of another to his audience. The primary reality that determined the speech of Amos was the call of Yahweh: 'Go prophesy to my people Israel' (7.14). Following the messenger's style Amos often spoke in the first person of the sender. These divine sayings are usually identified by messenger formulae such as the introductory 'This is what Yahweh has said' (e.g. 1.3, 6; 3.11, 12), the internal and concluding formula 'a saying of Yahweh' (2.11, 16; 3.10, 13, etc.), and the final 'said Yahweh' (e.g. 1.5, 8; 5.17). On occasion Amos begins with the proclamation formula which summons the folk to attend a herald's announcement ('Hear this [word]' 3.1; 4.1; 5.1; 8.4), and three times he uses an introduction to an oath ('Yahweh has sworn by . . .'; 4.2; 6.8; 8.7) to characterize Yahweh's word.

The basic message given to the messenger was 'The end has come for my people Israel' (8.2), and the content of the message determined the forms in which it was spoken. Appropriately most of Amos' oracles are in the form of an announcement of judgment, which is composed of reproach and proclamation of punishment (1.3–2.16; 3.2, 9–11; 4.1–3; 5.7, 10f., 12, 16f.; 6.1–7, 13f.; 7.16f.; 8.4–7). Some of his sayings contain only the second element and are oracles of doom (3.12, 13–15; 5.1–3; 6.9–11; 8.9f., 11–14; 9.9–10). Alongside such a categorical message of judgment instruction and appeal for change would have little place and Amos seldom exhorts his audience. When he does his imperatives are without exception qualified by the context of his basic message. They warn in expectation of judgment (5.4–6) or mimic the cult (4.4f.) or lay down the lines of living which the audience ought to have been following (5.14f., 24).

Such a messenger would hardly have been welcomed nor his message accepted at face value. The occurrence of disputation-sayings (3.3–8; 5.18–20; 9.7) and the frequency of elements of dispute in other forms (2.11; 3.2, 12; 5.25) are ample evidence for the clash and struggle between messenger and audience. At times Amos himself undertakes the defence of his words (3.3–8); the vision-reports were probably formulated and used publicly to vindicate his radical message (7.1–9; 8.1–3; 9.1–4). One of his favourite devices for engaging his hearers was to include in his sayings quotations which dramatize their point of view (2.12; 4.1; 5.14; 6.2, 13; 7.16; 8.5f., 14; 9.10). The confrontation and exchange with Amaziah (7.10–17) represents a situation which must have occurred at other times with different groups, and the stress of controversy over the message has entered into the formulation of the messenger's speech.

Beyond the primary forms determined by his message and the controversy which it provoked Amos knew the art of appropriating a variety of other speech-forms as the vehicle of what he had to say.

His speeches display a remarkable skill at using all the devices of oral literature available in Israel's culture. He sang a funeral dirge for Israel in anticipation of its doom (5.1–2), and formulated woe-sayings as a way of marking certain kinds of action as those which lead to death (5.18; 6.1; 5.7?). He used several forms that belonged to the priest to mimic and attack the cult of the nation (4.4f.; 5.4, 21–24, 14f.?). He was especially adept at the employment of forms of speech that appear in the riddles, comparisons, and popular proverbs of folk wisdom. He used the graduated numbers-saying in the oracles against the nations (1.3, 6, 9, etc.), argued with the logic of proverbs (3.3–6), used comparisons and riddles to make his point (2.9; 3.12; 5.2, 7, 19, 24; 6.12; 9.9). Many of his metaphors come from observation of the country life which he knew as shepherd and farmer (1.3; 2.13; 3.12; 4.1; 9.9). But countryman from Tekoa though he was, his rich and polished speech warn that he is not to be taken for a simple and uncultured person. No prophet surpasses him in the combination of purity, clarity, and versatility that characterize his language.

Perhaps his art is most apparent in the three composite sayings, in which Amos takes a form and, by using its structure in a series of sayings, creates a sequence of increasing emphasis and urgency that builds to a climax. The oracles against the nations lead up to the oracle against Israel (1.3–2.16). The recitation of the ineffective curses prepares for the announcement of a decisive intervention by Yahweh (4.6–12). The vision reports move in order from the forbearance of God to the revelation that the end has come for Israel (7.1–9; 8.1–3).

THE MESSAGE

Amos was Yahweh's messenger to Israel. His vocation belonged to the relation between God and people. But the message Yahweh gave him to announce was the end of Israel. The content of the message was in unbearable tension with the basis of his commission, and that tension played a decisive role in shaping the theology expressed in his words. Yahweh appears pre-eminently as God of the world, and his relation to Israel is viewed as an aspect of his total sovereignty. The old traditions of the salvation-history become more the revelation of Yahweh's power in history over all nations including Israel, and less the basis for security for Israel. The special relation of Yahweh to Israel comes into play solely as the ground of Israel's guilt and Yahweh's judgment. The picture of Israel in Amos' sayings takes the forms of an indictment, the articulation of Yahweh's categorical 'no' to the nation's life. The theology of Amos, then, is a function of his message. He knew the older theological traditions of Israel's religion, but he used them to vindicate and disclose the God of the new and unexpected word.

In the vocabulary of Amos the name Israel stands for two related entities. It designates the northern kingdom ruled by Jeroboam II, a state with its own history, culture, and prospects (7.9, 10; 3.12). Israel was also the name of the old sacral league, the people constituted by their relation to Yahweh, and it is this second identity which is operative when in the call and visions of Amos Yahweh speaks of 'my people Israel' (7.8, 15; 8.2; 3.1; 4.12; 9.7). Amos addressed the subjects of Jeroboam in their identity as the people of Yahweh, making them stand *pars pro toto*, putting their national life alongside the history and traditions of the Israel of faith.

Amos never speaks directly of a covenant between Yahweh and Israel. But it must have been some form of the covenant tradition which lay behind and gave content to the relation implied in 'Israel my people'. Amos knew and spoke of the themes of Israel's historical credo (see comment on 2.9–10), but he believed that Yahweh had also been active in the history of other nations (9.7), so that events like the Exodus could hardly be the basis for an exclusive bond between God and people. In the one text in which Amos speaks of a unique relation which Yahweh instituted between himself and Israel, an election that made Israel liable to Yahweh's punishment for every iniquity, the covenant seems to be in view (3.2).

It was this establishment of Israel's responsibility to Yahweh which furnished the basis for the pictures of Israel in Amos' indictments of his audience, and the norms by which Israel's life was measured belong to the tradition of Yahweh's requirement under the covenant (cf. 2.6–8). In one of the series sayings (4.6–12) Amos used the curses which enforced the covenant as clues that showed how Israel's immediate past was already a record of Yahweh's wrath at Israel's failure to maintain their relationship to him. It is thus apparent in the places where elements of the covenant tradition do come into view that it is understood and used only in terms of its threatening side. It comes into play only as the basis for the 'end' Amos has to announce and furnishes the basis for interpreting it as judgment. It is completely typical, and not accidental, that Yahweh is never called 'your (their/my) God' (4.12?). Israel is subject to Yahweh and measured by his will, but any claim that Israel might have had on Yahweh has receded and disappeared behind the divine wrath.

Since Amos' message means the end of the salvation-history, it is only appropriate that where its themes appear they receive a radical reinterpretation. He knew that Yahweh had been active in Israel's past; probably his audience never let him forget it. Yahweh had brought Israel up out of Egypt, led them in the wilderness, and won the land of their habitation for them (2.9–10; 9.7; 5.25; see comment on 3.1). Thereafter he had informed and warned them by Nazirite and prophet (2.11). But in Amos' sayings these themes have lost their character as proclamation of Yahweh's salvation. The historical credo has been drawn into the accusation against the nation (2.9–10; 5.25). The conquest discloses the irresistible might of the God who has turned against them (2.9). The Exodus manifests Yahweh's role as God of Nations, even of Israel's enemies (9.7). The popular hope in the extension of the salvation-history into the future, expressed in the yearning for the Day of Yahweh, is turned into a warning of disaster (5.18–20). Confident talk about Yahweh's presence and grace is abruptly contradicted by exhortations which uncover the basis for Yahweh's hostility (5.14f.). In Amos' sayings the salvation-history turns into a judgment-history. Indeed he sees that from the beginning it never was a manifestation of Yahweh's identification with Israel, but rather a disclosure of the sovereign power under whose terrible might they had been brought by the covenant. Yahweh's deeds in past and future were a Yahweh-history, and any understanding that made the nation an indispensable part of that history was a misunderstanding.

Israel, then, was Yahweh's people, but Yahweh was not Israel's God—not at least in any of the current interpretations put on the possessive by the popular theology in Israel. The Yahweh who speaks through Amos is God of the nations. Yahweh had acted in the history of the Philistines and Arameans as well as in that of Israel (9.7). He is patron of good and judge of evil in all the world; his eye is on the sinful kingdom (9.8), and he sends his punishing fire on every nation whose crimes oppose his authority (1.3–2.3). He can summon one nation to work his wrath on another (6.14). The world is subject to his command and serves his purpose even in disasters (7.1, 4; 4.6–11, etc.). No region of space is beyond his authority; his power reaches even to Sheol (9.2–4). The way in which Yahweh's status as world

God comes to the fore as a coordinate of his decision to destroy Israel's existence is clear in the oracles against the nations which reach their climax with Israel (1.3—2.16) and the assignment of the Exodus to an instance of Yahweh's general government of history (9.7). Israel had known its God as Creator and Lord of history from olden times, but it is only in the word that Yahweh had decreed an end for the people and therefore is God in sovereign freedom from Israel—only then does the radical meaning of Yahweh's lordship emerge.

As prophet Amos was faithful to the impelling visions. The consistent burden of his oracles is to announce the disaster that will fulfil Yahweh's decree of an end for his people. Descriptions of a military catastrophe dominate the future scenes upon which Amos raises the curtain. An enemy will ravish the land (6.14). Israel's troops will be decimated, its defences razed (3.11; 5.3), and the population carried away into exile with the leaders of the nation at the head of the pitiful procession (4.2f.; 5.5, 27; 6.7; 7.11, 17). Some of the oracles portray scenes of death, mourning, and gloom whose cause is not specified (5.16f.; 6.9.; 8.3, 9f.). Others hint at the terrors of earthquake (2.13; 6.11; 9.1). But all of these scenes probably belong to the primary drama, for Amos rehearses a calamity whose dimensions are not adequately filled by historical details. The entire panoply of gloom and doom will clothe a theophany of Yahweh's immediate presence and deed; the events will emanate a dreadful power that transcends the limits of the human and natural. Israel's future is the Day of Yahweh (5.18–20; 8.9), the time that is filled with Yahweh's self-vindication. Then the old Yahweh-history that must be told in verbs of which he is subject will resume; Amos' announcements are dominated by first-person verbs of Yahweh's action. He will no longer pass *by* (7.8; 8.2); he will pass *through* the midst of this people (5.17). The God who gave Israel its past will give them no future but the vindication of his will against theirs. The oracles that derive from Amos offer no hope for any other future to Jeroboam's Israel. The prophet did not speak of any time beyond the judgment. Occasionally he exhorts his audience, but his few imperatives offer no real alternative. They are either derisive (4.4f.), or lead up to the inevitable announcement of punishment (5.4f.), or simply serve to state the way of obedience that the doomed have long since deserted (5.14f., 24). The nation's death is so certain that Amos sings its funeral dirge (5.1f.).

The basis for this final judgment is established in the pictures of Israel's life sketched in Amos' oracles. In woes and reproaches he depicts his audience so that they may see themselves as deserving the punishment which he announces. As the audience and their setting changes, the prophet focuses on different situations in the variety of Israel's culture. Yet what he sees and reports at each point is not isolated; the various foci are interconnected so that the pictures merge into one mural of a basic evil at the centre of the nation's life. The crucial manifestation of evil in Israel is the oppression of the weak (2.6–8; 3.9f.; 4.1; 5.11f.; 6.6; 8.4–6). In his sayings Amos repeatedly refers to a group within the social structure which he names the 'weak', 'poor', 'afflicted', and 'righteous' (i.e. innocent). Their suffering is the arresting circumstance that discloses the situation of the entire nation before Yahweh. The weak are being sold into slavery (2.6), dispossessed (2.6; 8.6), exploited (8.5; 5.11), and ignored (6.6). The prophecy of Amos can be heard as Yahweh's response to their cry, for the weak and poor are the special objects of Yahweh's compassion and concern; the obligation of his people to protect and respect the weak in their helplessness is a theme of every survey of covenant norms preserved in the Old Testament (see the comment on 2.6–8; 5.11, 12).

The logic, then, of the reports to the audience about itself as indictments is the contradiction between the life depicted and the will of Yahweh. On occasion Amos uses normative concepts to identify the disparity. His favourite terms for what Yahweh requires of Israel —and because of the oppression of the weak does not find—are the word-pair 'justice' and 'righteousness' (5.7, 15, 24; 6.12). Righteousness is right conduct, ordered according to the commandments of Yahweh. What Amos has in mind specifically is the right way in the court which would provide justice for the weak. His use of the term 'good' shows how far he goes in concentrating the relation between Yahweh and Israel in the ethical sphere; Yahweh should be the goal of Israel's 'seeking', and that means seeking 'good' instead of 'evil' (cf. 5.6 and 14). 'Good' can be a surrogate for Yahweh himself in certain formulations of Israel's situation. But the way in which violence and destruction displace righteousness and justice in the dynamics of Israel's society shows that the nation 'does not know to do what is right' (3.10). The pictures of Israel's life drawn by Amos are documentation of that failure of right among Yahweh's people. The basic structure of Israel's responsibility under the covenant to Yahweh and a tradition of the stipulations of Yahweh's will for his people are everywhere presupposed. Amos assumes that what he describes in

Israel's society is evil and that his audience will have to agree. But he does not proceed as a witness against Israel so much by quoting laws and commandments, as by holding up a mirror before his audience so they can see the reflection of a folk whose corporate image is in stark contradiction to that of the righteous man.

The pictures catch Israel primarily in three spheres of public life: the administration of justice in the court, the confident affluent life of the upper classes, and the worship of God in the sanctuaries.

In Amos' eyes the court in the gates seems to have been the most crucial institution in Israel's life (see comment on 5.10, 15). It was the place where righteousness should bear its fruit and justice be established (6.12; 5.15). There the weak and poor should have their defender and find their right; how they fared in the court was the acid test of the soul of the society. But in the legal proceedings which Amos observes righteousness is discarded and the justice offered the poor is a bitter draught (5.7f.). The judicial process had been corrupted by the powerful and rich, and was used as instrument of oppression (5.12; 2.7). Courts were no more than markets to enslave the needy and wring the last bit of land and produce from him. His rights were violated with impunity (2.7). The source of the little man's right had been turned into a spring of injustice.

In shocking contrast to the plight of the poor, the leaders of society lived in pride and luxury (3.15; 5.11; 6.4–6). The affluence of the rich does not enter into Amos' portrait of evil because he was an ascetic by faith, a primitivist in cultural outlook. The wealth he denounces was specifically the result of oppression of the poor and corruption of the court (3.10; 5.11); it was detested by Yahweh (6.8). Estates had grown by dispossessing the peasants; the lofty elegant residences were no more than robber's dens (3.10). The managers of economy were infected with a greed that knew no bounds (8.4–6). The leaders of the nation were intoxicated with a heady pride in their status and the achievements of the nation (6.1, 13). What was worst of all, they celebrated their own prosperity in an incredible insulation from the suffering on which it was based (6.7; 4.1).

The religion of Israel had become a celebration of this national optimism and preoccupation with themselves. It was an idolization of what they themselves loved (4.5). The cult prospered with their prosperity (5.21–23), indeed, the gains from the corruption of the court and oppression of the poor fed the fires of their ardent celebration (2.8), and they hoped for a future in which Yahweh would provide more of the success and security they enjoyed (5.18). The priest Amaziah claimed that Bethel was the shrine of the king and his rule; he was right (7.14). In visiting Bethel Israel had not sought Yahweh (5.4f.). He vehemently rejected their entire cult because the basic requirement of their relation to him was missing (5.2–24). They had failed in the courts so their cult was worthless (5.15). Yahweh would not hear the praise of a congregation deaf to the anguish of their neighbours, nor should the practitioners of oppression count on his grace.

Taken as a whole this testimony of Amos says that the crimes of individual Israelites against their fellows had risen to the level of the nation's rebellion against God. In times past any man who did such things was condemned in the courts, reckoned unfit for participation in the congregation of worship, and rejected as unrighteous by those devoted to Yahweh's will. Amos spoke for Yahweh when the crimes had become those of the nation to such measure that Yahweh could no longer pass by.

THE BOOK

The book of Amos is composed primarily of material of three distinct types: (1) sayings spoken by a prophet in carrying out his commission; (2) first-person narratives told by the prophet; (3) a third-person narrative about the prophet. In the present form of the book these major types of material are distributed in this fashion. True to its title, 'The words of Amos' (1.1), the book begins with a large block of sayings (1.3–6.14). Then comes a section composed of four vision reports in first-person style (7.1–3, 4–6, 7–9; 8.1–3) with the only third-person narrative about Amos set between the third and fourth vision reports (7.10–17). The sayings resume in 8.4–14, then comes a fifth first-person vision report (9.1–6), and a final sequence of sayings closes the book (9:7–15). The three major types of material do not quite exhaust the book; there are a few bits of material scattered through the book which belong to other categories: the title (1.1), sections of hymnic poetry (1.2; 4.13; 5.8f.; 9.5f.; 8.8?), an observation of the kind characteristic of wisdom (5.13).

The larger part of the material can be attributed with confidence to Amos. Most of the sayings and the five autobiographical narratives fit appropriately into a coherent picture of his prophetic activity in Israel just before the turn of the eighth century. In the process of the formation and use of the book there were some additions to the prophet's own words. Sympathetic contemporaries, probably disciples, provided the narrative in 7.10–17 and furnished the information in the earlier form of the title (1.1). The oracles against Tyre (1.9–10), Edom (1.11–12), and Judah (2.4–5) reflect the circumstances of the exilic period, and, in the case of the Judah oracle, the outlook and vocabulary of Deuteronomistic circles. The work of this group is also apparent in the synchronistic dating in 1.1 and the theory of prophecy expressed in 3.7. The hymnic sections in 1.2; 4.13; 5.8f.; 9.5f. (and 8.8?) came from a cultic source in Judah. The observation in 5.13 is the comment of one of the wise. The oracles of salvation at the end of the book (9.11–15) presuppose a different time and situation from that of Amos, probably the exilic period. The reservation concerning Yahweh's judgment in 9.8b would stem from a time that saw that the fulfilment of Amos' message did not involve the whole Israel of God. These are the significant expansions of the material. In the redaction of Amos' sayings other minor elements have entered the material—probably the divine title 'God of hosts', some annotations and explanations such as the time spent in the wilderness (2.10; 5.25) or the identification of the deities mentioned in 5.26. These are noted in the commentary.

The final form of the book was thus the result of a process of formulation that reached from Amos down at least into the exilic period. A precise and detailed reconstruction of the course which that process took would have to be conjectural in large part. But at least an outline of the stages along the way can be suggested. Amos himself was responsible at least for the two series compositions found in the oracles against the nations (1.3–2.16) and the four similarly formulated vision reports (7.1–9 and 8.1–3). Whether he was also responsible for collecting and recording small groups of his oracles cannot be said. The third-person narrative (7.10–17) points to the existence of a person or group, probably disciples, who had a first-hand acquaintance with Amos' career. They (let us say) composed the account in relation to 7.9 and inserted it after the third vision report. This group was most likely the collector of Amos' sayings and responsible for the arrangement of the book. They used the two series compositions as a framework and set a large block of sayings (3.1–6.14) after the oracles against the nations and the rest of the material available to them (8.4–9.10) after their revision of the quartet of vision reports. The oracles against the nations perhaps

seemed to be a good introductory piece and the sayings that followed
represented Amos' typical words at Bethel and Samaria. The oracles
following the vision reports seem to be chosen to emphasize the
character of the end for the nation revealed in them. An arrangement of the sayings in 3.1–4.16 into subgroups seems apparent in the
spaced recurrence of certain formulae: 'Hear this word' (3.1; 4.1;
5.1) and 'Woe to. . .' (5.18; 6.1; see comment on 5.7). The collectors
apparently took oracles which had the same introductory words and
used them as headings of small sequences of approximately equal
length. Beyond this there is no demonstrable scheme to the arrangement, historical, geographical, or thematic. Another sequence (8.4–
14) introduced by 'Hear this. . .' (8.4) follows the vision quartet.
The collectors had a fifth vision report (9.1–4) which did not belong
to the similarly formulated series, and they used it as a heading for
the final brief sequence (9.1–10) whose sayings emphasize the inevitable character of Yahweh's decree of doom portrayed in the
vision; it made a fitting conclusion. The best explanation, though
like all conjectural, for the form of the book is the assumption that
the first collectors developed its present form in something like the
manner sketched above.[a]

The further redaction and expansion of the book occurred in the
course of its adaptation and use in Judean circles, most probably in the
cultic community in Jerusalem. The hymn fragments may have been
added to equip the book for liturgical use. The overture (1.2)
furnishes an introduction that lets its words be heard as the terrible
sound of the God whose wrath emanates from Jerusalem. The other
hymnic fragments celebrate the theophany of Yahweh in natural
phenomena and seem to have been inserted at points where Amos'
language suggested the expectation of a theophany (4.13; 5.8f.; 9.5f.;
8.8?). During the exilic period the book passed into the hands of the
Deuteronomistic circles who were especially interested in preserving
the prophetic traditions; their touch is clear in 1.1 and 3.7; and the
oracles against Tyre, Edom, and Judah were probably added by
them to contemporize the book. After the Exile, when the prophetic
message of judgment had been fulfilled, the oracles of salvation in
9.11–15 were added to let the broken community hear the full counsel
of God.

[a] For different proposals see especially A. Weiser, *The Old Testament, Its
Formation and Development*, ET, 1961, pp. 243ff.; J. D. W. Watts, 'The Origin of the
Book of Amos', *ExpT* 66, 1954/55, pp. 109–112.

ABBREVIATIONS

ANET	*Ancient Near Eastern Texts Relating to the Old Testament*, ed. J. Pritchard, 1955²
ATANT	Abhandlungen zur Theologie des Alten und Neuen Testaments
ATD	Das Alte Testament Deutsch
BA	*Biblical Archaeologist*
BASOR	*Bulletin of The American Schools of Oriental Research*
BDB	F. Brown, S. R. Driver and C. A. Briggs, *Hebrew and English Lexicon of the Old Testament*, 1955
BH	Biblia Hebraica, ed. R. Kittel (refers to the critical notes)
BK	Biblischer Kommentar
BO	Biblica et Orientalia
BWANT	Beiträge zur Wissenschaft vom Alten und Neuen Testament
BZAW	Beiheft zur *Zeitschrift für die alttestamentliche Wissenschaft*
CAT	Commentaire de l'Ancien Testament
CB	Cambridge Bible
CBQ	*Catholic Biblical Quarterly*
EB	Études Bibliques
ET	English translation
ExpT	*Expository Times*
EvTh	*Evangelische Theologie*
FRLANT	Forschungen zur Religion und Literatur des Alten und Neuen Testaments
G	Greek
GK	Gesenius' *Hebrew Grammar*, ed. E. Kautzsch, English ed. by A. E. Cowley, 1910²
HAL	*Hebräisches und Aramäisches Lexikon zum Alten Testament*, W. Baumgartner with B. Hartmann and E. Y. Kutscher, first part 1967
HAT	Handbuch zum Alten Testament
HUCA	*Hebrew Union College Annual*
IB	*The Interpreter's Bible*

ICC	The International Critical Commentary
IDB	*The Interpreter's Dictionary of the Bible*
Interpr.	*Interpretation*
JBL	*Journal of Biblical Literature*
JNES	*Journal of Near Eastern Studies*
JSS	*Journal of Semitic Studies*
JTC	*Journal of Theology and Church*
JTS	*Journal of Theological Studies*
KAT	Kommentar zum Alten Testament
KB	L. Köhler and W. Baumgartner, *Lexicon in Veteris Testamenti Libros*, 1958
KuD	*Kerygma und Dogma*
MT	Massoretic Text (as printed in BH)
NF	Neue Folge
OS	*Oudtestamentische Studiën*
RSV	The Revised Standard Version of the Bible
S	Syriac
SBT	Studies in Biblical Theology
TB	Torch Bible Commentaries
Th. Büch.	Theologische Bücherei: Neudrucke und Berichte aus dem 20. Jahrhundert, Altes Testament
TLZ	*Theologische Literaturzeitung*
TZ	*Theologische Zeitschrift*
VT	*Vetus Testamentum*
WMANT	*Wissenschaftliche Monographien zum Alten und Neuen Testament*
ZAW	*Zeitschrift für die alttestamentliche Wissenschaft*
ZTK	*Zeitschrift für Theologie und Kirche*

BIBLIOGRAPHY

COMMENTARIES IN SERIES

W. R. Harper, 1905 (ICC)
A. van Hoonacker, 1908 (EB)
S. R. Driver, 1915[2] (CB)
E. Sellin, 1929[2, 3] (KAT XII/1)
T. H. Robinson, 1954[2] (HAT 14)
H. E. W. Fosbroke, 1956 (IB VI)

J. Marsh, 1959 (TB)
A. Weiser, 1964⁵ (ATD 24)
S. Amsler, 1965 (CAT XIa)
H. W. Wolff, 1967 (BK XIV/6, first fascicle only)

INDIVIDUAL COMMENTARIES AND BOOKS

J. Wellhausen, *Die kleinen Propheten* (Skizzen und Vorarbeiten V), 1893²
G. A. Smith, *The Book of the Twelve Prophets* Vol. I, rev. ed., 1928
A. Weiser, *Die Profetie des Amos* (BZAW 53), 1929
K. Cramer, *Amos – Versuch einer Theologischen Interpretation* (BWANT 51), 1930
R. S. Cripps, *A Critical and Exegetical Commentary on the Book of Amos*, 1955²
A. Neher, *Amos. Contribution à l'étude du prophétisme*, 1950
V. Maag, *Text, Wortschatz und Begriffswelt des Buches Amos*, 1951
J. D. W. Watts, *Vision and Prophecy in Amos*, 1958
A. S. Kapelrud, *Central Ideas in Amos*, 1961²
H. Reventlow, *Das Amt des Propheten bei Amos* (FRLANT 80), 1962
H. W. Wolff, *Amos' geistige Heimat* (WMANT 18), 1964

ARTICLES

S. Amsler, 'Amos, prophète de la onzième heure', *TZ* 21, 1965, pp. 318–328
R. Bach, 'Gottesrecht und weltliches Recht in der Verkündigung des Propheten Amos', in *Festschrift für G. Dehn*, 1957, pp. 23–34
C. Howie, 'Expressly for Our Time. The Theology of Amos', *Interpr.* 13, 1959, pp. 273–285
J. P. Hyatt, 'The Book of Amos', *Interpr.* 3, 1949, pp. 338–348
A. S. Kapelrud, 'New Ideas in Amos', *VT Suppl.* 15, 1966, pp. 193–206
J. Morgenstern, 'Amos Studies', *HUCA* 11, 1936, pp. 19–140; *HUCA* 12/13, 1937/38, pp. 1–53; *HUCA* 15, 1940, pp. 59–305; *HUCA* 32, 1961, pp. 295–350
W. Schmidt, 'Die deuteronomistische Redaktion des Amosbuches', *ZAW* 77, 1965, pp. 168–192
R. Smend, 'Das Nein des Amos', *EvTh* 23, 1963, pp. 404–423
S. Terrien, 'Amos and Wisdom', in *Israel's Prophetic Heritage*, 1962, pp. 108–115
E. Würthwein, 'Amos-Studien', *ZAW* 62, 1950, pp. 10–52

II

COMMENTARY

1. THE TITLE: 1.1

1¹ The words of Amos, who was among the herdsmen of Tekoa, which he saw concerning Israel, in the days of Uzziah, king of Judah, and in the days of Jeroboam son of Joash, king of Israel, two years before the earthquake.

[1] Verse 1 is the title of the book, placed at its beginning by the collectors of Amos sayings. The title tells the reader that the book is composed of sayings ('words'), who spoke the sayings, to whom, and when. The words come from Amos, who was one of the shepherds from Tekoa. They are meant for Israel. They were spoken during the time of Uzziah and Jeroboam ben Joash, more specifically, two years before the earthquake. The title has passed through several stages of development. The basic phrase ('the words of Amos') is modified by two relative clauses; the first identifies Amos, the second names the addressee of the sayings. There are also two dates; one places the sayings in the reigns of certain kings of Judah and Israel, the other dates the sayings in a time 'two years before *the* earthquake'. The synchronistic dating by reigns of Judean and Israelite kings is the work of the Deuteronomistic editors of the book; its form resembles the synchronization of reigns in the Deuteronomistic historical works (e.g. II Kings 14.23; 15.1; cf. also Isa. 1.1; Jer. 1.2; Hos. 1.1; Micah 1.1; Zeph. 1.1), and the fact that Uzziah's name precedes Jeroboam's betrays a Judean point of view. The first relative clause ('who was among the shepherds of Tekoa') interrupts the connection of the second with the basic phrase which it modifies, and may also be an addition to the original title. The original title given by the first collectors may have been: 'The words of Amos . . . of Tekoa which

18

he saw concerning Israel . . . two years before the earthquake.'

'Word' is used here in the technical sense of 'saying', what is spoken by a prophet in one oracle; as elsewhere in the Old Testament the plural is simply a title for a collection of sayings, e.g. Eccles. 1.1; Prov. 30.1; 31.1; Neh. 1.1; Job 31.40. The term is an accurate classification of the book's contents, for it is made up primarily of a collection of speeches in which Amos delivered the message sent to Israel by their God. The name Amos (*'āmōs*) does not occur outside the book, though a longer form, Amasiah, is mentioned in II Chron. 17.16. Like Jeremiah (Jer. 1.1) Amos is identified in terms of the circle and locale from which he comes: he was one of the herdsmen (*nōqᵉdīm*) of Tekoa. *Nōqēd* probably means 'breeder and tender of small cattle (sheep and goats)'. The word is used in only one other text in the Old Testament; Mesha, king of Moab, is called a *nōqēd* (II Kings 3.4). The term appears once in the Ugaritic texts as the title of herdsman who served the cultic establishment;[a] it has been proposed that the term means hepatoscoper, so that Amos was a cultic functionary who practised augury,[b] but the proposal is hardly justified.[c] In 7.14 Amos called himself a 'breeder of large cattle' (*bōqēr*), who was following the flock when Yahweh called him. He lived a secular life as a landed peasant before his prophetic activity. But the use of *nōqēd* in the Old Testament and at Ugarit does suggest that Amos was no ordinary shepherd, but a breeder of sheep who would have belonged to the notable men of his community.

Tekoa was a village located directly south of Jerusalem within distant sight of Judah's capital (cf. II Sam. 14.2; Jer. 6.1; and II Chron. 11.6 which reports that it was a site where Rehoboam constructed fortifications). That Amos was a Judean is confirmed by 7.12. Yet his mission was to the northern kingdom. Since the prophetic office as manifested in Amos was a function of Yahweh's lordship over his people, the political boundary that had been set up between Judah and Israel was utterly irrelevant. Amos was concerned with Israel in their identity as the people of the Lord; the sphere of his activity was the realm of the old tribal league, all Israel under Yahweh, and not the state cult with its orientation to the current king and his kingdom.

That Amos 'saw' (*ḥāzāh*) his words is a conventional way of saying

[a] *ANET*, p. 141b (colophon to 'Baal and Anath').
[b] M. Bič, *VT* 1, 1951, pp. 293–296.
[c] A. Murtonen, *VT* 2, 1952, pp. 170f.

that his words were received as revelation before they were spoken
(cf. Isa. 1.1; 2.1; Micah 1.1). The conventional idiom rests on the
visionary experience which underlay the activities of older seers and
prophets (e.g. Balaam in Num. 24.2f., 15f.; and Micaiah ben Imlah
in I Kings 22.17) and the canonical prophets. Amos reports five
visions (7.1–9; 8.1–3; 9.1–4) through which he received his basic
message.

The reigns of Uzziah (783–742) and Jeroboam II (786–746) span
the middle years of the eighth century BC. 'The earthquake' is
mentioned elsewhere only in Zech. 14.5, which looks back on it as a
memorable catastrophe of the distant past. The excavators of Hazor
found traces of an earthquake in the eighth century which they dated
around 760.[a] If the date is correct, it would place Amos' activity late in
the fourth decade of the eighth century. The reference to a point two
years before a catastrophic disaster gives the impression that those
who remembered the connection thought of Amos' activity in Israel as
having been short, not more than a year. The connection may have
been triggered by sayings of Amos which appear to allude to an
earthquake as the coming punishment (2.13; 3.14f.; 6.11; 9.1).

Thus the title is primarily concerned to introduce the book as the
sayings of a man who is carefully identified by name, home, vocation,
and time. That his words were of divine origin is recognized by the
note that he 'saw' them, and this fact is repeatedly emphasized by the
recurrent 'This is what Yahweh has said' which introduces many of
the oracles within the book. But the title stakes out a crucial herme-
neutical principle; the sayings are to be read and understood as
words for a particular time and place through one individual man.
Rather than an embarrassment, their historicity is a key to their
meaning.

2. THE VOICE OF YAHWEH: 1.2

1 [2]He said,
  'When[b] Yahweh roars from Zion,
    from Jerusalem utters his voice,

   [a] Y. Yadin and others, *Hazor II, An Account of the Second Season of Excavations
1956*, 1960, pp. 24ff., 36f.
   [b] For this construction of Hebrew imperfect verbs followed by perfects, cf.
G. Beer, R. Meyer, *Hebräische Grammatik*, 1952–55, par. 101. 6. b.

the pastures of shepherds dry up,[a]
and the top of Carmel withers.'

[2] The title (1.1) is followed by this poetic couplet which serves as an overture to the entire book. The couplet describes the awesome voice or noise of Yahweh and its devastating effect; when Yahweh utters his voice from his residence in Jerusalem, it reverberates across the earth, searing the landscape, and reaching even to the summit of Carmel in the north. The last editor of the book connected the couplet with the title by the transitional phrase 'and he said', and so indicated his opinion that it was a saying of Amos'. But the style and theme of the verse are those of the hymn, not the prophetic saying. Yahweh does not speak in the first person; his voice is portrayed as a devastating phenomenon. The two bi-cola are perfect synonymous parallelisms in 3+3 rhythm. The notion that Yahweh is resident in Zion is a Jerusalem cultic tradition; and the only other allusion to specifically Jerusalem tradition in the book appears in 9.11f., an oracle of salvation which is secondary. The couplet has been placed at the beginning of Amos' sayings by an editor who understood the oracles to be anticipations of the destructive 'sound of Yahweh'. The selection of his hymnic couplet may have been provoked by Amos' use of the lion's growl as an illustration of the compelling power of Yahweh's speech in 3.8a. The reference to Carmel, a mountain on the coast of Israel, as the target of Yahweh's voice, makes the couplet appropriate as an introduction; Amos came from Judah and proclaimed Yahweh's judgment against Israel.

Verse 2a appears in Joel 3.16 (MT 4.16) and with variations in Jer. 25.30 (cf. also Isa. 66.6). All three texts are celebrations of the appearance of 'the voice of Yahweh' (*nātan qōlō*), locate its source in the divine residence (Jerusalem/Zion, or its heavenly counterpart), and depict the dolorous consequences of its appearance. The three are variant formulations of a basic theme; their similarity is not due to literary dependence but to common use of a significant motif from the Jerusalem cult. In each case the motif is used to depict the initiation of Yahweh's action against his enemies in history. This suggests that the motif had this function in the cult. The 'voice of the Lord' is not, as in Deuteronomic texts (e.g. Deut. 8.20; 9.23; 13.4, 18) the articulate communication of the Lord's covenant will. It is rather an awesome, dreadful noise, a phenomenon with a distinctive significance.

[a] For 'dry up' instead of 'mourn' as the meaning of '*bl* cf. KB.

The characteristics and setting of this *qōl* Yahweh are to be found elsewhere only in the ancient hymnic portrayals of Yahweh-theophanies (cf. *nātan qōlō* in Ps. 18.13 = II Sam. 22.14; Ps. 68.33; 46.6; and *qōl* Yahweh in Ps. 29), where the divine appearance is clothed in the imagery of the thunder-storm. The roaring of the Lord is a stylized metaphor based on the sound of rolling, growling thunder (Ps. 18.13; Job 37.4). The notion that thunder was the voice of a deity who manifested himself in the rainstorm came to Israel from old Canaanite sources; in the texts from Ugarit it is Baal who 'utters his voice' in the thunder.[a] The effect of Yahweh's voice is depicted as a searing drought, withering pastures and scorching the verdant garden ridge of Carmel; the imagery of drought is used here to represent the work of Yahweh's wrath, a frequent motif in the prophets (e.g. Isa. 5.6; 11.15; 19.7ff.; 42.15; Jer. 12.4; etc.).

A hymnic overture presents Amos as a herald announcing the advent of Yahweh whose earthly residence is on Zion, the God whose ancient appearances wrought terror and defeat on his enemies, whose glory in judging all that resist his authority was celebrated in Jerusalem's temple.

3. ORACLES AGAINST THE NATIONS: 1.3—2.16

In 1.3—2.16 there are eight oracles announcing the imminent action of Yahweh against the nations of Syria-Palestine. The first seven are constructed on the same pattern. This use of repetition gives the series a quality of unrelieved menace as the roll call of the nations unfolds. One after another Israel's neighbours are included on Yahweh's list of judgment—until finally Israel alone remains. Then the pattern of the series is broken and expanded as Israel hears its own name added to the list of those whom Yahweh will devastate.

In type the oracles are all examples of the announcement of judgment. Yahweh's words in the first person are introduced by the messenger-formula: 'This is what Yahweh has said.' The oracle itself is made up of two parts: a specification of the crime of which the concerned nation is guilty, and an announcement of the punishment

[a] Cf. *ANET*, p. 135a ('Baal and Anath', col. vii, lines 29–33); on this problem and the larger question of the history of the portrayal of Yahweh's theophany, see Jörg Jeremias, *Theophanie, die Geschichte einer alttestamentlichen Gattung* (WMANT 10), 1965, especially pp. 73ff.

which Yahweh will enact. Amos has developed this basic structure by filling it out with formula-like sentences. The resulting pattern is constructed of these constants:

(a) *The messenger formula*: 'This is what Yahweh has said. . .'

(b) *The indictment*: 'For three crimes of (name) and for four I will not revoke it, because they have (specification of one crime)'

(c) *The announcement of punishment*: 'I will send fire on (name), and it shall devour the strongholds of (name)'

(d) *Concluding messenger formula*: 'has said Yahweh'

Element *d* is omitted in the oracles against Tyre, Edom, and Judah (1.10, 12; 2.5). The Israel oracle begins with elements *a* and *b*, but the indictment is expanded and the pattern is abandoned in the rest of the saying (see the comment on 2.6–16). Otherwise this pattern is used as though it were a form whose blank spaces need only to be filled in with the appropriate crimes and names. It is obviously significant for the message and theology which the prophet articulates.

(a) The prophet announces what he has heard Yahweh say. The nations are not directly addressed, but are referred to in the third person. The audience for the series must have been a group in Israel; either Bethel or Samaria are possible settings. But even Israel hears of its indictment and punishment in the third person; the departure from the third-person style within the Israel oracle is a clue that they are the actual audience (2.10–12). The style is that of reports for general announcement from a court which has already deliberated and reached its verdict.

(b) The crime which has provoked Yahweh's judgment is introduced by the opening formula of a graded numerical saying: 'For three . . . and four. . . .' Examples of the formula appear in Prov. 6.16–19; 30.15f., 21–23, 29–31; Job 5.19ff.; 33.14ff.; Ecclus. 23.16–21; 25.7–11; 26.5f., 28; 50.25f.; outside biblical literature see 'The Sayings of Ahiqar'[a] and 'Baal and Anath'.[b] In these examples various numerical sequences are used in the pattern $X/X+1$ (they range from 1/2 to 9/10), in order to establish a framework for a following list of things which always reaches the larger number. The formula is a device of speech to organize a number of items into a coherence for consideration and reflection. In some cases the interest of the saying is focused on the final item, and that seems to be the way in which Amos employs the formula; he does not itemize the

[a] *ANET*, p. 428b.
[b] *ANET*, p. 132b (col. iii, lines 17f.).

first three crimes, but rather jumps to the fourth, which in this context is the one which has provoked the action of Yahweh. There are others, but the one named has finally broken the patience of Yahweh. The distribution of the formula in biblical literature shows that the device was a favourite of Wisdom; by its very nature it is suited for reflection and instruction. Amos is the only prophet to employ it and he may have adopted it from the style of folk-wisdom in order to present the coming action of Yahweh as a response to an accumulation of offences that has outrun the tolerance of God.[a] Within element *b* the masculine singular pronoun in the expression 'I will not revoke *it*' has no antecedent, and hangs suspended in mysterious and threatening ambiguity. In the present arrangement of the material in Amos 1—2, a possible antecedent could be found in the hymnic bi-cola in 1.2. The 'voice of Yahweh' has gone forth, the terrible sound which does the work of his wrath; that awesome force will not be recalled! Doubt about the originality of v. 2 calls for another solution. In Num. 23.20 the same verb and suffix are used in a context in which 'it' stands for the blessing which Yahweh has decreed for Israel. By contrast the pronoun in Amos represents the curse, the decree of judgment which Yahweh has announced in the heavenly court. It then refers forward to the announcement of judgment in *c*. Yahweh's decision is irrevocable. The certainty that Yahweh has already initiated the punishment of his foes and cannot be restrained is the foundation of Amos' entire message.

(*c*) Element *c* appears in other prophetic books (Hos. 8.14; Jer. 17.27; 21.14; 49.27; 50.32; Ezek. 39.6) as a formula for announcing Yahweh's action against his foes. This suggests that Amos adopts a conventional formula which was already in use for oracles against foreign nations as Yahweh's enemies. The one variation in this element appears in 1.14 where 'I will send' shifts to 'I will kindle'; the variant appears in the same formula in Jer. 17.27 (cf. also Ezek. 20.47; Lam. 4.11). The agent of Yahweh's wrath in the formula is a divine fire which consumes the defences of the nations. This notion of the divine fire which consumes the enemy is a feature of the vocabulary of Yahweh's Holy War; it usually appears, as here, in the context of descriptions of military catastrophe worked by Yahweh.[b] There are other features

---

[a] On the formula see among others: W. M. Roth, 'The Numerical Sequence $X/X+1$ in the Old Testament', *VT* 12, 1962, pp. 300–311; G. Sauer, *Die Sprüche Agurs* (BWANT 84), 1963.

[b] See P. D. Miller, Jr., 'Fire in the Mythology of Canaan and Israel', *CBQ* 27, 1965, pp. 256ff.

in the material used to fill out element *c* that also stem from the features of the Holy War tradition, as it was used in the portrayal of the day of Yahweh. See the exegesis below (1.14; 2.2, 14–16). The formula is the vehicle of Amos' expectation of the imminent visitation of Yahweh on his day for defeating his foes, a fundamental clue to the way in which he expected Yahweh to act in judgment. The description consistently portrays a military catastrophe in which the defences of the nation are removed and its political leadership destroyed. This conception is not the product of historical observation, an anticipation of Assyria's intrusion into the area, but a dramatic portrayal of the revival of Holy War brought off by theophanic manifestation of Yahweh. Where Amos came by this specific tradition is difficult to say. The tradition could have lived on among the people of the land who cherished the heritage of the tribal league; it appears again in Deuteronomic material. It was also taken up in some Yahweh hymns of the Jerusalem cult (cf. Pss. 46, 29, 18) and put to a quite distinct use.

The pattern common to these oracles against the nations seems then to be the creation of Amos. In its construction he shows the capacity to assimilate forms and motifs from a variety of spheres and traditions to fashion a speech appropriate for his message which is characteristic of his prophecy. He is a master of the oral style of his time, not bound to one background or tradition, adopting broadly from the available possibilities of communication, and fashioning original moments in the history of speech. Here he has used the long established form of the announcement of judgment cast in the messenger style, combining it with elements of the didactic and military tradition to shape an oracle form suited to a new moment in the history of Yahweh's word in Israel: the moment when it is made known that the people of Yahweh are now numbered among the foes against whom their God wages the warfare of his wrath.

Taken as a whole the sequence of eight oracles presents two problems. Are all eight from Amos? Is the series an original unit of speech or the creation of the collectors who formed the book?

First, if the analysis in the commentary on the individual oracles is correct, the sayings against Judah and Edom, and probably Tyre, are later additions to the series, composed in the interest of contemporizing the book of Amos for use in Judah during the exilic and post-exilic periods. The original group included only Damascus,

Gaza, Ammon, Moab, and Israel. This leaves any geographic pattern incomplete. It is of course impossible to say whether the additions displaced other original oracles, and it is fruitless to speculate why Judah and Edom should be omitted. The four which appear original do cover the international region around Israel and include the nations with which that kingdom had struggled in the previous century. One could conclude that Amos had no word concerning the others and did not expect them to be destroyed in the imminent catastrophe.

The series appears to be a rhetorical unit, including the Israel oracle. If the groups of oracles against foreign nations in other prophetic books are a guide for judging, then we should have to think about a collection (Isa. 13—23; Jer. 46—51; Ezek. 25—32; Hab. 2.5–19; Zeph. 2.4–15). But the analogy does not apply; Amos' oracles are quite unlike those found in these collections. The powerful repetition of the formula and the motifs with which it is filled out bind the sequence into a unity. Then, there are two other series in Amos where repetition of form occurs and where the point of the sequence is clear only when the series is heard to the end (4.6–12; 7.1–9 plus 8.1–3). The series is a feature of Amos' style. Moreover, it would be difficult to imagine a setting for the oracles against the nations apart from the Israel oracle. In the reign of Jeroboam II, these nations were no threat to Israel. The oracles against the nations create the setting for the announcement of Israel's judgment. This is not to say that they were a homiletical trick, not to be taken seriously. They are announced as a word from Yahweh and portray the scheme of events which Amos looked for—an action of Yahweh against the sinful nations in the immediate area.

In form, intention, and content these sayings are unlike the oracles against foreign nations in the collections in the other prophetic books. The others are often implicit salvation-oracles for Israel and Judah, and function as powerful curses spoken against the enemies of God and people. Usually they contain simply a portrayal of the nation's downfall. A reproach is seldom used; and where it is, it is an accusation of pride and arrogance or of hostility against Israel. Here, Amos charges the nations with crimes and cites quite specific indictments which put little emphasis on injury to Israel as the people of Yahweh. The basic form of the oracles is that of the proclamation of judgment used by the earlier prophets against individuals in Israel and by Amos and his successors against Israel and Judah.[a] Amos uses this form because it is the appropriate one for Israel which stands at the climax of the series, and because he thinks in terms of a theology of Yahweh as world God who judges the sinful nation (see the commentary on 9.8 and 3.2). There is then no need to try to construct a cultic ritual situation or background for the announcement of these oracles. A. Bentzen in a much cited article[b] saw an analogy in the execration texts from the Egyptian court. The Egyptian texts were used in a ritual in which curses were announced against the enemies of Pharaoh, first in foreign lands and then at home. Bentzen saw no more here than a suggestive analogy. H. Reventlow has extended the suggestion and sees Amos practising a regular routine ritual of proclaiming curses against the enemies of Yahweh.[c] The earlier prophets delivered announcements of judgment against individuals in situations that had no cultic setting. Amos stands in that tradition, only the addressee is now the entire nation.

Finally, there is the problem of the norms by which the nations are indicted. On what grounds are they accused of offences against Yahweh?[d] In the sequence Amos ranges Israel alongside the nations, *and* the nations alongside Israel. Both relations are significant. Israel is put in the general category of sinful kingdoms (9.8) subject to Yahweh's wrath. They are as vulnerable as the rest to punishment (3.2). And the nations are spoken of with a formal structure that is appropriate for Israel. They are subject to Yahweh's norms, can be indicted by him for misconduct, and their punishment justified in terms of a system of responsibility to him. Their deeds can be called 'crime' (*pešaʿ*) just like those of Israel; so much is simply a fact of the text. Amos specifies the basis of Israel's responsibility to Yahweh in 3.2, the election of Israel. But in 9.8 Amos ranges the Exodus from Egypt, the great event of salvation in the historical credo, along with the migrations of the Philistines and Syrians. Yahweh also brought them from their original home to their present abode. Amos sees Yahweh as the sovereign of history who moves nations in their national careers and can remove them to their earlier spheres (1.5). By analogy with Yahweh's relation to Israel, that sovereignty in the nations' history furnishes the foundation for their responsibility to him. It seems clear that for Amos the ethos over which Yahweh

[a] See C. Westermann, *Basic Forms of Prophetic Speech*, ET, 1967, *passim*.
[b] 'The Ritual Background of Amos 1.2–2.6', *OS* 8, 1950, pp. 85–99.
[c] *Das Amt des Propheten bei Amos*, 1962, pp. 62ff.
[d] For surveys and discussions of this issue see A. S. Kapelrud, *Central Ideas in Amos*, 1956, pp. 25ff.; H. Reventlow, *Das Amt des Propheten bei Amos*, 1962, pp. 67ff.

28 COMMENTARY

watched was not exhausted in or confined to a particular covenant legal tradition which was Israel's possession by special revelation. That tradition was important and Israel was responsible to its mandates (cf. 2.6–12). But Amos regards Yahweh as enforcer of all standards for distinguishing between good and evil known and used in the culture area. An ethic for conduct did not originate with the Yahweh-Israel relation. That was certainly not the opinion of the theological traditions which date before Amos—the Yahwist, Elohist, and early Wisdom. It is conceivable that Israel was aware that many of its legal traditions were held in common with other peoples. In Amos' theology the nations were subject to indictment for acts that violated the mores which established the moral quality of an act. The word *peša'* is thus appropriate in the indictment of the nations. The basic meaning of *peša'* is rebellion, revolt; it connotes the flaunting of authority. The term belongs pre-eminently to the language of politics rather than the cult.[a] The implication of the term is that these nations in their conduct are in revolt against Yahweh's authority over them. The deeds which Amos cites are excessive cruelty in warfare, stealing men for the slave trade, and desecration of the dead. The opinion that these acts were wrong is neither a judgment of Amos' unique creative moral sensitivity, nor an application of covenantal ethics to world history. They are the sort of deeds which the general *mores* of the time would question. These particular ones were chosen because Amos had to select items from the historical memory available to him and his audience. The particular act is not so much the issue; it serves as illustration of the kingdom's guilt. These items are simply material to fill out the basic formula which carries the message and theology. Yahweh as sovereign of history is about to bring the sinful kingdoms into judgment. These nations belong to the list of the condemned—and Israel also.

(a) AGAINST DAMASCUS: 1.3–5

1 [3]This is what Yahweh has said:
'Because of three crimes of Damascus,
  and because of four I will not turn it back—
because they threshed Gilead
  with iron threshers.
[4]I will send fire on the house of Hazael,
  and it shall devour the strongholds of Ben-hadad.

[a] G. von Rad, *Theology of the OT* I, ET, 1962, p. 263.

⁵I will cut off the inhabitants from the valley of Aven,
    and him who wields the sceptre from Beth-eden.
ᵃI will break the bar of Damascus' gate,ᵃ
    and the people of Aram shall go in exile to Kir,'
said Yahweh.

[3] The subject of the first oracle is Damascus, whose name stands
in the appropriate blank in the form. Damascus was the capital of
Aram, the city-state to the north-east of Israel which was the chief
adversary of Israel in the incessant border wars that stretched from
the middle of the ninth century down to the beginning of the eighth.ᵇ
The oracle is concerned with this state, for which Damascus stands as
identifying name. It contains more historical detail than any of the
subsequent oracles. It speaks of a specific military campaign in the
reproach (v. 3) then, of particular persons and places in the announcement of punishment (4f.). One might expect to gain from the
convergence of these details some specific clue to the date of Amos.
But when they are set in historical perspective, an interesting result
emerges in the light of the fact that the tradition in the book of Amos
fixes his mission in the reign of Jeroboam II (1.1; 7.9–11) whose
dates are 787/6–747/6.

[4] Ben-hadad and the house of Hazael are mentioned. At least
two and perhaps three Ben-hadads of Damascus appear in the Old
Testament (I Kings 15.18, 20; 20.1ff.; II Kings 6.24; 8.7, 9; 13.3).
Hadad was the name of the ancient god of the storm whose cult was
established in Damascus, among other places. Ben-hadad is undoubtedly a throne name assumed by a succession of kings who ruled
Aram. Only one Hazael of Damascus is known; he gained the throne
of Aram through the murder of the reigning Ben-hadad (II Kings
8.7–15) and ruled from about 842 to 806. He founded a new dynasty
referred to in Assyrian documents as the 'house of Hazael'.ᶜ His son
and successor was named Ben-hadad (II Kings 13.3), following the
royal tradition of Damascus; he is probably the Ben-hadad of our
text.

[3] The military campaign against Gilead, the traditionally

ᵃ⁻ᵃ In MT this sentence comes at the beginning of v. 5; its rearrangement
restores the parallelism in the two lines; cf. the similar line in v.8.
    ᵇ For a description of the course of these wars, see J. Bright, *A History of Israel*,
1959, pp. 211, 221ff., 235f.; and M. Noth, *The History of Israel*, ET, 1960², pp.
238ff., 229f.
    ᶜ See the discussion in B. Mazar, 'The Aramean Empire and Its Relations with
Israel', *BA* XXV 4, Dec. 1962, pp. 98ff.

Israelite territory to the east of the Jordan and touching Aram's southern borders, must be the one reported in II Kings 13.3–7. During the reign of Jehoahaz of Israel (815–801) the king of Aram defeated the soldiers and chariotry of Israel and 'made them like the dust of the threshing'. The metaphor is quite similar to that of Amos. This campaign must have occurred shortly before 800, for that was the year in which the Assyrian king Adadnirari III completely broke the power of the Aramean state. After 800 there were no further Assyrian incursions into Syria-Palestine for more than half a century. During that respite Jeroboam II reoccupied Transjordan (II Kings 14.25) and the state of Hamath expanded into the northern territories held formerly by Aram. If this estimate is correct, Amos is not citing an event that is contemporary with his mission. Other hints in Amos portray Israel as having already reached the zenith of power and prosperity which it achieved under Jeroboam II (cf. 6.1; 3.13). Probably Gilead had already been reunited with Israel, and the Aramean campaign belonged to history. This shows that the oracle against Damascus is not concerned with a current situation or a recent offence. The real motif is not the provocation of contemporary history, but the form of the series and the total conception behind it. Amos is portraying a catastrophe which Yahweh will send upon the entire region of Syria-Palestine; to fill out the fixed form which he employs, he reaches back into the available tradition for an illustrative event to use in the oracle against Damascus. It is a theology of the history which will occur as the act of Yahweh, rather than external events, which moves the oracle series. It may well be that Jehoahaz's defeat by Aram was the occasion for the other incursions against the weakened state which are cited in the rest of the oracles.[a] In any case one does not have to seek for contemporary events in the others, for the historical evidence here shows that the incidents can be any events of the past which were available to Amos in the tradition which he knew.

[5] Besides Damascus, Amos names *Biqʻat-'āwen* and *Bēt-ʻeden* as places marked for destruction. *Biqʻat-'āwen* means 'valley of evil'; *'āwen* is probably a revocalization of the consonants of the name *'ōn*, a derogatory pun after the fashion of the change of *Beth-'ēl* to *Beth-'āwen* (Josh. 7.2; 18.12; I Sam. 13.5; 14.23; Hos. 4.15; 5.8; 10.5). The LXX has *Ὤν*='ōn (cf. Ezek. 30.17). '*ōn* is probably to

---

[a] J. Bright, *op. cit.*, p. 236.

be identified with Baalbek, a city not far to the north of Damascus where the cult of the sun-god was practised. If this is correct, then the site could lie within the territory still controlled from Damascus in the time of Amos. This is not the case with Bēt-ʿeden. It is apparently the place called Bit-adini in Akkadian texts, an Aramaic city-state between the Euphrates and Balikh rivers.[a] The predicted action of Yahweh will remove the reigning king of Eden, so the expected catastrophe will strike another Aramean state in the same geographic quarter. Amos thinks not just in terms of Damascus, but in terms of a region. The oracle in 1.6–8 speaks only of a crime of Gaza in the reproach, but goes on to include the other cities of the Philistine pentapolis in the judgment. Once again here is evidence that it is the form which predominates; Amos is describing a general catastrophe which encompasses the entire region and he furnishes no precise correlation between guilt and punishment as he does in the Israel oracles. There is little likelihood that the rulers of Eden had anything to do with the campaigns against Gilead.

The crime which illustrates the guilt of Aram is described by a metaphor; Aram's armies had raked across Gilead as though it were grain on a threshing floor, chopping and grinding like a threshing sledge.[b] The reference could be quite literal, describing a method of torturing prisoners, but it is more likely to be a metaphor drawn from the agrarian life known so well to Amos (cf. II Kings 13.7; Isa. 41.15). As punishment for the Aramean states Amos expects a military defeat, the overthrow of the reigning dynasties, and a deportation of the population to Kir, a site in Mesopotamia near Elamite territory. Amos considered Kir to be the original home of the Arameans from whence Yahweh had brought them (9.7). Their punishment amounts to a reversal of their history. Yahweh, who brought them out of Kir, will send them back, after obliterating what they have achieved in the meantime. Once again it is apparent to what extent in Amos' prophecy the sphere of international history is the theatre of Yahweh's dominion, and how the patterns of events are an expression of Yahweh's actions. Yahweh himself makes history in a positive sense, and cancels the history which men make in acts of rebellion.

[a] See IDB III, p. 389; cf. ʿeden in II Kings 19.12; Ezek. 27.23.
[b] On the various types of sledges used to prepare grain for winnowing, see IDB IV, p. 636.

(*b*) AGAINST THE PHILISTINES: 1.6–8

1 ⁶This is what Yahweh has said:
'Because of three crimes of Gaza,
  and because of four I will not turn it back—
because they deported an entire population
  in order to hand them over to Edom.
⁷I will send fire on Gaza's wall,
  and it shall devour her strongholds.
⁸I will cut off the inhabitants from Ashdod,
  and him who wields the sceptre from Ashkelon.
I will turn my hand against Ekron,
  and the last manᵃ of the Philistines shall perish,'
said Lordᵇ Yahweh.

[6–8] Here the form is filled out as in the foregoing oracle. One
specific act is mentioned in the reproach (v. 6) while the announcement of punishment (vv. 7f.) ranges beyond the city named in the
reproach to cover a much broader group. Several of the expressions
in the announcement of punishment repeat those used in v. 5. The
name which appears in the blank for the subject of the oracle is
Gaza, but this one name is only representative, because the names
of Ashdod, Ashkelon, and Ekron are added in v. 8. The names cover
four of the five cities composing the Philistine pentapolis. The
fifth, Gath, is missing. The series thus moves from the north-east to
the south-west of Israel to deal once again with a region. The crime
specified as an illustration of Gaza's guilt is an isolated border raid
of the kind for which there would hardly be any historical attestation.
Gaza captured and deported the entire population of some place and
handed the captives over to Edom. Whose territory was raided is not
said, though the geographic probability points to Israel's or Judah's.
Such a raid could be carried out with impunity only when the state
concerned was in a rather defenceless condition. The episode, if
Israel is concerned, could have occurred during the period when
Jehoahaz was sorely pressed by Aram. See the comments on 1.3–5.
The raid undoubtedly had the purpose of securing slaves to be sold
in the markets of Edom from where they possibly were resold to the
south (cf. Joel 3.6, 8). From the viewpoint of Israel's legal traditions,
this raid would have been a case of stealing men (cf. Ex. 21.16). For
their crime the Philistine system of city-states would be completely

---

ᵃ For this translation of *šeᵉērīt* (usually 'remnant'), cf. Ezek. 36. 3, 4 and J.
Wellhausen, *Die kleinen Propheten*, 1893, p. 69.
ᵇ The title is missing from G and the other concluding formulae in chs. 1–2.

annihilated by Yahweh. By his hand their defences would be breached, their kings cut off, and the population slain to the last man. The omission of Gath has led to the suspicion that this oracle presupposes the destruction of that city by Sargon in 711,[a] and so must be a later addition to the series. But there are other possibilities which offer better explanations for the absence of the name. The omission may be due to Gath's frequent inclusion in the Judean territory (I Sam. 21.11–16; 27–30; II Sam. 15.18ff.; II Chron. 11.8–10; 26.6), or to Gath's having come under the rule of Ashdod in this period,[b] or perhaps to the current ruined condition of Gath resulting from the raid of Hazael (II Kings 12.18). Gath is not mentioned in the other prophetic oracles against the Philistines (Jer. 25.20; Zeph. 2.4; Zech. 9.6–7), and its absence here is hardly serious evidence against the authenticity of the saying.

(c) AGAINST TYRE: 1.9–10

1 ⁹This is what Yahweh has said:
    'Because of three crimes of Tyre,
      and because of four I will not turn it back—
    because they handed over an entire population to Edom,
      and did not remember the covenant of brothers.
  ¹⁰I will send fire on Tyre's wall,
      and it will devour her strongholds.'

[9–10] The saying against Tyre continues the set pattern for these oracles against foreign nations, but the pattern is filled out in a way that is different from the sayings against Damascus and Gaza. In length and proportion it is similar to the oracles against Judah (2.4–5) and Edom (1.11–12). There are three bi-cola instead of five. The announcement of punishment (v. 10) is reduced to the basic formula, without any descriptive enlargement to portray the action of Yahweh or to include other sites in the Phoenician area besides Tyre. The reproach (v. 9) contains not only a citation of the culpable act, but a normative elaboration as well, which tells why the act was wrong ('violation of a covenant of brothers'). The concluding formula is missing.

Tyre was the chief city of the Phoenicians in the mid-eighth

---

[a] *ANET*, p. 286 ab.
[b] *IDB* III, p. 794.

century, having supplanted Sidon as the dominant urban centre of the region. It was located on the Mediterranean coast, just north of the traditional territory of the tribe of Asshur. Its fame and prosperity as a commercial centre with a far-reaching trade were eloquently described by Ezekiel (Ezek. 26–28). The crime with which Tyre is charged is 'handing over an entire population to Edom'. Obviously, the charge repeats the immediately foregoing accusation against Gaza (1.6). 'Covenant of brothers' refers to a treaty between Tyre and some other state; brotherhood was an integral element of international treaties because they inaugurated mutual obligations between the parties similar to those belonging to kinship relations.[a] The treaty-partner of Tyre is not named. If Israel were the injured partner, then the covenant might have been the pact concluded between Solomon and Hiram of Tyre (I Kings 5.12; 9.13), or the relations established between Tyre and the kingdom of Israel during the reign of the Omrides by the marriage of Ahab and Jezebel (I Kings 16.29ff.). But these relations had been violently interrupted by Jehu's purge. The identity of the nation involved remains uncertain.

Did the Tyre oracle belong to the original series? Since the last half of the nineteenth century critical commentaries have raised questions about its authenticity. The standard formula is filled out in a different way from the undisputed oracles against Damascus, Gaza, Moab, and Ammon, as is noted above. The other protests against Tyre's slave trade appear in exilic and post-exilic texts (Joel 6.6; Ezek. 27.13). The charge against Tyre is in fact an echo of the one against Gaza. The oracle could have been added at a later time to make the series more inclusive of Israel and Judah's neighbours. Of course, the shift of the series to the north-west is exactly what one expects if Amos is moving from one point of the compass to another; the next three lie to the south-east. But there is no way of being certain that this pattern underlay the original conception of Amos. In a series where form so strongly defines the content, and where Amos simply seeks characteristic illustrations of crimes, the repetition of the charge against Gaza cannot carry too much weight. The most serious count against the Tyre oracle is its formal similarity to the Judah and Edom oracles against whose originality more significant evidence is available.

[a] Cf. J. Priest, 'The Covenant of Brothers', *JBL* 84, 1965, pp. 400ff.

(*d*) AGAINST EDOM: 1.11–12

1 ¹¹This is what Yahweh has said:
'Because of three crimes of Edom,
    and because of four I will not turn it back—
because he harassed his brother with the sword,
    and violated his obligations of kinship.
Endlessly his wrath tore,
    his anger kept watch relentlessly.
¹²I will send fire on Teman,
    and it will devour the strongholds of Bozrah.'

[11–12] With the Edom oracle the series moves to the fourth geographic quarter, the south-east. Edom was situated along the Arabah from the lower end of the Dead Sea southward. The Edomite kingdom of Israelite times was organized in the thirteenth century, and throughout biblical history was involved in the destiny of Israel. Teman was Edom's largest city in her southern region, located on the King's Highway just east of Sela. Bozrah was Edom's stronghold in her northern territory. The two cities thus encompass the nation.

The charge against Edom is hostility against 'his brother', an enmity which Edom nourished and cultivated with zeal, and put into action by the constant harassment of military raids. Edom's wrath is pictured as the carnivore that worries and tears its captured prey, then crouches over it watching against scavengers. The specific crime cited is violation of the customary ethos of kinship obligations. The 'brother' could hardly be any other than Israel; the kinship of 'Esau' and 'Jacob' was the subject of patriarchal saga (Gen. 25.19ff.; 36.1); Edom is frequently referred to as the brother of Israel (Num. 20.14; Deut. 2.4; 23.7; Obad. 10, 12). Beginning with the events represented by the Jacob-Esau saga, the relation of the two had been strained. David added Edom to his empire (II Sam. 8.13f.; I Kings 11.15–17). During the reign of Jehoram of Judah (849–842), Edom threw off Judahite control (II Kings 8.20–22), but was subjugated again by Amaziah and Uzziah in the first half of the eighth century (II Kings 14.7, 22). So by the reign of Jeroboam II and the time of Amos, Edom was firmly under Judah's control.[a] What then was the period of Edom's persistent and vindictive hostility against 'his brother'? There is of course the possibility that Amos draws on unknown traditions about Edom's conduct during the struggle for power between Judah and Edom in previous centuries. On the other

[a] J. Bright, *A History of Israel*, 1959, p. 238.

hand, there is a cluster of texts in the Old Testament lamenting and condemning the conduct of Edom against Judah. The two that can be most certainly dated (Obad. 10–12; Lam. 4.21f.) belong to the period after the fall of Jerusalem to the Babylonians in the first decades of the sixth century. Obadiah makes precisely the same complaint against Edom—that he betrayed his obligations to his brother. The other texts most probably come from the same period and later (Isa. 34.5ff.; Jer. 49.7ff.; Joel 3.19; Ps. 137.7). Edom exploited the collapse of Judah to the fullest extent, acted with vindictiveness against refugees, and steadily appropriated Judean territory in the south. The indictment in this oracle fits the conduct of Edom in that time so closely that it must have been formulated in the same period. Its formal correspondence to the Judah oracle also indicates that it did not stand in the original series. The corpus of Amos' sayings has been expanded so that it fits a later time in which it was read and heard with respect. What was true for Gaza in the eighth century was also true for Edom in the sixth. The word did not exhaust itself, but lived on into a later age.

(e) AGAINST AMMON: 1.13–15

1 13This is what Yahweh has said:
'Because of three crimes of the Ammonites,
  and because of four I will not turn it back—
because they ripped open the pregnant women of Gilead
  in order to enlarge their borders.
14I will kindle a fire on Rabbah's walls,
  and it shall devour her strongholds,
with a war-cry in the day of battle,
  with a tempest in the day of the whirlwind.
15Their king shall go into exile,
  he and all his officers together,'
said Yahweh.

[13] The Ammonite kingdom lay on the east side of the Jordan along the upper courses of the Jabbok, between Moab on the south and Gilead on the north. Ammon had belonged to David's empire; he himself wore its crown. But it became independent with its own king soon after Solomon's death. The illustrative crime with which Ammon's guilt before Yahweh is established is a border war conducted to expand the northern frontier of Ammon into Gileadite territory. From the time of the tribal league (Judg. 3.12–14) the Ammonites on

every favourable occasion had pressed west and north into Gilead whose fertile grazing land was a constant lure (Judg. 10.7ff.; 11.4ff.; I Sam. 11.1–11; 14.47f.). The particular case which Amos mentions probably occurred contemporaneously with the campaigns of Hazael against Israel in the last third of the ninth century (see the comment on 1.3–5). Though there is no historical notice of the event, Ammon would have seized the opportunity to annex the territory on her northern borders up to the Jabbok.[a]

The indictment against them cites their terrible cruelty in victory, as well as their insatiable hunger for Israel's territory. The practice of ripping open pregnant women in captured places was sometimes a feature of war in that day (II Kings 8.12; 15.16), especially in the case of border wars where the purpose was to terrorize and decimate resident populations.[b] The crime of Ammon was this heartless murder of defenceless women for the sake of *Lebensraum*.

Here also it appears that Amos reaches back into the previous century to find an indictment with which to fill out the reproach. We know from the short notice in II Kings 14.25 that Jeroboam II re-established Israelite hegemony east of the Jordan. The notice says he controlled the territory as far south as the Sea of the Arabah. What this geographic notice means exactly is unclear. At the very least it means that Ammon had been pressed back within its original boundaries, and possibly brought under Jeroboam's control. In the time of Amos, Ammon was no threat to Israel, and her territorial conquest had been cancelled. Once again it is clear how the formula of the oracles draws from out of the past the material which it uses to announce the grand conception of a general judgment upon the area by Yahweh.

[14] The name of Rabbah (elsewhere Rabbath-ammon) stands in the formula sentence of the announcement of judgment. The old capital of the Ammonites lay at the present location of modern Amman, the capital of Hashemite Jordan. The execution of Yahweh's judgment is described, as is usual in the series, in military terms. The fire of Yahweh will break out and consume the defences of Ammon to the accompaniment of the war-cry on the day of battle. The *terū'āh* is the shout of the attacking army as they fall on their victims. The word occurs in Jer. 4.19; 49.2; for its use see Josh. 6.5, 20. The term appears again in 2.2 where it is accompanied by the sound of the

---

[a] Cf. M. Noth, *The History of Israel*, 1960[2], p. 249.
[b] Cf. the extra-biblical sources cited by W. R. Harper, ICC, p. 36.

war trumpet. Tempest and whirlwind are elements of the traditional portrayal of a Yahweh theophany. Yahweh appears in them (II Kings 2.1, 11; Job 38.1; 40.6; Ezek. 1.4). The tempest of Yahweh is the form which Yahweh's wrath against his foes and enemies takes (Jer. 23.19; Ezek. 13.13; Isa. 40.24; 41.16; 29.6). For whirlwind see Nahum 1.3; Isa. 66.15. Psalm 83 is a lament of the people to Yahweh in time of danger from attack by enemies; in this lament the petitioners appeal to Yahweh to pursue his enemies with his tempest and terrify them with his whirlwind (v. 15) as he did to Midian at the river Kishon (v. 9). The combination of themes is an unmistakable appeal for a theophany as it was known in the ancient tradition of the Holy War.[a] 'Day of battle' and 'day of whirlwind' are terms formulated as variants of the basic pattern 'Day of Yahweh'. (See comment on 5.18–20; and the other 'day of . . .' formulations in 5.20; 6.3; 8.10; 3.14.) The relation between the tradition of the Holy War and the motifs used to formulate the conception of the Day of Yahweh has been worked out by von Rad.[b]

Amos thinks in terms of this military-theophanic conception of Yahweh's intervention in history. Behind the oracles against the nations with the repeated use of military terminology and with Yahweh as subject of the action is the fundamental expectation of a specific historical time when Yahweh will bring war as catastrophic judgment against the area of Syria-Palestine. What remains mysterious is the historical configuration of that time. In the Holy War, Yahweh's wrath clothed itself with the armies of Israel, but in this oracle there is no prospect of a military campaign prepared by Israel. **[15]** The exile of Ammon's king and his officers is announced. As in the oracles against Damascus and Gaza, the displacement of royal power and the destruction of military defences are chief features of the judgment. And once again the motif of exile appears. The judgment of Yahweh will be a quite specific reality within the sphere of political and military reality. Its result will be a complete vacuum of power, an absence of the customary rule and might by which the usual events of history were determined.

(f) AGAINST MOAB: 2.1–3

2 [1]This is what Yahweh has said:
'Because of three crimes of Moab,

[a] See G. von Rad, *Der Heilige Krieg im Alten Israel* (ATANT 20), 1951, pp. 12f.
[b] 'The Origin of the Concept of the Day of Yahweh', *JSS* 4, 1959, pp. 97–108.

and because of four I will not turn it back—
because he burned the corpse
of Edom's king to lime.
²I will send fire on Moab,
and it shall devour the strongholds of Kerioth.
Moab shall die with tumult,
with war-cry, with trumpet blast.
³I will cut off the ruler from his midst,ᵃ
and slay all his officersᵇ with him,'
said Yahweh.

[1] The series remains in the same geographic quarter, and moves southward to Ammon's neighbour, Moab, whose northern border lay along the Arnon. Moab had been a vassal state in David's empire and passed into control of Israel after the schism. In the latter years of the Omride dynasty, King Mesha of Moab withheld tribute and success-fully withstood the campaign of Jehoram and Jehoshaphat against him (II Kings 3.4ff.). The inscription on the stele of King Mesha, which was found in Dibon in 1868, reports details concerning Moab's acquisition of territory north of the Arnon in the same period. To what extent Jeroboam II had reclaimed this territory for Israel cannot be determined from the cryptic notice in II Kings 14.25. The oracle mentions only one other name, the city Kerioth (v. 2). The Mesha stele refers to a Kerioth as a site where there was a shrine to Chemosh,ᶜ the god of the Moabites (I Kings 11.7, 33; II Kings 23.12). In v. 2 the name stands in parallel with Moab, and it could be an alternative name for Ar of Moab (Num. 21.28; Isa. 15.1), the chief city of the state.

The illustrative crime cited against Moab in the reproach is that 'he burned to lime the bones of an Edomite king'. The historical circumstances of this deed against the kingdom to the south of Moab cannot be determined. The exact nature of the deed is also obscure. Did the Moabites desecrate a royal tomb in Edom (II Kings 23.16)? Perhaps the Moabites burned the body of a captured Edomite king until the bones were calcified. In the culture area such treatment was an outrage reserved for contemptible criminals (Gen. 38.24; Lev. 20.14; 21.9). In spite of the obscurity of the deed, one thing is clear and of primary interest; the deed did not injure Israel or concern them in any way. It was in Amos' view none the less a crime (*pešaᶜ*)

ᵃ Read *miqqirbōh*.
ᵇ Read *śārayw*.
ᶜ *ANET*, p. 320b.

against Yahweh. The sphere of Yahweh's authority as divine judge included the relation of other states to one another; the norms which he enforced were valid in the international realm. Yahweh's suzerainty was not concerned only with the conduct of Israel and the acts of other nations against them. In the theology of Amos Moab clearly is subject to Yahweh's normative will.

[2–3] Once again the motifs of the announcement of punishment are military defeat (2b) and removal of royal power (v. 3). The first bi-colon (2b) elaborating the basic formula of the announcement (2a) is composed of sound-words drawn from the vocabulary of battle. The terse line evokes the tumult and noise of an army on the attack. In the midst of uproar, with the battle cry (cf. war-cry in 1.14) and the blast of the trumpet ringing in his ears, Moab shall die. Ruler and officers will be eliminated. Instead of *melek* = 'king', Amos speaks here of Moab's *šōpēṭ*. But the term is a synonym for *melek* and carries the basic meaning which often belongs to *šāpaṭ*, 'to rule'.

(g) AGAINST JUDAH: 2.4–5

2 ⁴This is what Yahweh has said:
   'Because of three crimes of Judah,
      and because of four I will not turn it back—
   because they rejected the instruction of Yahweh,
      and did n ot keep his statutes.
   Their lies dec eived them,
      the ones their fathers followed.
   ⁵I will send fire on Judah,
      and it shall devour the strongholds of Jerusalem.'

[4–5] With this oracle the series moves into the geographic centre of the circle which the preceding oracles have drawn. In the area defined by the series only the two Israelite states are left, and Judah is the first to be included in this progressive announcement of Yahweh's judgment. The set formula is filled out in the same way as the oracles on Tyre and Edom. The announcement contains only the basic form-sentence with the names of Judah and Jerusalem s et in the appropriate blanks; there is no descriptive development of Yahweh's action. It is the announcement of punishment which receiv es emphasis, with the addition of the prosaic sentence in 4c. And the re is no concluding messenger formula.

In the opinion of most critical scholars the Judah oracle did not belong to the original series. The judgment is probably right. However, the conclusion cannot be established on biographical or psychological or formal grounds alone. It can hardly be objected that Amos had no commission to speak against Judah, but was authorized only to prophesy against Israel. So far as one knows, he had no call to prophesy against the rest of the nations in the series. To say that he would not have included a Judah oracle because it would have anticipated the Israel oracle and left it an anti-climax, or would have included a Judah oracle because he did not want to seem partial to his own land—both call on psychological presuppositions which cannot be established. Nor can we say that, because the formula is filled out in a different way from the majority of the oracles, the Judah oracle is spurious. The statistics show four long forms (Damascus, Gaza, Ammon, Moab) against three short (Tyre, Edom, Judah); out of seven only one type could have the majority. And who can be certain that Amos was bound to a rigid consistency of form? The decisive evidence must come from the stuff with which the form is filled out. The vocabulary and general conception of the indictment against Judah points to a period after that of Amos. First, 4b: 'they have rejected the law of Yahweh, and have not observed his statutes.' *Tōrat* Yahweh is not out of the question for Amos as an expression. One can call on the undoubtedly authentic *tōrat 'elōhēnū* of Isa. 1.10, for instance. But in Isaiah the expression means the instruction of Yahweh delivered as *dābār* by his spokesman. Here the synonym is the plural *ḥuqqīm*. *Tōrā* means a body of stipulations, is used as a collective concept which comprehends a corpus of statutes by one term. What is at issue is a collection of law established as Yahweh's *tōrā*. The verb *šāmar* with the singular object *tōrā* along with plurals like *ḥuqqīm* and *miṣwōt* is a feature of Deuteronomic style. (Deut. 4.40; 6.17; 7.11; 11.32; 16.12; 17.19; etc.) One has to ask whether this particular protest is likely to have been formulated before the Deuteronomic reform. From then on, the *tōrā* was the Deuteronomic corpus and the *ḥuqqīm* were its specifications. Second, v. 4c: 'Their lies, which their fathers followed, have led them astray.' *Kāzāb* is used only here for 'false gods' or 'idols', but in the context that is clearly its sense. The expression is similar to the use of *hebel* in Jer. 2.5; 14.22; 8.19 and in Deuteronomic literature (II Kings 17.15; I Kings 16.13, 26; Deut. 32.21). 'Follow other gods' is again a feature of Deuteronomic style (Deut. 4.3; 6.14; 8.19; 11.28; etc.). In a word, not only the vocabulary, but the entire conception of rejecting Yahweh's law to follow other gods is a basic preoccupation of the

Deuteronomic tradition. Finally, there is the general character of the indictment. Instead of citing one specific act as an illustration of guilt, a sweeping theological accusation is made, which is out of character with all the other indictments in the series. Disobedience and apostasy in general, not a concrete case of either. The evidence indicates, then, that the Judah oracle is an addition to the series, prepared and inserted by the Deuteronomic editors of Amos. By its inclusion these later theologians contemporize the prophecy of Amos for their time and situation. The announcement of Yahweh's action against the rebellion of the nations strikes Judah also. Even Jerusalem stands under the threat of annihilating judgment because of disobedience and apostasy. One sees here how the editors of the prophetic literature understood and treasured its validity as relevant word. The theme and form of Amos is taken up and brought to speech again as an act of theology, as a reformulation of the earlier word in a new situation.

If this conclusion is correct, certain consequences follow. Since the distinctive way in which the form is filled out in the Judah oracle is shared by the oracles against Tyre and Edom, the likelihood that they are also secondary is increased. All three are formulated in precisely the same way: abbreviated announcement of punishment, expanded reproach with some normative expression included to specify wherein the deed is wrong, and the omission of the concluding formula. Each has its own particular problems, as the above comment points out. But this common distinctiveness indicates that all three were produced and added by the same person, probably the Deuteronomic editor of the book of Amos in Jerusalem.[a]

(h) AGAINST ISRAEL: 2.6–16

2 ⁶This is what Yahweh has said:
'Because of three offences of Israel,
    and because of four I will not turn it back—
because they sell the innocent for silver,
    and the poor for a pair of sandals.
⁷They trample[b] (upon the dust of the earth)[c] on the head of the
                                                              helpless,
    and turn aside the way of the afflicted.

[a] On this question, see W. H. Schmidt, 'Das deuteronomistischen Redaktion des Amosbuches', *ZAW* 77, 1965, pp. 168ff.
[b] Taking *šōʾᵃpīm* as *šāʾpīm* from I *šûp* (*KB*, p. 956); cf. G.
[c] The prepositional phrase disturbs metre and syntax.

A man and his father go to the same maid
　　and so profane my holy name.
8They spread out (upon)ª pledged garments
　　beside every altar;
they drink wine from those who were fined
　　in the house of their God.
9Yet I myself destroyed the Amorite before them,
　whose height was like the height of cedars,
　　who were strong like the oaks.
I destroyed his fruit above
　　and his roots below.
10I brought you up
　　from the land of Egypt.
I led you in the wilderness for forty years
　　to possess the land of the Amorites.
11I made some of your sons prophets,
　　and some of your young men Nazirites.
Is that not so, O people of Israel?'
Saying of Yahweh.
12'But you made the Nazirites drink wine,
　　and commanded the prophets, "You shall not prophesy."
13Behold, I will make a shaking under you
　　as a wagon shakesᵇ
　　when it is full of sheaves.
14Flight shall fail the swift,
　　and the strong shall lose his strength.
The warrior shall not save his life,
　　15nor shall the bowman stand.
The swift of foot shall not escape,ᶜ
　　nor shall the horseman save his life.
16The bravest among the warriors
　　shall flee naked in that day,'
Saying of Yahweh.

In 2.6–16 the series reaches Israel, the actual audience of the prophet. The listeners had heard the proclamation of Yahweh's judgment on the neighbouring nations whose misfortune would be to their advantage. Amos seemed to predict the imminent occurrence of what they hoped for in their theology—Yahweh's Day against their enemies, a time of light for them and darkness for the others, the historical demonstration that the God of the Exodus was with them.

ª The verb *yaṭṭū* elsewhere takes a direct object, and is not used in a reflexive sense: 'stretch oneself (upon)'.

ᵇ So *KB* for the hapax *'ūq* whose meaning is uncertain; for another possibility ('furrow, groove') see the comment on v. 13.

ᶜ Read Niphal instead of Piel.

But the series does not conclude; it moves on, and now their name is heard. By the oracle they are thrust away from Yahweh across the line between him and his foes, and aligned with the guilty nations of history upon whom Yahweh's wrath will fall. Yes, he will be with them—as the God who punishes all their iniquities (3.2).

The Israel oracle is much longer than the others in the series, and in its course departs from the pattern whose structure shapes them. It contains only elements *a* and *b* (v. 6). After the indictment in v. 6b, instead of the expected announcement of judgment formulated according to element *c*, the reproach continues for four more lines (vv. 7f.) giving an extended list of Israel's sins. The announcement of judgment does not begin until v. 13, where the exclamation 'behold' introduces a proclamation of Yahweh's action against Israel, whose result is then portrayed in terms of the terrors and helplessness of a total military collapse (vv. 14–16). Between reproach and announcement stands a recitation of the deeds of Yahweh, the classic events of the salvation-history (vv. 9f.). The recitation covers not only Conquest, Exodus, and Wilderness, but adds the calling of prophets and Nazirites (v. 11a). The section reaches a climax in the insistent question of v. 11b, and is rounded off with the internal oracle formula 'saying of Yahweh'. The accusation that Israel has violated the offices of Nazirite and prophet (v. 12) turns the entire recitation of the salvation-history into an accusation and shows that it is to be reckoned functionally to the reproach. The long, rather complex oracle has thus the basic structure of reproach (vv. 6–12), and announcement of punishment (vv. 13–16), with two movements in the first division, the sins of Israel and the acts of Yahweh. The pattern is sprung, and the oracle-form expanded and shifted, because with Israel the series reaches its climax. The folk who are the ultimate concern of the entire sequence are finally in focus. The word to Israel breaks through the formal structure which has carried the series to this point.

The length and complexity in structure and style has raised suspicions about the rhetorical unity of 2.6–16. The major problem turns around vv. 10–12 which appear to some to be a redactional expansion of the theme of the conquest in v. 9.[a]

In v. 10 the pronouns referring to Israel shift from third to second person so that the style becomes that of direct address. The traditional

[a] See the arguments in A. Weiser, *Die Profetie des Amos* (BZAW 53), 1929, pp. 93ff.; and recently in W. H. Schmidt, *ZAW* 77, 1965, pp. 168ff.

order of events is not followed; Conquest precedes Exodus and Wilderness. The phraseology is said to be stereotyped, the conventional language for the salvation-history. The reference to prophets and Nazirites (vv. 11f.) hangs in the air in Amos' time, and presupposes his own experience (cf. 7.16). The positive reference to the Exodus conflicts with Amos' radical contradiction of its significance in 9.7. The problems raised are impressive. But none of them necessarily disrupts the unity of the oracle. The shift to direct address is presupposed by the announcement in v. 13, which continues the style. Rather firmly established phraseology is to be expected in the recitation of Yahweh's classic deeds, and this conventional character could account for the shift in style, since this recitation is often formulated as direct address (Ex. 20.2; Josh. 24.2–13). One must be prepared to prove that Amos could not have used the language of the classic tradition of the salvation-history, and that is out of the question in the light of 9.7; how he used it is another matter. The use of the recitation of salvation-history as indictment appears in other prophets (Hos. 11.1ff.; 13.4f.; Micah 6.3ff.; Isa. 1.2; Jer. 2.6f.). There were prophets before Amos who had been opposed and persecuted. The institution of the Nazirites is too little known to constitute a decisive factor either way. The section in its present order makes good sense as an indictment of Israel.

[6b] The first accusation against Israel is selling men for *the* money and a pair of sandals. Selling and buying (the same bi-colon is repeated in 8.6 with *qānā* in place of *mākar*) men refers to the institution of slavery. People became slaves in the ancient Near East by capture in war, and by being bound over in legal process in lieu of debts. A particularly pathetic example of the latter is told in the story in II Kings 4.1–7. The definite article before 'money' (*kesep*) indicates that a particular sum as debt is in mind. The parallel term to 'the money' in the second colon is 'a pair of sandals'; the expression could mean 'a very little' (cf. I Sam. 12.3 LXX); but the transaction was hardly a cheap one. Quite the contrary. The phrase is probably an idiom for the legal transfer of land. In the ancient Near East footgear was used as a probative instrument in the transfer of real property.[a] Men were sold either for money or land. The existence of slavery is reckoned with by Israel's oldest law collection (Ex. 21.2–11); the law did not found the institution, but sought to control it. Amos'

[a] Cf. R. de Vaux, *Ancient Israel*, 1961, p. 169; E. A. Speiser, *BASOR* 77, 1940, pp. 15ff.; R. Gordis, *JNES* 9, 1950, p. 45.

explicit accusation is that the *ṣaddīq* are sold. The term designates the
innocent party in a legal process, the man in the right whom the
court should vindicate (cf. *ṣaddīq* in 5.12; Ex. 23.7 where its synonym
is *nāqī*; Deut. 25.1). The perversion of the court by the rich and
influential is a constant theme of Amos (5.10, 12, 15). Legal process
was being used to exploit the poor and enslave them. Israelite courts
by their nature were susceptible to corruption, a tendency recognized by the admonitions in the legal code itself (Ex. 23.6: 'You shall
not pervert the justice due to the poor in his suit').

[7] 7a is a parallel restatement of 6b. On the surface it sounds like
a general charge that the poor and weak are oppressed. But 'turn
aside the way of the afflicted' is a locution for the perversion of legal
procedure. 'Way' (*derek*) is a synonym for 'justice' (*mišpāṭ*);[a] cf.
also *hiṭṭah mišpāṭ* in Ex. 23.6, and *hiṭṭah ṣaddīq* in Isa. 29.21. Both 6b
and 7a are charges that the courts are being used to oppress the poor
instead of to maintain *mišpāṭ*.

The maiden to whom both father and son go could be the cultic
prostitute who plays such an important role in the fertility cult of
Canaanite religion (Hos. 4.14). The institution of cultic prostitution
was strictly forbidden in Israel (Deut. 23.17). But maiden (*na'ᵃrā*)
is a neutral word that does not of itself mean sacred prostitute
(*qᵉdēšā*). Possibly v. 7b refers to the violation of the rights of a female
bond-servant by making her into a concubine for father and son,
prohibited in Ex. 21.8. (Cf. also Deut. 22.30.) The emphasis of the
line on father *and* son highlights the promiscuity involved. In Israel's
legal tradition the juxtaposition of related pairs in sexual relations to a
third is the subject of a number of laws (Deut. 27.20; Lev. 18.8, 15,
17; 20.10ff.). 'And so profane my holy name' describes the consequences of this promiscuity with technical terminology that makes a
quite professional theological judgment. The case cited in Jer. 34.16
shows that Yahweh's name could be profaned by breaking an oath
or covenant made in Yahweh's name. The terminology is characteristic of Ezekiel (20.39; 36.20–23) and the Holiness Code (Lev. 18.21;
19.12; 20.3; etc.). Such a theological evaluation of the cited deeds is
an exception in the sequence of vv. 6–8 and in the genuine oracles of
Amos. The phrase could be a redactional expansion of 7b, though it
may well be connected with altar and house of Yahweh in v. 8 so as
to create the sequence 'name—altar—house of God'.

[8] The two lines of v. 8 are formulated alike; the first colon of each

[a] See V. Maag, *Text, Wortschatz und Begriffswelt des Buches Amos*, 1951, p. 151.

cites the use of material acquired by legal process (pledged garments, wine of those who have been fined), and the second locates their use in a sanctuary (altar, house of God). Social practices are set in a cultic environment to illuminate their character. Garments were used as a legal instrument for securing a debt; the debtor left his cloak with the lender as a surety. The practice is mentioned in Israel's legal tradition, which does not establish it, but sets limits around it. Ex. 22.26f. requires that the pledged garment of a neighbour be returned to him 'before the sun goes down; for that is his only covering, it is his mantle for his body; in what else shall he sleep?' Amos does not say precisely that this limitation is being disregarded, though the use of the pledged garments for couches at the shrine seems to presuppose its violation. Fines required by the court as reparation for injury are known from legal texts (Ex. 21.22; Deut. 22.19). 'Wine gained from fines' must refer to a payment in kind exacted from debtors. The line between legality and illegality of these practices would be difficult to draw in a technical sense from the material available. What is certain is that they both involve the suffering of the poor under the power of the rich to use legal process to their own advantage. With 'beside every altar' and 'in the house of their God' Amos evokes a picture of cultic festivals in the sanctuaries of Israel where the rich recline and feast on the profits gained from the exploitation of the needy. The text does not say specifically that these proceedings are part of a Canaanite cultic festival where other gods are worshipped. 'The house of *their* God' has an ironic ring in the context, as though Amos would say that the deity of the shrine belonged to these Israelites, instead of *their* belonging to Yahweh. At the least, the portrayal shows that these worshippers felt no incongruity between what they did in the legal economic realm and the God worshipped with feasting and sacrifice.

These, then, are the examples of Israel's conduct which Amos cites as their crimes (*pešā'îm*) against Yahweh. In contrast to the accusations against the nations, which all came from the sphere of international relations, they stem from the social order of the national community. In the oracles against foreign nations Amos was dependent on the popular historical tradition known to him. In the case of Israel he has copious material before him in the life of his audience. He can cite what he has witnessed himself. By what norm are all these deeds *peša'* against Yahweh? Amos lists them with the obvious presupposition that they are all culpable acts before Israel's God.[a]

[a] On the question of the relation of vv. 6–8 to Israel's legal traditions, cf. R.

All the items can be placed under the general rubric of the oppression of the poor. This motif is clear in 6b and 7a. In v. 8 a surety is given by a debtor, fines taken from those under legal duress. 7b also belongs to the same rubric, if 'the maid' is a bond slave. The texts show contacts with the legal sphere of Israel's life. The specific acts cited are all related to matters under the jurisdiction of the court in one way or another. The highly probable conclusion is that all the actions cited stem from the corruption of justice for which the court in the gates was responsible (cf. 5.15). The social institutions under the court's supervision were being violated, and the courts used as instruments of exploitation. The concern of Israel's legal customs for justice had been displaced by a crass commercial spirit. The courts had become places for profit by the strong instead of protection for the weak.

In his indictment Amos does not proceed by assembling a list of laws which have been broken. The correlation between his language and particular statutes in the Book of the Covenant rest on allusions, on one word in some cases. The impression given is not so much that Amos itemizes one infraction of law after another, but rather that he throws together a montage of typical acts to portray the character of a society. The entire series could be brought under the rubric of one prohibition from the Book of the Covenant: 'You shall not pervert the justice due to the poor in his suit' (Ex. 23.6). And the concern which penetrates all the accusations is akin to the exhortations (in the style of a divine saying) which have been appended to certain prohibitions in the redaction of the collections in the Book of the Covenant. Ex. 22.22ff.: 'You shall not afflict any widow or orphan. If you do afflict them and they cry out to me, I will surely hear their cry, and my wrath will burn, and I will kill you with the sword' (cf. Amos 6.9; 9.1); Ex. 22.26f.: 'If he [i.e. the neighbour whose cloak is expropriated] cries to me, I will hear, for I am compassionate.' It is this will of Yahweh for justice, this divine concern for the weak, which constitutes the basic norm for measuring the life of Israel. Amos does not preach law in legalistic fashion, but represents the divine will and concern which lies behind it.

He knows this Yahweh who also comes to expression in the

Bach, 'Gottesrecht und weltliches Recht in der Verkündigung des Propheten Amos', in *Festschrift für Gunther Dehn*, 1957, pp. 23ff.; H.-J. Kraus, 'Die prophetische Botschaft gegen das soziale Unrecht Israels', *EvTh* 15, 1955, pp. 295ff.; E. Würthwein, 'Amos-Studien', *ZAW* 62, 1949/50, pp. 10–52.

commandments of the Book of the Covenant and its redaction, this Yahweh whose authority stands behind the norms of justice used in the courts in the gate, this Yahweh whose passion on behalf of the weak and compassion for their suffering issues in threats against their persecutors. Some of the characteristics of this view of Yahweh appear also in sayings collected in the non-cultic material in Proverbs where covenant is never mentioned. The same motif of concern for the poor is scattered throughout the collection (Prov. 14.31; 19.17; 30.14; 31.8f.). Prov. 22.22f. says: 'Do not rob the poor, because he is poor, or crush the afflicted at the gate; for Yahweh will plead their cause and despoil of life those who despoil them.' This saying is a parade example of the theological tradition under discussion. Here are commandment plus a basis in Yahweh's nature, the motif of the poor, the legal setting. There can be no question that norms and values which appear in the legal material also occur in proverbial sayings. These features may have been assimilated by both the legal collections and the wisdom collections from an earlier form of a general Near Eastern folk wisdom which has contributed also to extra-Israelite Wisdom collections. But in this particular text, there are elements in contact with the material in the Book of the Covenant which do not appear in Wisdom sayings: the legal rights of the innocent, promiscuous intercourse with a bond servant, the pledged cloak, and fines. Amos knows these norms as the requirement of Yahweh for the relationship he has inaugurated with Israel (3.2)[a]

In vv. 9–12 the indictment of Israel continues, but the tactic changes. The accusation shifts from a portrayal of what Israel does to a proclamation by Yahweh of what he has done as the real subject of Israel's normative history. The history which Israel makes when the autonomous folk are the real actors is set in contrast to the history of which Yahweh was the subject. Appropriately, the dominant stylistic feature of the recitation becomes a series of emphatic first-person pronouns and verbs. Israel now appears, not as subject as in vv. 6b–8, but as the object of Yahweh's action. This reversal of roles for Israel is a restoration of reality, the presentation of the structure of their history as it was and ought to be. The third-person pronoun 'them' of v. 9 for Israel continues the third-person plurals of vv. 6–8 and furnishes a transition to the second-person pronouns of vv. 10ff. Israel is set in the position of those who hear the word of Yahweh

[a] For a different opinion see H. W. Wolff, *Amos' geistige Heimat* (WMANT 18), 1964, pp. 40ff.

concerning his lordship in their past. Such first-person proclamation in which Yahweh recites what he has done as the subject of Israel's history seems to have been used in the cult of the tribal league (cf. Josh. 24.2–13; Ex. 20.2). It was the liturgical act in which the God of Israel laid claim to the loyalty and obedience of his people as their sovereign Lord. By this self-proclamation through the oracle of Amos, Yahweh sets the history of which he is subject against that in which Israel is the chief actor.

The order of themes is surprising; Conquest (v. 9) comes before Exodus and Wilderness (v. 10). This unusual order has its own logic; it emphasizes that Israel's existence in the land of the Amorites is the result of Yahweh's work. Because this is uppermost in Amos' mind the conquest is listed first, and then emphasized again at the end of v. 10 as the goal of the acts of Yahweh.

[9] The focus of v. 9 is not so much the acquisition of the land as the incredible power of Yahweh in the destruction of its inhabitants. These Amorites were giants, tall as cedars, strong as oaks. No army could possibly have overwhelmed them. Israel's penetration into Canaan was the manifestation of Yahweh's irresistible power in battle by which he is able to overthrow the greatest of men. Amorite is a name used loosely in various strands of Old Testament tradition as the designation of the inhabitants of the territory conquered by Israel in the thirteenth century.[a] The 'memory' that some of the original inhabitants of Canaan were gigantic is noted in other texts: Num. 13.22–33 refers to the Anakim or Nephilim; Deut. 2.10, 20f., to the Emim, Rephaim, and the Zamzummim.[b] Amos is unique in extending this characteristic to the Amorites as a whole; the notion is probably a free individual formulation of tradition. The metaphors for great size (cedar and oak) and total destruction (fruit and root) are of general provenance. For the first see II Kings 14.9; Ps. 80.10; Isa. 2.13; etc.; for the second, Ezek. 17.9; Job 18.16; and the Esmunazar Inscription ('May he have no root underneath, or fruit above . . .').[c]

[10] The Exodus from Egypt and the passage through the wilderness move toward possession of the land. Yahweh led Israel out of Egypt and through the wilderness in order to establish them in the

[a] Cf. M. Noth, 'Der Gebrauch von '*mry* im Alten Testament', *ZAW*, 58, 1940/1, pp. 182ff. (appended to 'Num. 21 als Glied der "Hexateuch"-Erzählung')·
[b] See G. E. Wright, *Biblical Archaeology*, 1962², pp. 29ff.
[c] Cited by W. R. Harper, ICC, p. 55.

land of the Amorites. As in v. 9, Israel's existence in the place where they now live is interpreted as the sole achievement of Yahweh. Verse 10a is simply a statement of the conventional formula for the Exodus (e.g. Ex. 20.2; Micah 6.4; and more loosely at many other places); the formulation appears also in 9.7 where the significance of the Exodus as a guarantee of salvation is radically deflated (see the comment there), and in 3.1 where its originality is questionable. Yahweh's care for Israel in the wilderness is further evidence of the way in which their existence is founded on Yahweh's action. A similar use of the theme is made in Jer. 2.6; Deut. 29.5; Ps. 136.16. The motif of 'forty years', found elsewhere in Num. 32.13; Deut. 2.7; 8.2; 29.4, may be an expansion; see the comment on Amos 5.25.

[11] In order to fill the interval between Conquest and the present, and to bring the sequence of Yahweh's acts for Israel to a contemporary climax, Amos adds to the classical sequence of Exodus, Wilderness, and Conquest, the calling of prophets and Nazirites. Yahweh continued to act upon Israel by summoning to action prophets and Nazirites from among the young men of the people. The fact that Yahweh called and sent prophets to Israel is used as a complaint against the people in Hos. 6.5; 12.10; Jer. 7.25; 25.4; 26.5, but never elsewhere as an item in the proclamation of Yahweh's action in Israel's normative history. This extension of Yahweh's acts to the vocation of prophets and Nazirites is peculiar to Amos, a free formulation of the tradition known to him. The record of prophetic activity preserved in Samuel and Kings is so fragmentary that one can only speculate about whom Amos and Hosea have in mind. One can think of figures like Elijah (I Kings 17) and Micaiah ben Imlah (I Kings 22.8) who had struggled and suffered in their vocation as messengers from Yahweh. Amos knows of $n^e b i' i m$ whose careers were in his view a continuation of Yahweh's action within the existence of Israel, whose words and work were the contemporary manifestation of Yahweh's power. It is altogether likely that Amos understood his own vocation and mission in these terms. He was one of these prophets, called into existence by Yahweh's direct action, whose oracles were the deeds of Yahweh to implement the original purpose behind the normative history. The Nazirite is cited as a parallel to the prophet, a clue that Amos thinks of men whose consecration of life was the response to vocation, the effect of a charisma to manifest in a special life the zeal for Yahwism against its corruption by life

in Canaan.[a] Figures like Samson (Judg. 13–15) and Samuel (I Sam. 1.1ff.) could serve as illustrations. The law for the Nazirite preserved in Num. 6.1–21 applies to a later development of the institution, when its character had become a basic asceticism practised in the context of cultic regulation.

In 11b the proclamation of Yahweh's deeds is abruptly concluded with a challenging question: 'Is all this not so, ye Israelites?' Stylistically, the question is a feature of a dispute-saying and it therefore interprets the proclamation as a weapon in a controversy between prophet and audience. Amos uses the 'salvation-history' here in precisely the way he employs the election theme in 3.2a. The recitation of Yahweh's deeds in history is unfolded only to bring Israel under judgment. The events of that history were the constant themes of Yahwist orthodoxy recited by the Israelites in the cult[b] as their claim upon Yahweh and in pious hope that Yahweh would continue to protect and prosper them (5.14, 18). But Amos does not employ the proclamation as salvation-history; he brings it as indictment. In its events the God Yahweh discloses himself as the terrible God of war whose unlimited power for destruction overwhelmed the Amorites. He is the God in whose hands Israel has been from the beginning of her existence, the God who has not left them without his witnesses throughout all their life in the land. The message of this classical history becomes in his hands the word of Israel's smallness and vulnerability before the God whose will they flaunt in disobedience. The potential always latent in the salvation-history—that Israel is totally in the hands of a God whose power is unlimited and will is sovereign—emerges as dominant theme; and the salvation-history is proclaimed as judgment-history, not a reversal or contradiction, but in direct continuity with the past.

[12] By corrupting the Nazirites and silencing the prophets, Israel has rebelled against Yahweh. Faith in the God of the classical history does not consist of a belief in facts of the past, but humility and obedience before the manifestations of the God of that history in the present. Prophets and Nazirites were the contemporary acts of Yahweh. To reject them was to reject the reality of the classical history and to set their authority against the power of Yahweh. In effect,

---

[a] On the history of the Nazirite, which is known only in fragmentary fashion, see R. de Vaux, *Ancient Israel*, 1961, pp. 466f.; W. Eichrodt, *Theology of the Old Testament* I, ET, 1961, pp. 303ff.

[b] See G. von Rad, *Theology of the Old Testament* I, 1962, pp. 121ff.

Israel has set its own commands and will against the rule of Yahweh. Abstinence from wine was one feature of the Nazirite's consecration (Judg. 13.14; Num. 6.3f.). Opposition to the word of Yahweh brought by a prophet was common enough among the kings of Israel (I Kings 13.4; 18.4; 19.2; 22.8, 26f.; II Kings 6.31). The command 'You shall not prophesy' is identical with Amos' quotation of Amaziah's order to him (7.16), which explains the similarity. Amos puts Amaziah in the ranks of those who forbid the prophet his mission. The indictment is thus complete; Israel has disobeyed the will of Yahweh (vv. 6–8) and set itself against his power and authority (vv. 9–12).

[13–16] The announcement of judgment in vv. 13–16 discloses what action Yahweh will take against Israel. He will come upon them as foe in an awesome irresistible onslaught; the scene is portrayed with impressionistic phrases which blend into a picture of terror and helplessness before the attack. The announcement unfolds in two movements: the direct action of Yahweh against Israel interpreted by a metaphor (v. 13), and the result of the onslaught described in terms of a military catastrophe (vv. 14–16). Yahweh's action is introduced by 'Behold' (cf. 6.11, 14; 9.9) followed by a first-person pronoun and participle; the very style evokes the impending nearness of the next event in the history which Yahweh makes. The pronoun resumes the emphatic 'I' in vv. 9f. and marks this coming judgment as a direct continuation of the old classical history. It is precisely the God of the Exodus and Wilderness, the God whose terrible power vanquished the mighty Amorites, who comes upon them. This new event is not the denial or contradiction of the events which Israel celebrated as their salvation-history, but their contingent fulfilment. The reality of those events had never been simply and only salvation for Israel; their actuality was the person and will of Yahweh, and he now vindicates himself in the next act of the drama. In dread and despair Israel will learn that the salvation-history is in fact a Yahweh-history, that its centre and continuity lies in him and not in the people. Yahweh's intervention is depicted by the verb *hēʿîq*, found only here; its meaning is uncertain (see p. 43 n.*b* above). The one thing that is clear about v. 13 is that Yahweh's action upon Israel is compared to the effect of a wagon, overloaded with sheaves of grain. The metaphor may seem less than adequate for its subject, but it is quite typical of Amos to select an image from the life of the shepherd and farmer to portray the most awesome divine reality (cf. 3.8, 12;

5.19). H. Gese thinks that the verb means 'cleave/furrow'[a]: Yahweh will cleave the ground under Israel as a laden wagon furrows the soft earth of a field. The imagery describes an earthquake that furrows the earth and throws the populace into a panic. The earthquake motif appears in 4.11, perhaps in 3.14f.; 6.11; 8.8; 9.1a; and a particular earthquake is used to date Amos in the superscription of the book (1.1). The power of Yahweh will split the very earth of the land which he gave them, leaving Israel no security in the encounter.

There follows in vv. 14–16 a panoramic portrayal of men seized by horror in awareness of confrontation by the divine. The picture is that of an army arrayed and ordered for battle. The mighty warrior (*gibbōr*), the swift and strong among the men of Israel, bowman and horseman are all there. Amos draws on a traditional motif of 'holy war' in which divine dread fell upon the enemy when Yahweh led the forces of Israel against their foes.[b] The gripping picture of terror and collapse does not envision some specific historical battle, but actualizes the experience of Yahweh's hostile approach. Yahweh alone is named as enemy. The Israelites who longed for the 'day of Yahweh' (5.18) hear from the prophet that the day will come upon them. 'In that day' when Yahweh appears to judge the nations, Israel will know that they who have not followed their God now confront him in terrible nakedness (4.12; 5.17). The drama is the clothing of Yahweh's theophany against his enemies, and in that role he is the future of Israel.

4. ELECTION TO JUDGMENT: 3.1–2

3 ¹Hear this word which Yahweh has spoken against you,
O children of Israel, against all the family which I brought
up from the land of Egypt:
²'You alone have I known
from all the families of the earth;
therefore I will punish you
for all your iniquities.'

This brief oracle has been placed at this point in the collection as a kind of introduction to the following sayings. Since it bases Yahweh's

[a] *VT* 12, 1962, pp. 417ff.
[b] Cf. G. von Rad, *Der Heilige Krieg im alten Israel* (ATANT 20), pp. 10f., 62f.; L. Toombs, *IDB* IV, pp. 797ff.

punishment on the special relation to Israel which he himself inaugurated, the word furnishes a theological framework within which other announcements of coming judgment can be understood. The particular sins which Amos itemizes in the subsequent oracles are to be seen within the context of Yahweh's relation to Israel if the passion and significance of the divine decision to judge is to be understood. The unit is composed of introduction (v. 1) and divine saying (v. 2). The introductory proclamation-formula summons a group to hear the word, identifies the divine speaker and addressees (1a) and then elaborates further the identification of the audience by referring to the deliverance from Egypt (1b). The two members of the divine saying are joined by 'therefore', which throws Yahweh's statement of his unique relation to Israel (2a) into the role of a basis for his announcement that he will punish all their iniquities (2b).

[1] The proclamation formula was used by Amos to introduce divine and prophetic sayings (4.1; 5.1; 7.16; 8.4; cf. 2.13). It creates a situation in which hearing is the commanded response; an otherwise occasional accidental group is constituted and identified as those for whom the following message is meant. Yahweh has sent a word to them! Amos calls his hearers 'the children of Israel' (2.11; 3.12;4.5; 9.7), members of the historical political entity that bears the name Israel. Undoubtedly he addresses citizens of Jeroboam's kingdom, but in Amos' usage 'Israel' bears the overtones of its classic significance as the designation of the tribal league, the confederacy constituted by Yahweh's action and defined by his will. All the perspectives of the following word are drawn from that sphere. The claim of the word upon their hearing does not rest upon their existence as the northern kingdom of Israel, but upon their identity as 'my people'. 3.1 is the longest example of the proclamation formula in Amos; the status of 1b as part of the original is a bit precarious. It shifts to divine first-person style within the introduction, which has begun with a reference to Yahweh, before the word proper is reached; and the Exodus theme seems to anticipate 2a and make it an anticlimax (W. H. Schmidt). In the light of 9.7, which ranges the Exodus along with the immigrations of other peoples, the Exodus as Yahweh's deed cannot be synonymous with the exclusive relation described in 2a. The shift in style may be due to the fixation of the sentence in the first person in cultic usage (e.g. Ex. 20.2; Josh. 24.17) and equation of the Exodus with 2a may not be intended. Amos uses the Exodus theme formulated similarly against Israel in 2.10 and 9.7, and

interprets it as a basis for Yahweh's claim upon and sovereignty over Israel. If it is original here, it puts the basic redemption act of the 'historical credo' alongside the exclusive relation stated in 2a, a juxtaposition of Exodus and covenant.

[2] The divine word itself, as concerns mere form, has the structure of a word of judgment. The first part makes an assertion which serves as the basis for the following announcement of Yahweh's intention. The two sentences are connected by the conjunction 'therefore', frequently used to join indictment and announcement of punishment. But the content of this formal structure is surprising. The indictment does not point to a failure of Israel, but rather to an act of Yahweh; instead of announcing a specific imminent punishment by Yahweh, the announcement promulgates a general policy of Yahweh's conduct *vis-à-vis* Israel. Yahweh's unique relation to Israel is the basis for culpability; it establishes a special sphere of jurisdiction. The unusual construction of the word of judgment produces an assertion that comes as close to being theological formulation in principle as anything found in the speeches of Amos. It is virtually a paradigm of his prophetic faith, compressing the radical significance of Israel's election into a terse summary of the theological basis of his message.

The interpretation of 2a involves two distinct problems: what its words mean; and what significance that meaning has in the prophecy of Amos. First, the sense of the sentence. The affirmation points twice to the selectivity of Yahweh's 'knowing'. 'You only' stands at the beginning in an emphatic position. 'From all the families of the earth' sets this particular status of Israel in the context of world history. Out of all the nations of the world Israel alone has been the object of the action of Yahweh expressed in the verb *yādaʿ*. Within this context, 'to know' must have a relational meaning, instead of a cognitive sense. That Yahweh knew about Israel alone would be a limitation upon his nature which was unlikely as a viewpoint of Amos' audience, and impossible in the mouth of the prophet in the light of the oracles against the nations (chs. 1–2) and of the assertion in 9.7f. that Yahweh was active in the history of other peoples. *Yādaʿ* means 'to watch over, to care for' in a series of texts, e.g. Ps. 1.6: 'Yahweh knows the way of the righteous' (cf. also Nahum 1.7; Ps. 37.18; 144.7). There are several other texts in which *yādaʿ* with Yahweh as subject means 'to establish a relation, to select for a purpose', and comes very close to the technical term *bāḥar* ('elect') used by the Deuteronomist. Jer. 1.5, for instance: 'Before I formed you in the womb I *knew* you, and before you were born I consecrated you; I appointed you a prophet to the nations.' See also II Sam. 7.20, which speaks of Yahweh's relation to David, and Deut. 9.24; Hos. 13.5, where the object of *know* is Israel. The most interesting example is a sentence, usually attributed to a redactor of J, where God speaks of his relation to Abraham: 'I have *known* him, that he may command his children and his household after him to keep the way of Yahweh by doing righteousness and justice' (Gen. 18.19). In the immediate context the motif of 'all the families of the earth' appears (v. 18), as it does in Amos 3.2a. Moreover, the concepts of righteousness and justice which constitute the purpose of Abraham's selection are fundamental themes of Amos' conception of Yahweh's requirement of Israel (5.24). Structurally, the notion of Yahweh's relation to Israel is the same in Amos and R^J. The latter is reading back into the epic of Abraham the claims of the Sinai covenant so that the reader will see that God's promise to Abraham (J's theme) all along intended to bind his seed to the requirements of justice and righteousness. An analogy between the use of *yāda'* in the texts mentioned above and the meaning of the verb 'know' in Hittite and Akkadian vassal-treaties has been pointed out;[a] in such contexts the verbs mean the legal recognition of the other, i.e. 'recognize by covenant'. Such a construction furnishes the presupposition of 2b; because Yahweh has recognized Israel *alone* as covenant partner, he will punish them for *all* their iniquities. It is the covenant binding Israel to explicit responsibility, not the Exodus, which is in view when Amos speaks 3.2a.

The question has been raised whether 2a actually represents the faith of Amos (the problem is 9.7), or is no more than an ironic, scornful response to hearers who lay claim to the dogma of a special relation to Yahweh as a defence against Amos' message of judgment. If the line is only a mimicry of the faith of his audience flung at them in scorn to destroy their false security, then it need reveal little of Amos' position. Other evidence is too strong to suppose that Amos stood completely outside the normative theological traditions of Israel (cf. the Introduction on 'The Message' of Amos) and did not regard Israel as Yahweh's people in a special sense. However, Amos does seem to take up the themes of the theological tradition from his audience and use them in a way that was completely 'unorthodox' and unexpected (see comment on 2.9f.; 5.14f., 18–20; 9.7) and

[a] H. Huffmon, 'The Treaty Background of Hebrew YĀDA'', *BASOR* 181, 1966, pp. 31–37.

frequently quotes his hearers. It is quite possible here that he picks up a remark or opinion of his hearers, formulates it to introduce v. 2b, and traps them in the consequences of their own defence.

'Therefore' joins 2b to 2a in an inseparable sequence: '*only you, therefore all your iniquities*'. Israel's special position means that they especially have special reason to expect judgment upon their iniquities. What these iniquities are is not said here. For the particulars of Amos' indictment of Israel one has merely to listen to the indictments which are the basis of most of his announcements of judgment. They furnish the background for this saying and one must suppose that it was spoken after at least some of these oracles had raised the theological issue of whether Yahweh would act against Israel to the level of a crisis between prophet and audience. The one message of this word is the strict correlation of Yahweh's choice and Israel's culpability. The formulation is radical, breathtaking. It is the proclamation of the Old Testament gospel as a word of judgment; the grace of Yahweh discloses itself as an inexplorable struggle with sin. Certainly the notion that Yahweh punished iniquity was not new with Amos in Israel's religious history. Israel's oldest theological traditions knew Yahweh as a God whose wrath could break out against those who flaunted his will. What is new here is the radical way in which this potential of Yahweh emerges as the express purpose of his dealing with Israel. To be chosen is to be put under judgment. Israel is the folk in whose history the will of Yahweh for righteousness becomes visible in that all their sins are punished. Amos will have nothing to do with a mere salvation-history, only a righteousness-history. And it ought to be added that unless a man has heard that word seriously he cannot really understand why the gospel of the New Testament is founded on the crucifixion. Paul understood when he said: 'I have been crucified with Christ, and it is no longer I that live, but Christ. . . .' The old Israel had no future, precisely because its God in supreme sovereignty meant to live in their history.

5. THE WORD IS THE WORK OF YAHWEH: 3.3–8

3 ³Do two walk together,
   unless they have made an appointment?
⁴Does the lion roar in the forest,
   if he has no prey?

Does the young lion raise his voice (from his lair),[a]
    unless he has caught something?
[5]Does a bird fall to (the trap of)[b] the earth,
    if a net has not snared it?
Does the trap spring from the ground,
    when it has caught nothing?
[6]If the trumpet is sounded in a city,
    are the people not afraid?
If misfortune occurs in a city
    has Yahweh not done it?
[7]For Lord Yahweh carries out no decree, unless he has revealed
his counsel to his servants, the prophets.
[8]The lion has roared!
    Who is not afraid?
Lord Yahweh has spoken!
    Who will not prophesy?

The words of Amos are an echo of the word of Yahweh. The prophet speaks because God has spoken; that is the burden of this
saying. It is not itself a message but a defence of the messenger's
work; the prophet himself speaks to justify his commission.

The saying is constructed with an amazingly artful deftness.
In vv. 3–6 a series of questions is developed. All of them ask about the
relation between an event and its cause. Each presses toward the
agreement of the audience: 'It is true! This thing would not happen
were it not preceded by the other.' In the first five lines the event is
stated first, followed by the question about its necessary cause. In 6a
the order is reversed, first the cause and then the inevitable result,
because of the nature of the event. Then in 6b, the prevailing sequence
is resumed. Verse 8 has two lines which begin with an assertion and
conclude with a question whether the appropriate result must not
follow. This final variation in structure of v. 8 marks the climax of
the saying. After v. 3, which stands alone, the questions come in
pairs: first the beasts of prey (lion and young lion), then the craft of
the hunter (throw-net and spring-net), next the city in crisis (the
danger signal and the calamity), and finally the parallelism between
the lion's roar and the utterance of Yahweh. Verse 7 interrupts the
pattern; its form, vocabulary, and meaning suggests that it is a later
insertion.

In function this passage is a dispute-saying. With it Amos responds

[a] The phrase overloads the metre, is a gloss added to correspond to 'in the
forest' in the previous line.
[b] Omit *paḥ, metri causa*; cf. G.

to protests against his radical message of Yahweh's total punishment. The setting is a hostile encounter between speaker and audience. The report of one such encounter appears in the story of Amos' confrontation with Amaziah (7.10–13), where his right to speak is rudely denied in the name of Israel's king. There are other indications that Amos carried out his vocation in the midst of bitter resistance (2.12; 6.3; 9.10), a fate which was the lot of more than a few spokesmen for God in later times (Hos. 9.8; Jer. 20; Isa. 50.4–9; Luke 6.22f.; II Cor. 11.24ff.) But here Amos does not proceed as he does with the priest Amaziah, whose orders are answered with a divine word foretelling his doom. Instead, he attempts to persuade his audience; he carries out what in his culture was an authentic apologetic. Not content to shake the dust of this place from his sandals because his message is opposed, he wrestles with the mind and soul of this recalcitrant folk, reaching out for their understanding of his work and for their faith in his words. In his first two visions (7.1–6) he interceded successfully with Yahweh for their life; now he appeals to them for the perception on which their life depends. In order to persuade them he uses a kind of logic with which they were familiar. In style and theme the questions are folk-sayings of the kind formulated and passed on among the landed peasantry. The word-pictures in the questions come from the sphere of everyday life in the country. Practitioners of folk-sayings were accustomed to assemble comparable phenomena into series whose analogical reasoning disclosed the meaning of human life. And questions that elicit assent were a device of pedagogy practised from earliest times by the purveyors of Wisdom in the culture-area.[a] Here a window opens on Amos' own life in Tekoa, his observations as a shepherd following his flock across the Judean hill country (7.14), and his expertise with the materials and techniques of proverbial argument. Through this medium the lonely spokesman seeks to create a community of understanding for the word he proclaims.

[3–6] The first seven questions range across happenings which common experience and outlook would connect self-evidently with another event. When two men are seen making their way across the horizon of Judah's empty hill country, one knows they could hardly have met except by appointing a time and place (v. 3). The lion's distant roar announces that his stalk, during which a sound would

---

[a] On the background of the type in the world of Wisdom, see the materials gathered in H. W. Wolff, *Amos' geistige Heimat* (WMANT 18), 1964, pp. 3–12.

alert his quarry, is over; he has captured his prey (v. 4). If one sees a bird checked in his flight, tumbling to the ground, it is clear that a hunter's throw-net ensnared it; or a hunter who sees his spring-trap snap up knows something has tripped its trigger.[a] In 6a the sequence is reversed—the cause is the blast of the *šōpār* sounded in alarm, and the result is the hubbub of the city stirring in near panic—but the argument remains the same. Of more consequence is the progress of the series from the situations of normal life to one of crisis precipitated by nearing danger. The harmless argument to which no listener could object now grows ominous. Now the question is asked whether disaster strikes a city unless Yahweh wills it and does it. To this proposition the listeners might not so readily agree. Was not Yahweh their God, the deity who wrought weal and peace for them? But if disaster struck, would it not be also *his* work, for surely they were not in the power of another god. Yet if Yahweh worked woe as well as weal, how in principle could they object to Amos' prophecy that God had decreed disaster for them? The problem they found with Amos' message becomes more a problem with their God and less with the prophet!

[7] Verse 7 interrupts this tightly constructed sequence. It is prosaic, lacks the form of the other lines, and makes a dogmatic assertion, rather than advancing the argument. The verse is a didactic proposition reminiscent of the vocabulary and point of view expressed in Jer. 23.18, 22, but its flat claim is more dogmatic than the position of these authentic sayings of Jeremiah. 'His servants the prophets' is an expression which belongs to the vocabulary of the Deuteronomistic historical work (II Kings 17.13, 23; 21.10; 24.2) and to the prose sections of Jeremiah ('my servants the prophets', Jer. 7.25; 26.5; 35.15; 44.4). The verse undertakes to vindicate the authority of the prophet by basing his knowledge on a consistent policy of Yahweh who always discloses his decisions to a prophet before he acts. The theory is very close to the view of prophecy developed in the Deuteronomistic history.[b] As an explanation the sentence is out of order; it pertains to the following verse more closely than the preceding. And one must note that the necessity that revelation precede action binds Yahweh's sovereign freedom to a specific *modus operandi*. The prophet becomes a *sine qua non* of divine action. The theology

---

[a] On the type of traps and snares behind this imagery and the meaning of *paḥ* and *mōqēš*, cf. L. Toombs, *IDB* IV, 687f.; G. R. Driver, *JBL* 74, 1954, 125ff.

[b] Cf. G. von Rad, *Studies in Deuteronomy*, ET (SBT 9), 1953, pp. 78ff.

seems very unlike the thinking of Amos. Probably, the verse belongs to the redactional history of the book of Amos and is the work of Deuteronomic editors who strengthen Amos' original argument with an indisputable theological truth. The true prophet has stood in the divine council where Yahweh's policy is formulated and decreed before it is carried out in history. Because the heavenly counsel (*sōd*) has been revealed to the prophet, his messages are true and to be believed. The role of the prophet as messenger has become an institution of the divine government.

[8] In v. 8 the sequence reaches its climax. The style shifts from hypothetical illustration to statement of fact: 'The lion has roared ||Yahweh has spoken'. Now the cause is named first and is followed by its inevitable consequence, put in rhetorical questions: 'Who is not in awe?||Who will not prophesy?' The cause of Amos' dreadful prophecy of Israel's doom is the speech of Yahweh. No use to protest and resist the prophet as though he could be isolated! Decision about the scandal of Amos' mission is in fact decision about the word of the Lord. Amos cannot make Israel hear and accept his message, but he makes clear for his opponents what it is that they resist and reject. The parallelism between the lion's roar and Yahweh's speech (1.2; Jer. 25.30) is based on an early traditional identification of the growling sound of thunder with the voice (*qōl*) of Yahweh as he is manifested in the thunderstorm theophany. Yahweh utters his voice when he appears against his enemies and at its sound earth trembles and disaster sets in. Amos has heard the *qōl* of Yahweh and been given the knowledge that *Israel* is the foe against whom Yahweh is coming! (Cf. the commentary on 1.2.)

6. OPPRESSION WITHIN BRINGS PLUNDERING FROM WITHOUT: 3.9–11

3 9Call out to the strongholds in Ashdod,a
and to the strongholds in the land of Egypt,
(and say:)b 'Assemble upon the mountains of Samaria
and see the great tumults within her,
the oppressors in her midst.'

a G reads 'Assyria', probably because Ashdod seemed to make an inappropriate pair with Egypt.
b Probably an editorial addition.

¹⁰They do not know to do what is right, [a saying of Yahweh,]ᵃ
they who store up violence and destruction in their strongholds.
¹¹Therefore this is what Lord Yahweh has said:
'An enemy will surroundᵇ the land;
he will bring down your defences,
and your strongholds will be plundered.'

The oracle is addressed to the prominent citizens of Samaria and
announces that what they have done to others will be done to them.
The urban culture which they have built through violence will come
to a violent end. The plunderers shall be plundered. The oracle has
the form of an announcement of judgment with indictment (vv. 9f.)
and announcement of punishment (v. 11). The latter is a divine
saying in first-person style, introduced by a messenger formula ('thus
said Lord Yahweh'), addressing the audience directly ('your defence').
The indictment is spoken by the prophet; the oracular formula ('a
saying of Yahweh') in 10a is an editorial insertion to emphasize the
sentence which it concludes. The basic reproach is stated in v. 10.
Verse 9 opens with plural imperatives. No specific hearers are identified (cf. the opening summons in 3.13). Instead of thinking of a
group of prophets, or heralds of the northern state, or of persons in or
from Ashdod and Egypt (all have been proposed), it is better to take
the imperative as a rhetorical device, meant actually for the ears of
the Israelites in Samaria.

[9] Amos pretends to issue a summons to heralds authorizing them
to carry an invitation to the city-state of Ashdod and the great empire
of Egypt as a highly dramatic and ironic method of commanding the
attention of his listeners. This introduction creates the atmosphere of
preparation for a state visit. Prominent men from these neighbouring
states are to come and see what Samaria is like! The pride of the city's
residents to which Amos refers elsewhere (6.1) would respond to that
prospect. The leaders of Ashdod and Egypt, where the art of violence
and injustice was well developed, will be astounded at what they
observe in Israel's capital. The invitation is to be carried to the
'strongholds' of Ashdod and Egypt. This architectural term is the
theme-word of the saying, appearing three times. 'armōn appears to
have been a name for any building that was higher than the usual
house and contained several stories. It could be constructed so as to
be defensible (Prov. 18.19; Lam. 2.7) and was often part of the

ᵃ Probably an editorial addition.
ᵇ Reading yᵉsōbēb; cf. S.

defence system of a city (Pss. 48.13; 122.7). The king's house or palace could include an *'armōn* as part of its structure (I Kings 16.18; II Kings 15.25); and such buildings also served as residences (Jer. 9.21). These residential strongholds were a particular object of Yahweh's wrath in Amos' prophecy (1.4, 7, 10, 12, 14; 2.2, 5) and are associated with the pride of Jacob in 6.8. Such buildings obviously would be the residences of the richer and ruling class in a city. They are manifestations of the development of an urban culture based on an economy of trade and capital, the sign of the development within the populace of a class system which did not exist in earlier Israelite society. These are people whose luxurious life Amos describes in such oracles as 6.4ff.; 4.1–3. Since the invitation to Samaria is sent to the residents of strongholds in Philistia and Egypt, the upper classes from these foreign states are summoned *to Israel* to learn that these Israelites have outstripped them in the practices of their own culture. Like a great crowd of witnesses they are to assemble on the mountains around Samaria and see for themselves. The plural 'mountains of Samaria' refers to the region lying around the capital, perhaps the state itself. Elsewhere Amos uses 'mountain of Samaria' for the city itself (4.1; 6.1).

The real purpose of this dramatic setting is reached with Amos' description of what the visitors would see in Samaria—a city full of *tumult* instead of order, *oppression* instead of justice. In the preserved oracles of Amos there is a concentration on two cities in Israel. Bethel, the site of the most important state shrine, must have been the locale of his oracles against the cult; Samaria as the seat of the royal government was the setting for some of his oracles against the social order. He inveighed against the selfish, indulgent life of its women (4.1), the arrogant pride of its leading citizens (6.1); he knew it to be a doomed city (3.12). Its courts were corrupt (5.7, 10–12) and its commerce was an open form of extortion 8.4–6). What Amos describes in detail in these other oracles is here comprehended under the general terms of 'disorder and oppression'. And what was done in Samaria undoubtedly set the style for the lesser cities of the kingdom. Samaria was a special case, because the tune was called there and sung throughout the land.

[10] The prominent citizens of Samaria 'do not know how to do what is right (*nᵉkōḥā*)'. To specify what is missing in their conduct Amos uses a normative term by which actions can be measured. He transcends his usual procedure of simply stipulating deeds with the assumption that their culpability is self-evident and puts a criterion

over against their life. *Nᵉkōḥā* means 'what is straightforward, honest, right' in contrast to what is deceptive and false (Isa. 30.10). The term belongs to Israel's general vocabulary of words for 'right/good' as opposed to 'evil/bad', so it is of little assistance in determining what tradition of values Amos brings to bear on Israel's conduct. The word is used in Isa. 59.14 as a synonym of 'justice', 'righteousness', and 'faithfulness' in a sequence dealing with the theme 'Justice is far from us'; in II Sam. 15.3 along with 'good' as synonym, it applies to a legal appeal; and in Prov. 24.26 the word is used in a Wisdom saying concerning conduct in legal affairs. Its other occurrences do not offer a more precise orientation for its meaning (Prov. 8.9; Isa. 26.10; 57.2). In Amos' mouth the term signifies what was acceptable practice in court and trade. The norms which ought to govern the affairs of men in Israel under Yahweh had dropped out of sight and consciousness among Samaria's leading citizens. The older ways of social life in Israel had been displaced by Canaanite social custom. Amos is no ascetic in his attack on the residence-towers, nor simply an Israelite chauvinist attacking foreign ways. What is alone of moment to him is the departure from an order of society which was formed according to Yahweh's will and which maintained every Israelite one with the other in a system of mutual responsibility. In Samaria the strongholds had become treasuries in which the powerful stored away the profits of 'violence' against others and of 'destruction' of rightful custom (cf. violence and destruction in Jer. 6.7; 20.8; 48.3; Ezek. 45.9; Hab. 1.3. This series of texts which combine the words indicate that the two synonyms became a single expression in the prophetic vocabulary for the collapse of normal conditions).

[11] 'Therefore this is what Lord Yahweh has said' introduces the decision of Yahweh against Samaria. 'Therefore' binds the city's deeds to its doom. What Samaria's leading citizens perpetrated within their own city will be visited upon them within the international society. The punishment is described by a little narrative of defeat. A foe will encompass the land, bring down the city's defence system, and plunder its residences. The three measures of the line sketch in terse staccato sentences the stages of a military campaign: invasion, siege, and looting. The foe is not identified. It is generally assumed that the Assyrians are in mind. But Amos never mentions Assyria in his preserved speeches. Were the hearers to assume that Egypt and Ashdod who come to inspect would remain to conquer a city whose internal condition portrayed a fatal weakness? In any case, the foe is

the instrument of Yahweh's announced decision, the fulfilment of his word. It is Yahweh who makes himself the foe of his people Israel in judgment on the enmity of Israelite against Israelite. What matters in the prophetic view is that history transacts the judgment of Yahweh who rules over all nations (9.7f.).

7. YOUR DELIVERANCE WILL PROVE THE DEATH OF YOU: 3.12

3 ¹²This is what Yahweh has said,
    'Just as the shepherd rescues from the lion's mouth
       two legs or a piece of ear,
    so shall the people of Israel be rescued—
    the ones who loll in Samaria
  ^aon splendid beds
    and couches from Damascus.^a'

[12] Verse 12 is a *māšāl*, a saying which illuminates one thing by comparing it to another whose character is generally known. The formulation of comparisons is a feature of Amos' style. Frequently he takes images from everyday life to make his message vivid and clear. The trembling of the earth in the day of punishment will be like the reverberations made by the overloaded wagon at harvest time (2.13). Justice and righteousness should be as constant in Israel as the brook that never goes dry (5.24). The conduct of Israel is like those who ride horses on cliffs, or plough the sea with an ox, or turn the good into poison (6.12; 5.7; cf. also 9.9). The style is that of popular proverbs; such comparisons are scattered throughout the sayings in Proverbs (e.g. Prov. 25.25f.; 26.21; 5.4). But a messenger formula introduces the comparison as a divine saying. The message of Yahweh is clothed in the style of Amos. The voice is the voice of the shepherd from Tekoa, but the word is the word of the Lord.

The imagery of the comparison is drawn from the work of the shepherd who, in pasturing his flocks across wide, uninhabited hill country, had frequently to face the raids of marauding wild beasts

^{a-a} So *KB*, reading *pᵉ'at* as *pē'ā* III from *yph* (p. 750), revocalizing *dammešek* and putting it after *'ereś* (p. 214). The text is corrupt. H. Gese finds the names of parts of a bed of Mesopotamian type in *pē'ā* ('footpiece') and *dᵉmešek* ('headpiece'; corrupted from *'āmešet*), and points to Accadian cognates ('Kleine Beiträge zum Verständnis des Amosbuches', *VT* 12, 1962, pp. 427ff.).

(e.g. I Sam. 17.34f.). According to the customary legal tradition of Israel and the surrounding cultures, a shepherd had to give evidence to the owner of the sheep, when any of the flock had been captured, by producing what was left of the carcass. He had not stolen or sold it, for here was proof! In the collection of legal stipulations in Ex. 21—23, there is a case-law which deals with the responsibility of a shepherd or herder to the owner (22.10–13). 22.13 says: 'If it [one of the sheep or cattle] is torn by beasts, let him bring it as evidence; he shall not make restitution for what has been torn.' A similar law appears in the Code of Hammurabi: 'If a visitation of god has occurred in a sheepfold, or a lion has made a kill, the shepherd shall prove himself innocent in the presence of the god, but the owner of the sheepfold shall receive from him the animal stricken in the fold.'[a] This legal custom lies behind the saying. Israel's deliverance will be like that of the poor beast whose remains only serve as evidence of destruction. The rescue of evidence proves that rescue came too late— surely an ironic thrust! The saying does not promise the survival of a remnant, however small and wounded, after the coming judgment, but rather shatters any hope of rescue. The oracle may well have been given in answer to those who disputed the doom prophesied by Amos in the name of the deliverance which Israel expected from Yahweh as a matter of course. 'Is it deliverance you expect, O Israel! Well, here is what your "deliverance" will be like—the rescue of a corpse's shredded remains, a deliverance that means nothing to you!' For other instances of the dispute-saying in Amos, cf. 3.2, 3–8.

The prophetic *māšāl* ends with a participial sentence which identifies the Israelites concerned as the residents of Samaria who enjoy the luxurious life of the privileged rich. Verse 13 opens with plural imperatives addressed to unidentified listeners; some (Weiser, Robinson, and Maag) attach this conclusion to v. 13 to furnish addresses for these imperatives. But the result is a saying opening with a participle, a forced order; the imperatives of v. 13 are similar to the beginning of vv. 9–11 where there is also an imperative without an identified addressee. The description is similar to 6.4a; the line is an expansion of the *māšāl*-form to specify the group at whom this word is levelled. It was probably from the confident upper class of Samaria that the 'theological' rejoinder came (6.1–3); their irresponsible luxury was especially odious to Amos because their heedless affluence was the rejection of their responsibility to Yahweh (6.4–8). They could loll

[a] Law 266, *ANET*, p. 177a.

on their couches and dismiss Amos' message with a prattle about a theology of redemption. But the divine shepherd (Ps. 23), on whose protection they presumed, now only wanted the evidence of their death. On the portrayal of Yahweh's judgment as the work of a savage lion, cf. Hos. 13.7f.; 5.14.

8. THE FALL OF THE HOUSE OF JACOB: 3.13–15

3 ^{13}'Hear and testify against the house of Jacob,'
    a saying of Lord Yahweh, God of hosts,[a]
  ^{14}'that on the day when I punish Israel for his crimes,
    I will punish the altars of Bethel.
The horns of the altar shall be cut off
    and fall to the earth.
  ^{15}I will smite the winter-house
    along with the summer-house.
The houses of ivory shall perish,
    and the great houses come to an end,'
    a saying of Yahweh.

The messenger formula in vv. 13, 15 and the first-person style of the entire passage mark it as a divine saying. Yahweh himself issues the summons to hear as part of his word. The message proper (vv. 14–15) contains only an announcement of punishment describing the action of Yahweh. There is no preceding indictment to establish the basis for Yahweh's action.[b] However, an indictment-motif does appear within 14a ('when I visit the crimes of Israel upon him . . .').

[13] Who are the unidentified addressees of this summons from Yahweh to serve as witnesses against the house of Jacob? Not a company of prophets; Amos always appears alone, and the saying is not a private message from God to prophet. Hardly the Israelites, or any group of them, since the witnesses are to testify to the verdict announced against Israel. The summons to serve as witness is more likely a rhetorical device to provoke the attention of an audience (cf. the imperative in 3.9). By this device the atmosphere of legal proceedings is created. Witnesses are being constituted. Their role is not

    [a] This full title ('Lord Yahweh God of hosts') appears nowhere else in the book; 'God of hosts' is probably an expansion of the original.
    [b] For a discussion of this form and the proposal that the saying of a single element is a development from the two-element form, see C. Westermann, *Basic Forms of Prophetic Speech*, 1967, pp. 128f.

to bring evidence, but to hear and be the guarantors of the court's verdict. Israel is called the *bēt yaʿaqōb*, that is, the household, the family of Jacob. Amos uses the patriarchal names of Jacob (6.8; 7.2, 5; 8.7), Isaac (7.9, 16) and Joseph (5.15) to put Israel in the role in which they stand as the recipients of his message from Yahweh. Before him these Israelites are less the kingdom of Jeroboam II, and more a corporate person whose real identity was established in their father's relation to Yahweh in the early times of clan life. As Jeroboam's nation they worship at Bethel and build houses of royal magnificence in Samaria; but as Jacob's family they have to do with the sovereign will of Yahweh.

[14] Verse 14a is a temporal clause designating the time when the action of Yahweh described in 14b–15 will occur: 'the day when I punish Israel for his crimes'. The style assumes it is a matter of course that Yahweh punishes Israel's rebellions and that there will be 'a day' for the execution of this judgment. Behind this phrase lies the concept and expectation of 'the day of Yahweh' (see the commentary on 5.18–20). It is a fundamental element of Amos' theology, a basic element of his understanding of Yahweh's relation to the history of man in general and to Israel in particular. Time and history articulate the role of Yahweh as the divine judge who punishes *pešaʿ*. The word has a very specific flavour; its orientation is political and connotes transgression against the will of established authority (see commentary on 1.3–2.16). Yahweh is the divine suzerain who punishes his refractory subjects for crimes against his sovereignty. That Yahweh punishes Israel for sin is a conviction in every earlier tradition preserved in the Old Testament—Yahwist, Elohist, older Wisdom, and the covenant tradition. Therein Amos says nothing particularly new. But he stands forth as messenger to announce that the day is near for this transaction and how this action will occur.

The judgment of Yahweh will strike two foci—temple and mansion. The two furnish a virtual paradigm of Amos' conception of Yahweh's incursion against Israel. The temple is the centre of religious life; the mansions are the incarnation of Israel's social economy of luxury built on exploitation. Indeed the entire saying turns on the catchword 'house': house of Jacob, house of God (Beth-El), winter house and summer house, ivory house and great house. What Israel had built stands as the manifestation of the nation's rebellions. The devastation of these houses is the actualization of Yahweh's 'no' to Israel's cult and culture. Bethel was the pre-eminent religious centre of Israel in the time of Jeroboam II (7.10–13). It draws the prophet's denunciation in a special way (cf. the commentary on 4.4f.; 5.5f., 21–24; 7.9; 9.1–4). Because the very worship carried on at Bethel was at root a rebellion against Yahweh (4.4) the central focus of its cult, the altar (9.1; 2.8) was doomed. The 'horns of the altar' were little stakes or pillars rising at each corner above the flat surface of the altar's top, and the holiness of the altar was connected with them in a special way.[a] A fugitive might gain sanctuary and enjoy the protection of the deity by coming to the shrine and 'laying hold of the altar horns' (I Kings 1.50; 2.28). This sacral security of last resort would be removed; Israel would find no sanctuary from the enemy who was coming against her. The altar would be deconsecrated, and thereby the cult brought to an end.

[15] Not only 'the house of God' (*Beth-El*) but also the houses of men were doomed. Kings built 'houses' whose architecture was adapted to the two climatic seasons of the Palestinian year (Jer. 36.22). 'Ivory houses' were mansions decorated with ivory inlay.[b] Ahab built such a house in Samaria; all the Old Testament references are to a royal residence (I Kings 22.39; Ps. 45.8). It is possible that with these terms Amos refers only to royal buildings. But the greater probability, in view of the collectives (winter and summer house) and the plurals, is that the prosperity of the rich had allowed them to fulfil their pride by constructing residences like those which earlier only kings could build (cf. 6.11). Note Amos' description of the indulgent life of the privileged in 4.1; 5.10f.; 6.1–6, and his reiteration that such luxury was the profit of unrighteous oppression. The judgment which Amos announces is no ascetic primitivism, growing out of simple hostility against a commercial culture and its affluence. The houses were built, beam by beam and stone by stone, from a store of crimes.

In this description of punishment, Yahweh is the subject of the verbs. No historical instrument is mentioned; Yahweh will act directly; he will 'smite'. The same act of 'smiting the houses' is put indirectly in 6.4; there Yahweh commands and the houses are smitten. What kind of catastrophe is in mind must remain uncertain. In 9.11 the divine command to smite seems to result in an earthquake (cf. 1.1). Whether earthquake or destruction by enemy (3.11),

[a] Cf. R. de Vaux, *Ancient Israel*, 1961, p. 414.
[b] Cf. the illustrations in *IDB* III, pp. 774f., and the expression 'beds of ivory' in 6.4.

the calamity will be the work of Yahweh on the day he has already set to hold Israel responsible for its rebellions.

9. THE LADIES OF SAMARIA: 4.1-3

4 ¹Hear[a] this word
    you Bashan-cows on mount Samaria,
  who oppress the needy, crush the poor,
    saying to their[a] lords, 'Bring that we may drink.'
²Lord Yahweh has sworn by his holiness:
  'Behold! Days come upon you[a]
    when they will remove you[a] with hooks (?),
    the last one of you with fish hooks (?).
³Through breaches you shall go out, one after another,
    and you will be cast out[b] on Hermon,[c]'
  a saying of Yahweh.

The luxury and debauchery of urban affluence in Israel was a scandalous offence to the God for whom Amos spoke (6.4-7; 3.10, 15). The offence lay not just in its stark contrast to the condition of the poor, but in the fact that the affluence was built on the suffering of the needy. In this saying Amos uncovers the role of Samaria's women in the social dynamics of the state's economic aristocracy. The saying is composed of accusation (v. 1) and announcement of Yahweh's punishment (vv. 2f.). After the introductory summons to hear the message of a herald (cf. 3.1; 5.1; 8.4) the addressees are named and their guilty conduct described. The announcement of judgment is formulated as an oath which Yahweh has sworn (cf. 6.8; 8.7). The theme and formal structure of 8.4-8 is similar. The opening imperative is masculine (cf. *GK* 145 p) and in the following lines pronouns revert to masculine gender three times (cf. note *a*) while the vocative and the rest of the forms in the text are feminine. This mixed gender led to an early opinion (Targum, followed by Jerome) that the addressees were the leaders of Israel and 'their lords' were pagan gods. Uncertainty about the identity of the addressees may have produced the mixed pronouns in the text tradition. Isaiah's

---

  a The saying is addressed to the Bashan-cows (fem.), but this imperative and some of the other words are masculine.
  b Reading a Hophal with G's passive.
  c The text is corrupt; see the comment.

scathing attack on Jerusalem's fashionable females (Isa. 3.16–4.1) is a companion piece to this saying. The streets or markets of the capital city are the likely setting for the oracle.

[1] Amos calls the wives of the rich 'Bashan-cows'. The epithet was not in itself an insult. Bashan in Transjordan was noted for rich forests and pastures, and particularly for fine cattle (Deut. 32.14; Ps. 22.12; Ezek. 39.18); Bashan was a hallmark of quality. Nor in the idiom of ancient eastern flattery would women be offended at being called 'cows'; one has only to remember the terms used for compliments in the Song of Songs. The Bashan-cows are the women of quality in Samaria, the pampered darlings of society in Israel's royalist culture. On behalf of Israel's God Amos brings the same charge against them that is made against the officials and those who control Israel's wealth: ruthless exploitation of the helpless poor (cf. 2.6f.; 5.11; 8.4). Not that the women are the direct perpetrators of oppression! Rather, they make their lords (husbands) the instruments of their own desire, ruling the society of Israel from behind the scenes with sweet petulant nagging for wealth to support their indolent dalliance. The power behind the corrupt courts (5.10f.) and odious business practices (8.4ff.) is theirs. On the normative basis for the critique, see the comment on 2.6f. and 5.11.

[2a] The use of the oath as a way to announce the verdict upon the women of Samaria shows the vehemence of Yahweh's reaction. Their punishment is certain, for Yahweh has sworn 'by his holiness'. 'Holiness' is the dynamic, awesome, threatening power of the divine; the oath in 6.8, which Yahweh takes 'upon himself', bears the same meaning. God has committed the entire reality of his personal being to his decision to judge. 'Behold! Days are coming . . .' is one of the formulae of prophetic 'eschatology' (8.11; 9.13; I Sam. 2.31; II Kings 20.17; Jer. 7.32 and 12 other times in Jer.) used to designate the imminent inbreaking time when Yahweh would effect his great setting-right, whether for woe (8.11) or weal (9.13). In Amos 'the coming days' are the 'day of Yahweh' (5.18) in which the one true Lord will be the terrible circumstance exclusively determining Israel's experience.

[2b–3] The meaning of 2b and 3 is not clear. The gruesome doom prepared for Samaria's privileged darlings is hidden by obscure words and an uncertain text. The two Hebrew feminine nouns translated by 'hooks' do not appear elsewhere in the Old Testament with this meaning. The first (ṣinnōt) usually means 'shields'; it occurs in a masculine form (Prov. 22.5; Job 5.5) which probably means 'thorns'. The second (*sīrōt*) means 'pots', and has a masculine form which also means 'thorns' (Isa. 34.13; Hos. 2.6). G. R. Driver has proposed the translation: 'They will lift you high on shields, and your children in fish baskets.'[a] Most commentators assume that both nouns refer by extension from the meaning 'thorns' to some sort of hook used either to drag away corpses or to fasten captives in line for march. The last word in v. 3 is a locative and appears to be the name of a place, but MT's *harmōn* is unknown, and the variants in the versions look like guesses. Most emend to read 'Hermon', which if correct would give an ironic twist to the line, because Mount Hermon is in the Bashan range. The Bashan-cows will end up as carrion(?) on the mountains of Bashan! Do these verses portray captives led Assyrian style in a roped single file out through the breached wall of their city to be carried away into exile? Or is the picture one of bodies being dragged through the ruins to be cast in some place for corpses? All proposals involve unsolved problems. One thing is clear. The women whose present is enriched by the suffering of the poor have a future more terrible than the agony of the needy.

10. WORSHIP THAT IS REBELLION: 4.4–5

4 ⁴'Come to Bethel and rebel
    at Gilgal multiply rebellion!
  Bring each morning your sacrifices,
    on each third day your tithes.
  ⁵Burn[b] a thankoffering of leaven,
    proclaim freewill offerings, announce them;
  for so you love it,
    you Israelites!'
  a saying of Lord Yahweh.

Biting sarcasm and an abrupt separation between Yahweh's will and Israel's worship are characteristic of all Amos' words concerning Israel's cult (cf. 5.4f., 21–24, 25–27). The paradoxical irony of this word is more shocking than any. 'Come to the sanctuaries—and sin! Sacrifice and sacrifice—though it is your own pleasure, not Yahweh's,

---

[a] In a letter cited by Robinson in HAT *ad loc.*
[b] The imperative in MT is singular, where a plural is expected.

that is served!' The four lines are formulated in the style of priestly exhortation. Speaking in divine first person 'the priest' addresses the people with plural imperatives, setting forth instructions concerning the cultic ritual to be performed at the shrines (vv. 4, 5a).[a] Amos usurps the role of the priest and exhorts the congregation in a shocking parody of ecclesiastical language that must have sounded like irreverent blasphemy. The prophetic intrusion irrupts with the second imperative, in which an expected ritual term is displaced by 'rebel'! At the conclusion some declaratory formula spoken as the basis for the summons to worship would be expected: 'for I am Yahweh your God' or a reference to Yahweh's will or pleasure in the cult. But instead Israel's own pleasure in the cult is thrust into the place of the divine. The saying is an exhortation that contradicts every instruction the congregation was accustomed to hearing; it says nothing positive, only tears at comfortable customs, and leaves confusion in their place. It must have been spoken during a festival assembly at Bethel.

[4] When Amos took up the chanting rhythmic summons 'Come ye to Bethel . . .,' the pilgrims would have thought he was one of the cultic functionaries playing his usual role! (Cf. the similar Hos. 4.15.) But hardly had the summons begun than it struck a shocking dissonance: 'Come to Bethel!—and rebel!' The Israelites who had come for at-one-ment, to establish peace with their God by sacrificial communion meals and to receive his blessing to secure their welfare, were told that their piety was in fact the very opposite—an offence against, a breach with (*peša'*) the God whose community they sought.

Bethel was one of the two state shrines established by Jeroboam I as an alternative to Jerusalem (I Kings 12.28–32). A site of ancient sanctity, it was taken over from the Canaanites as a shrine for the cult of the God of the fathers (Gen. 28.10ff.) and later played a role in the religious life of the tribal league (Judg. 20.18). So it was a religious centre which Israelites had been visiting from time immemorial and it enjoyed in the middle of the eighth century the status attributed to it by its priest Amaziah of being the 'king's sanctuary' and a 'temple of the kingdom' (Amos 7.13). The Gilgal of this text and 5.6 is the shrine 'on the east border of Jericho' (Josh. 4.19), probably the mound called *Khirbet Mafjar*. Gilgal was a sacred site with an important role in Israel's traditions about her entry into the land (Josh. 4–5); Saul was anointed king there (I Sam. 11.14–

[a] Cf. J. Begrich, 'Die priesterliche Tora', *Gesammelte Studien zum Alten Testament* (Th. Büch. 21), 1964, pp. 243ff.

15). In the eighth century it continued to be used for pilgrimages and offering sacrifice (Amos 5.5; Hos. 12.11). Clearly, one could not name two more hallowed and venerable places for the worship of the Lord![a]

The list of rituals to which Amos invites his hearers sounds like a catalogue of normal cultic acts which would have been performed in the cult of that time. 'Sacrifice' (*zebaḥ*) is a general term for any offering in which an animal was slain, though here it probably refers to the 'sacrifice of peace offering' (Lev. 3; 7.11ff.) in which part of the offering is eaten as a sacred meal of communion with the deity. The 'tithe', which had an ancient connection with the shrine of Bethel (Gen. 28.22), was a tenth of the annual yield of the land which the Israelite was to bring to a sanctuary and use in the festival meals before the Lord (Deut. 14.22-29). 4b may simply describe what was current practice; the *zebaḥ* was offered on the morning of the pilgrim's first day at the shrine and his annual tithe presented on the third day. 'Multiply rebellion' in 4a may, however, govern the sense of 4b; then the time expressions are distributives: 'Sacrifice every day; give tithes every third day' (so RSV). **[5]** The thank-offering (*tōdā*) was not a different kind of sacrifice, but the use of the 'sacrifice of peace offering' as a ritual of offering praise to God for blessings, answers to prayers (Lev. 7.12-15; 22.29-30). In later Israelite practice leavened bread could be used in sacred meals except at Passover, but was forbidden as an offering by fire (Lev. 2.11; 7.11-14). The technical expression for 'offer' here is *qṭr* which means 'to burn and send up in smoke'. It is, however, unlikely that Amos is sarcastically charging Israelites with a breach of ritual regulations. The later prohibition of burning leaven was probably not in force at Bethel; the other items named belonged to normal ritual procedures. The 'free will offering' was a voluntary sacrifice which the worshipper made on his own initiative to express devotion; it too was a specialized use of the sacrifice of peace offering (Lev. 7.16-17; 22.18-23).

'For so you Israelites love it' takes up again the shocking dissonance of the opening invitation to come and rebel. In the usual priestly *tōrā* the series of imperatives would be followed by a 'for' clause, basing the proclaimed ritual in the person and will of the deity. The shift is in effect a charge that the sacrificial cult has nothing to do with Yahweh. It is not the Lord, but the self of Israel which is the ground of their worship. The people themselves have displaced the

[a] On Bethel and Gilgal see H.-J. Kraus, *Worship in Israel*, ET, 1966, pp. 146-65.

Lord as the central reality of cult. However pious and proper all their religious acts, the sacrifices and offerings are no submission of life to the Lord, but merely an expression of their own love of religiosity. The cult of Bethel and Gilgal has become a breaking with Yahweh because it evades rather than enforces the Lord's rule over the nation. It flourishes on an affluence gained by violence against the poor (2.8); it produces a passion for neither justice nor righteousness (5.24).

11. THE BROKEN QUEST: 4.6–13

4 ⁶ᵃI myself gave you
    empty mouths in all your cities,
    and lack of food in all your places;
but you did not return to me,'
    a saying of Yahweh.
⁷ᵇI withheld the rain from you
    while it was yet three months till harvest.
I would send rain on one city,
    but on another city I would not send rain.
One field would get rain,
    and a field that got no rainᶜ would dry up.
⁸Several cities would stagger to another city to drink water and
    not be satisfied;
but you did not return to me,'
    a saying of Yahweh.
⁹'I smote you with withering and blight;
    I ravagedᵈ your gardens and vineyards;
    the locust ate your fig and olive trees;
but you did not return to me,'
    a saying of Yahweh.
¹⁰'I sent on you a pestilence (in the manner of Egypt);ᵉ
    I slew your young men with the sword (along with capture of
        your horses);ᶠ
    I let the stench of your camps rise in your nostrils,ᵍ
but you did not return to me,'
    a saying of Yahweh.

ᵃ Omitting *weḡam*, an editorial transition to connect vv. 6ff. with what precedes.
ᵇ Omitting *weḡam 'ānōḵī*, an insertion to make v. 7 similar to v. 6.
ᶜ MT's verb is Hiphil and lacks a sensible subject; read Niphal and omit *'āleyhā*. G reads 'the field upon which I sent no rain'.
ᵈ Emending MT's infinitive (*harbōt*) to *heḥᵉrabtī*.
ᵉ A gloss identifying the pestilence more precisely; cf. Deut. 28.60; 7.15.
ᶠ An addition to fill out the picture of military disaster.
ᵍ Taking the *waw* in *ūbeᵉappᵉkem* as an emphatic *waw*.

11'I overthrew some of you as Elohim overthrew
   Sodom and Gomorrah;
   you were like a log snatched from burning;
   but you did not return to me,'
   a saying of Yahweh.
12'Therefore, thus I will deal with you, O Israel!
   Because I will do this to you,
   prepare to meet your God, O Israel.'
13For behold! he who forms thunder[a] and creates storm,
   and declares his works[b] to man;
   who turns the dawn to darkness,
   and treads on earth's high places—
   Yahweh, God of hosts, is his name.

This unusually long composition unfolds an amazing story. It contains a narrative of the deeds of Yahweh who sought the response of his people by bringing all manner of catastrophe upon them. But all in vain. There has been no answering repentance from Israel. The quest having failed, things are at an impasse which Yahweh will break. He himself will come to the people who refuse to return to him. Let them make ready to encounter the Lord of Hosts whose might is manifest in the storm! The composition contains three movements: the recitation of Yahweh's acts against Israel in the past (vv. 6–11), the declaration of what Yahweh is about to do (v. 12), and a doxology of praise to Yahweh, the God of Hosts (v. 13). The first movement contains five distinct divine sayings, each concluded by repetition of the refrain 'But you did not return to me,' and the formula 'a saying of Yahweh' (vv. 6, 7f., 9, 10, 11). Each saying has its own theme: hunger or famine in v. 6, thirst or drought in vv. 7f., loss of crops in v. 9, disaster in warfare in v. 10, and a calamity defined by comparison to Sodom and Gomorrah in v. 11. The oracles are all formulated in a similar way. Each opens with a perfect verb in the first person reporting some punishing act of Yahweh. Except for the second (vv. 7f.), all are constructed of three stichoi plus the refrain and concluding formula. The second is expanded by situational descriptions of drought where rain comes in one part of the country but fails in another. It is difficult to say whether the expansion is secondary; v. 8 is the most suspicious because of its prosaic style. The phenomena described in v. 7 are the kind of things which a shepherd-

---

[a] Reading *hāraʿam* for MT's 'mountains' (*hārīm*); cf. G. The description in v. 13 portrays Yahweh's theophany in the thunderstorm.
[b] Reading *maʿaśēhū* for MT's *mā-śēḥō*.

farmer would be likely to notice and could well derive from Amos'
own life in the country. It is possible that he simply was not able to
incorporate all that he wanted to say on the theme of drought into
three stichoi. After all, the units formed by the refrain appear to
have been his own creation and he was neither guided nor bound by
any formal law in this respect.[a]

There is no perceptible development in the sections, no heighten-
ing of the disasters' intensity. Each is terrible in its own right, no
worse than the previous one. The sequence gains its effect from
repetition, the recollection of one disaster after another as though
the narrative meant to exhaust the catalogue of human misery. The
sequence is not the work of a collector assembling units of similar
form. The individual sections have no point as isolated sayings. The
art of repetition is a feature of Amos' own style and is to be seen also
in the oracles against the nations (1.3–2.16) and the vision narratives
(7.1–9; 8.1–3). The refrain interprets the disasters as Yahweh's quest
for Israel's return to him and rings like a lament in its reiteration of
the failure of the quest. Only when the sequence is heard as a whole
does the repetition create the tension which prepares for the climax
that comes in v. 12. 'Therefore' breaks the tension and leads the
narrative into the future. The strategy of punishment has misfired so
often that it will be broken off and replaced by a different kind of
history. The narrative in vv. 6–11 then functions as an indictment
against Israel and serves as a basis for the announcement of judgment
in v. 12. The doxology in v. 13 is a hymnic fragment which rounds
off the whole with a portrayal of the power of the God whose terrible
greatness is inescapable.

[6–11] The catalogue of calamity is based upon episodes of disaster
through which Israel had passed. The validity of citing these events
as deeds of Yahweh rested, first of all, upon their actuality in the
experience of the audience. By their nature nothing can be said about
them as historical occurrences except that they all represent the type
of misfortune which happened from time to time in Syria-Palestine.
Famine, drought, crop-failure, war, contagious disease, natural
calamity, all punctuate the story of peoples in that region. The Old
Testament records recurrent famines when a shortage of food threat-
ened the population. Such famines were often caused or accompanied by drought. A shortage of rain in the late winter and spring

[a] See the formally exact reconstruction by H. Reventlow, *Das Amt des Propheten
bei Amos* (FRLANT 80), 1962, pp. 75ff.

was terrible enough in itself in a land where water has to be stored in cisterns during that time for the long dry season. The phenomenon of partial drought, when rain fails only one region in a land, is not uncommon. When the dry blasting sirocco-wind out of the Arabian desert blew too long during the growing season, the crop would yellow and wither (Hag. 2.17; I Kings 8.37; Deut. 28.22). The classic description of the ravaging locust swarm is given in Joel 1. Recurrent war brought suffering and death. During its course populations were crowded into walled cities and assembled in camps; contagious disease was more likely to break out and spread. The catastrophic overthrow of a part of the population (v. 11) leaving only a fraction of those concerned could be a reference to an earthquake, or to conflagration in a city. The raw material for Amos' narrative certainly lay at hand in the experience of a people for whom life was often nasty, brutish, and short. One need not assume that these misfortunes were either contiguous or contemporary. The audience would remember such calamities in their own time or in the days of their fathers.

The striking feature of the narrative is its presentation as a Yahweh-history. The God of Israel speaks in first-person style and proclaims these disasters as his own deeds in the past. Amos uncovers and articulates a dimension of Yahweh's dealing with Israel which stands in stark contrast to the deeds of the classical salvation-history which was proclaimed in the cult and heard as a message of salvation. The proclamation of the Exodus, the leading through the Wilderness and the Conquest was heard as a promise of protection and benevolence. But Amos' history spoke of the very opposite of security and blessing. His oracular narrative takes the separate sporadic hardships of Israel's life in Canaan and makes them coalesce into a continuous cohesive record in which Yahweh's personal dealings with Israel are disclosed. And it is a history with a rationale. Its purpose is insistently stated in the refrain which interprets the disasters as Yahweh's quest for Israel's return to him. The cogency of reciting this narrative as a record of Israel's failure to respond to Yahweh presupposes that Amos had a basis for recognizing the blows as the personal overtures of Yahweh, and that the people should have recognized them as such and responded.

The context in which these disasters could possess such significance is the covenant tradition. These hostile acts of Yahweh were in fact the implementation of curses for breach of covenant obligations. Lists of curses had a fixed place within the treaty form used to organize international relations in the ancient Near East; they functioned as divine sanctions against a possible breach of the treaty.[a] With Israel's use of the treaty-form as a way of thinking about the covenant with Yahweh, the curses acquired theological gravity and meaning. Leviticus 26 and Deuteronomy 28 contain long, detailed descriptions of the curses which Yahweh would enact against Israel in case of disloyalty, and there are convincing connections between the themes and motifs of those compositions and the formulations of Amos. Compare v. 8 and Lev. 26.26; v. 9 and Deut. 28.22; v. 10 and Lev. 26.25. Famine, pestilence, and sword are the basic categories for the covenant curses. Amos' first three oracles fall with the rubric of famine (hunger, drought, crop-failure); pestilence and sword appear in v. 10.[b] The catastrophe like that which befell Sodom and Gomorrah is not included in the preserved lists of covenant curses. But its repeated occurrence in the Old Testament, often as part of a malediction, shows that it belonged to a traditional reservoir of curses (Deut. 29.3; Isa. 1.9 [cf. BH]; Jer. 20.16; 49.17f.; 50.39f.; Zeph. 2.9). Of course there is no literary dependence of Amos on the later compositions preserved in Deut. 28 and Lev. 26. All three simply work from a basic conception of the place of the curse in Yahweh's relation to Israel and draw freely on the general reservoir of traditional curses to develop their descriptions of Yahweh's sanctions against unfaithfulness. Indeed, this tradition of covenant-curses furnished many motifs for most of the classical prophets when they formulate announcements of Yahweh's punishment.[c] Amos' narrative of disasters is a rather free construction using some traditional curses and depending on the general tradition that Yahweh acts in typical ways to punish those who are disloyal to the covenant.

In using the curse tradition to tell a narrative Amos makes a distinctive and new use of the curse materials. The treaty curses of the ancient Near East and those collected in the Pentateuch are oriented toward the future. They warn the participants in the covenant of the measures that will be taken against them by suzerain or deity for disloyalty. Amos sees in the sporadic disasters which have befallen Israel the actualization of the divine curses. Measures have

[a] See, among others, G. Mendenhall, *Law and Covenant in the Ancient Near East*, 1955, pp. 31ff.; K. Baltzer, *Das Bundesformular*, 1960, pp. 24ff.
[b] See the detailed analysis of correspondences in H. Reventlow, *op. cit.*, pp. 82ff.
[c] See D. R. Hillers, *Treaty Curses and the Old Testament Prophets* (BO 16), 1964.

already been taken against Israel's disobedience, and yet Israel goes its accustomed way unchanged. In the record of disasters and the perseverance of Israel in disobedience, the prophet has a kind of empirical material before him. In dealing with this material, he works from the dominant presupposition of the revelations given him in his visions. The time of Yahweh's forbearance is over (7.1–6); the end has been decreed for Israel (7.7–9; 8.1–3). In the light of this shift in Yahweh's conduct he can interpret the misfortunes of the past as Yahweh's attempt to bring Israel back to him. The enforcement of the curses was not mere punishment, but the quest of Israel's God for the return of his people. The repeated refrain reiterates this theme *and* discloses the failure of the curses to hold Israel in the covenant.

The failure of requisite repentance in Israel does not imply the absence of any religious response at all, a bland ignoring of the disasters as Yahweh's work. In Amos' time Israel's cult was flourishing and popular; and it was a worship offered to Yahweh (4.4f.; 5.21–24). Nor would religious cultic reaction have been wanting in the past; in time of famine and disaster there would have been private and public lamentation, prayers, and sacrifices to propitiate their god. But Amos' message condemned this cult precisely because it did not represent 'a returning to me'. It failed to express and to realize the stipulations of the covenant which the curses were intended to enforce. To 'seek Bethel' was not to 'seek Yahweh' (5.4f.; cf. the parallel of 'seek' and 'return to Yahweh' in Isa. 9.13). Amos sets the person of the deity in place of the sanctuary as the required object of the religious act. As concepts to connote the significance and reality of 'returning' he speaks of 'good', 'justice', 'righteousness' (cf. the comment on 5.14f., 24). 'To return to me' means something like 'to resume a past relationship in which I as revealed will am truly sovereign partner'.

[12] 'Therefore' normally introduces the announcement of punishment and the following sentence seems to prepare for Yahweh's declaration of some final action against his unresponsive people: '*thus* will I deal with you'. 'Thus' points forward and 'this' backward; where the lines indicated by the demonstratives intersect, the space is empty. Possibly a section of text describing the way in which Yahweh will confront an Israel that will not return to him has been lost. The sense of the sequence of the text in its present form is difficult to follow. As it stands, the call to prepare to meet the God of Israel is the

only element of specific content in the verse. Perhaps encounter with Yahweh is the concrete moment of judgment for which the opening 'therefore' prepares, and to which the demonstratives point. The summons in the final clause raises two questions of meaning. What kind of activity is involved in 'prepare' (*hikkōn*)? What kind of event is meant by 'meet your God'? Both expressions are used in the Sinai pericope where Israel's encounter with the theophany of Yahweh is reported (Ex. 19). 'Prepare' deals with the qualification of persons for cultic participation in the ritual of covenant making (vv. 11, 15; cf. Ex. 34.2). 'To meet God' is used for the location of the people over against the holiness of the mount where Yahweh appears (Ex. 19.17). The language in Ex. 19 belongs to the cultic situation of approach to the *deus praesens*. It is appropriate, and was probably used, for any ritual that centred on the presence of the deity. In the light of Amos' unqualified rejection of the cult and denunciation of every important sanctuary in Israel, it is unlikely that he summons Israel to a ritual of covenant-renewal.[a] One more cultic ceremony, even of covenant-renewal, would not fulfil the requirements of 'return to me'; Amos says as much in the plainest language possible. Not covenant-making but covenant-keeping! In some of his sayings Amos points to his expectation that in the impending judgment Yahweh will act directly and personally, that its central reality will be a theophany. The day of Yahweh would be a climax whose finality transcended the ineffective chastisements of the past (5.18–20). Yahweh would pass by his people no more (7.8; 8.2); instead he will pass through their midst (5.17). In his identity as Lord of the covenant, 'your God', Yahweh will confront his people. They will not return to him, so he will come to them in a terrifying historical theophany so inexorable that no Israelite can avoid it (9.1–4) and so awesome that none can mistake it (2.13–16)—not in a sanctuary, but in history—not for covenant-making, but for judgment. The cultic summons is displaced and applied to history, just as the curses were in vv. 6–11. The summons to 'prepare to meet your God' is in actuality an announcement of judgment day.

[**13**] The form of v. 13 is different from the oracular first personal address of vv. 6–12; it is composed in typical hymnic style, using predicative participles to glorify the God whose name is Yahweh. This fragment is clearly similar to 5.8f. and 9.5f. All three are additions

---

[a] For the contrary opinion, see W. Brueggemann, 'Amos iv 4–13 and Israel's Covenant Worship', *VT* 15, 1965, pp. 1ff.

to the Amos-material as it was passed on in tradition; the problems of
their source and place in the book of Amos are discussed below. The
descriptive measures of v. 13 recreate one of the oldest traditional
pictures of Yahweh's ways of manifesting himself. The approach of a
violent frontal thunderstorm with its awesome lightning and freshen-
ing wind, turning the early morning back to eerie darkness, its low
black clouds touching the tops of the high hills and shaking the
ground with reverberating thunder, is the phenomenological basis
for the picture. But *who* is it that so appears and announces in such
overwhelming flashing and shaking his works? None else but Yahweh,
God of hosts! Set just after the summons, 'prepare to meet your God',
the hymnic lines evoke the awareness of the frightening majesty of
Yahweh as he appears, coming to present himself to Israel. When
Amos' oracle sequence was spoken or read in later times to test Israel's
response to Yahweh's chastisement, this conclusion served to recreate
for the people just what encounter with Yahweh is like.

THE HYMNIC SECTIONS IN AMOS

Amos 4.13; 5.8f.; 9.5f. all stand distinct from their immediate
context in style and subject. All three use predicative participles and
refrain in the style of the hymn-form. They depict the majestic might
of Yahweh upon which earth and its inhabitants utterly depend—he
is Creator and establisher of earth's order—and the one whose
power can shake the world to recall its subjection to his sovereignty.
It seems likely that all three passages come from the same hymn.
Each concludes with the refrain: 'Yahweh (God of hosts) is his name!';
the final lines of 5.8 and 9.6 are identical; their metrical structure is
homogeneous; and their themes similar. There is no way to tell whether
the entire original hymn has been used, so any reconstruction could at
best only suggest a possible form and order for the available material.
Nothing in the form or content of the hymn indicates that it could not
have been current in Amos' day. The texts have no exact parallels
elsewhere in the Old Testament. The sentence, 'Yahweh is his name'
(which sounds like an early polemical confession used to claim powers
and manifestations attributed to other deities for Israel's God), does
not occur elsewhere as a refrain, but does appear in the early hymns,
Ex. 15.3 and Ps. 68.4. In these hymns Yahweh is praised in his
mighty appearances in storm-wind and thunderstorm; and motifs of
this theophanic tradition (Pss. 144.5; 104.32; 97.5; 29; 46.7;

Nahum 1.5) appear in Amos 4.13; 9.5; and perhaps 5.9. If Amos did use a line from the original hymn in his oracle ending in 8.8 (parallels 9.4), that would explain the attraction of this specific hymn to the Amos-material. Why portions of the hymn text were placed where they now stand in the book of Amos is another question. Their location is hardly due to the process of collecting the Amos-material and arranging it, for the hymns do not mark or conclude any discernible collections. In the case of 4.13 and 9.5f. the hymns follow hard on passages which announce the intervention of Yahweh in direct, personal fashion. This would be true of 5.8f. also if they belong after v. 6 instead of 7. The earliest tradents of Amos-material may have inserted the hymnic descriptions of Yahweh's supernatural might on which earth depends at the climax of Amos' oracles which seemed to them to involve a coming theophany.[a]

12. FUNERAL RITES FOR THE NATION: 5.1–3

5 ¹Hear this word
    which I deliver against you,
    a dirge, O house of Israel!
²'She has fallen! She shall never arise,
    the virgin Israel.
She is left prostrate upon her land;
    There is none to raise her up.'
³For this is what Lord Yahweh has said:
'The city that goes forth with a thousand,
    shall have left a hundred;
and the one that goes forth with a hundred
    shall have left ten (to the house of Israel).'[b]

[1] This saying is another example of the versatility with which Amos employs a variety of traditional forms of expression to clothe his message. It is introduced by the messenger's summons to his audience (cf. 3.1; 4.1 and 8.4), but the 'word' (*dābār*) is sung in the form of a dirge. The fall of Israel, usually announced as coming in the future, is treated as a judgment already executed; the calamity is

---

[a] On the problem of the doxologies, see F. Horst, 'Die Doxologien im Amosbuch', *ZAW* 47, 1929, pp. 45–54; J. D. W. Watts, 'An Old Hymn Preserved in the Book of Amos', *JNES* 15, 1956, pp. 33–39.

[b] The phrase does not fit the syntax or metre of this sentence; perhaps it has been displaced from the introductory formula at the beginning of the verse.

celebrated as though it had already occurred by singing a funeral song
for the nation (v. 2). The mourning song (*qīnā*; cf. 8.10) was the chief
funeral ceremony in Israel; it was a poem of grief portraying the
death of a kinsman, friend, or leader, traditionally cast in the 3 + 2
metre. A particularly lovely example is David's *qīnā* for Saul and
Jonathan (II Sam. 1.17–27); other prophets besides Amos used it
with compelling effectiveness, especially Jeremiah (e.g. Jer. 9.17–19,
20–22). While the 'word' clothed in the *qīnā* is the message of Yahweh,
the qualification in the introductory sentence ('which I deliver
against you as a dirge') indicates that the form is Amos' own contribution in which he self-consciously speaks concurrently with the divine
dābār. The choice of the form is not merely dramatic; it testifies to the
prophet's own grief at what his words foretell. He does not foresee the
doom hanging over 'the house of Israel', the northern kingdom, with
unconcern or hostility or scorn, however much these sentiments may
colour his speaking to specifically guilty persons. In his visions of the
doom threatening Israel, he twice besought God to spare a Jacob so
humanly weak and small (7.1–6).

[2] The mourning song laments the irrevocable fall of Israel. Its
effect on Amos' hearers would have been something like the shock of
reading one's own obituary in the newspaper. Behind the past tenses
of the dirge is the inexorable decree of judgment upon the Northern
Kingdom that the time of her end has arrived (8.2). The title 'virgin
Israel' (Jer. 18.13; 31.4, 21) personifies the nation as a maid cut off
before the consummation of her life, a girl violated by the ravaging
assault of a military foe. The personification is similar to Isaiah's
'daughter of Zion' for Judah (Isa. 1.8; 10.32). The fall of the nation
is tragically hopeless; there is none to help, for her no national
'resurrection'. Since Yahweh is the one 'who raises up' those in need
of help (I Sam. 2.6–8; Hos. 6.2; Amos 9.11), the lament that there
is none to do so is a disclosure of the coming dereliction. The very
land which was the gift through the promise to the fathers and was
viewed in the Yahwist epic as the sacrament of the fulfilment of the
election of Israel is the scene of Israel's death—the gift of blessing
becomes the site of the curse. The hymns of Yahweh's salvation will
turn into laments over the death his judgment brings (8.3, 10;
5.16–17).

[3] Verse 3 has its own messenger formula introducing a word of
Yahweh. It could stand separately as an independent saying, but it
continues the theme and rhythm of the previous two verses and is

probably a second movement in the oracle by which Yahweh
portrays the calamity that sets the stage for the dirge. The two bi-cola
portray in terse brevity a scene of military disaster. In the face of
invasion each city and town sends out the units of conscripts which it
supplies for the royal army, and they return—decimated! The
numbers are not arbitrary. The military forces of Israel were organized into units of 'thousands' and 'hundreds' (I Sam. 17.18; 18.13;
22.7; II Sam. 18.1).ᵃ Translated into modern terms, Amos is saying
that a battalion would be left a company, and a company reduced to
a platoon. The decimation of each city's conscript force would be a
disaster; the remaining tenth is no remnant of hope left for the future
but the statistical symbol that the nation was left with no future. They
would be helpless and hopeless. The prophecy (v. 3) is the forecast of
the death lamented by the dirge (v. 2).

13. THE HOLY ONE, NOT THE HOLY PLACE: 5.4–6

5 ⁴Forᵇ this is what Yahweh has said to the house of Israel:
'Seek me and live.
⁵Don't seek Bethel,
  nor enter Gilgal,
  nor go over to Beersheba.
For Gilgal shall go into exile
  and Bethel shall come to grief.'
⁶Seek Yahweh and live,
  lest he ᶜsend fire onᶜ the house of Joseph,
  and it devour with none to quench it (for Bethel).ᵈ

Yahweh, but not the sanctuaries—that is the astounding alternative with which Amos confronts Israel. Verses 4f. make up a divine
saying, introduced by a messenger-formula (4a) and formulated in
the first person as the speech of Yahweh. It begins quite positively
with a summons to seek Yahweh as the way to life (4b). But the

---

ᵃ On the organization of armed forces in Israel, see R. de Vaux, *Ancient Israel*,
1961, pp. 216ff.
ᵇ MT's *kī* is probably an editorial link connecting this oracle to the foregoing
one, or possibly an exclamatory word ('Yea').
ᶜ⁻ᶜ Reading *yešallaḥ 'ēš be* as in 1.4, 7, 10, etc. MT's verb *ṣlḥ* makes little sense
in this context.
ᵈ A gloss narrowing the threat to Bethel; G reads 'house of Israel'.

following prohibitions of pilgrimages to the shrines (5a) and the announcement of their imminent destruction (5b) changes the initial invitation to a message of doom for the shrines. Verse 6 is a prophetic saying; Yahweh is referred to in the third person. It begins with a sentence similar to 4b (6a) but then adds a warning to obey lest Yahweh consume the people in fiery punishment (6b). The prophetic saying could have been spoken along with the first, but probably it was placed here by the collectors because of the similarity of 4b and 6a.

The sentence 'Seek me that you may live' is a form of priestly *tōrā*.[a] In the mouth of the officiating priests the exhortation was an instruction to turn to Yahweh as the source of life, to come to the sanctuary where he was present to receive the dispensation of the blessing that conferred security and prosperity. Note the use of 'seek' in Ps. 27.8 ('You have said, "Seek my face!" Thy face, O Yahweh, do I seek'); 24.6; 105.4; Isa. 55.1 (*dāraš* and *biqqēš* are used synonymously). It was in the sanctuary as the sphere of the divine presence that life was available and was bestowed on the pilgrims who came there to seek Yahweh.[b] The polemical hardness of Amos' saying indicates that the priests in Israel's shrines were offering 'life' through the cult without pointing to the kind of living required of those who 'seek Yahweh' (Pss. 15; 24). They were offering an abbreviated *tōrā*, instruction concerning the way to 'cheap grace'; they were saying, 'Come to Bethel, that you may live' without confronting the worshippers with the will of the divine Lord from whom they expected the gift of life (see the comment on 5.14f., 21–24). Amos usurps the function of the priests of Bethel by giving *tōrā* himself in which he replaces shrine with the divine person, and then contradicts the priestly office by forbidding the Israelites to come to the shrines at all.

[4] *Seek* (*dāraš*) does not mean 'inquire about' or 'search for' something or someone lost or inaccessible. When Yahweh is the object, *seek* frequently means 'turn to Yahweh' (for help in a specific situation), and then by extension 'hold to Yahweh' (as a way of life). The prohibitions (5a) make it clear that *dāraš* involves a visit to a sanctuary; the Israelites were seeking Yahweh in Bethel and Gilgal. A

[a] J. Begrich, 'Die priesterliche Tora', *Gesammelte Studien zum Alten Testament*, 1964, pp. 243ff.
[b] G. von Rad, 'Righteousness and Life', in *The Problem of the Hexateuch and Other Essays*, ET, 1966, pp. 253ff.

series of texts in the Old Testament depict a specific procedural
context for seeking Yahweh; in a situation of need for help or instruction, one went to a man of God or a prophet to secure an oracle of
promise or direction (Gen. 25.22; Ex. 18.15; I Sam. 9.9; I Kings
14.1ff.; II Kings 8.8f.; Jer. 21.2; Ezek. 20.1ff., etc.).[a] When the
Israelites heard Amos exhort them to seek Yahweh, they would have
thought that this was precisely what they were doing in the sanctuaries. They were seeking Yahweh in expectation that he would
bestow upon them a secure and prosperous life. They were coming to
shrines at which Yahweh had been worshipped from ancient times to
carry out the required ritual, quite possibly in an attitude of personal
devotion, and they hoped to receive God's help for special needs and
blessing for their whole lives (for an idea of the content of 'life' as
blessing, cf. the long description of the effect of blessing on those in
covenant with Yahweh in Deut. 30). The radical distinction between
'Seek me' and 'Visit Bethel' would have left Amos' hearers, probably
pilgrims to the shrine, in puzzled shock—bid to seek Yahweh as a
matter of life itself, but forbidden the very holy places where they
believed the Lord willed that they find him. What 'Seek me' as a
word of Yahweh means when the shrines are excluded is left obscure
and provocative. The emphasis lies on the prohibition of the current
cult. What Amos had in mind as the right way to seek Yahweh
appears in the similar exhortation in 5.14, where 'Yahweh' is replaced
as object of the verb by 'good': 'Seek good that you may live.'

[5] Bethel had ancient and hallowed associations with Israel's
ancestor, Jacob; since the constitution of the northern tribes as a
separate kingdom under Jeroboam I it had enjoyed a florescence as
one of Israel's royal shrines. Gilgal in the Jordan Valley had a
significant place in the traditions of the conquest and enjoyed popula-
rity as a holy site from the times of the tribal league. On Bethel and
Gilgal, cf. the comment on 4.4–5. Beersheba was in the southern part
of Judah's territory (note the expression 'from Dan to Beersheba' as
the phrase which circumscribes Israelite territory); Amos' remark
here and in 8.14 indicates that Israelites still continued to 'cross over'
Judah's borders to worship there. In the patriarchal tradition the
founding of Beersheba's shrine was credited to both Abraham and
Isaac, and God had appeared to Jacob there (Gen. 21.31ff.; 26.23ff.;
46.1ff.); obviously its attraction for all who shared the patriarchal

    [a] Cf. C. Westermann, 'Die Begriffe für Fragen und Suchen im Alten Testament',
KuD 6, 1960, pp. 16ff.

traditions continued even after the schism. But the divine word bars the way to these famous shrines.

Why? Because these religious centres were themselves under the divine curse and had no future. The impending fate of Gilgal and Bethel is announced in sentences which play on sounds and words. 'Gilgal shall go into exile' (*haggilgāl gālōh yigleh*) builds an alliteration with the phonetic similarity between subject and verb; both contain *g* and *l*. Bethel, Amos says, will become *'āwen*, a word that means grievous trouble, religious perversion, and sometimes idolatry. The House of God (Beth-El) will become the place of trouble. Hosea goes so far as to nickname Bethel 'Beth-awen' (house of idolatry? Hos. 4.15; 5.8; 10.5). On the subject of the sanctuaries, Amos is always consistent; they are under judgment (Amos 3.14; 7.9; 8.3), rejected of Yahweh and therefore no longer a place to seek him. To do so is not only useless; it is a fatal error; for the devotees will invoke upon themselves the fate of the shrines.

[6] The prophetic saying in v. 6 begins with a repetition of the opening exhortation from 4b; once again the insistent connection between turning to Yahweh and life is heard. But this time instead of the prohibition of the sanctuaries and announcement of judgment, there follows the threat that Yahweh may destroy the entire people. The divine fire is the instrument of Yahweh's action against his foes (cf. the comment on the formula 'I will send fire . . .' in the structure of the oracles against the nations, 1.4, 7, 10, 12; 2.2, 5). When Yahweh's wrath breaks out there is no power left that can rescue because he who is the source of life will have become the author of destruction. Note the use of the same threat by Jeremiah to enforce his exhortations to Judah to return to a way of obedience (Jer. 4.4; 21.12). The formulation of the judgment of the people as threat instead of announcement means that Amos reckons in this saying with a possibility of life for Yahweh's people, the house of Jacob.

The warning that the outbreak of Yahweh's wrath is an imminent *possibility* stands in contrast to Amos' usual announcements of judgment as irrevocable decree. The offer of an alternative to judgment and death is explicit in all four cases of exhortation in the book of Amos (5.4, 6, 14f., and the jussive in 5.24). Exhortation is a marginal feature of Amos' prophecy, but it is present and offers an alternative to those Israelites who will hear its instruction. The way to Yahweh is the way of escape from death! Of course all the imperatives are fraught with the urgency of impending doom; their context is the prophet's knowledge of Yahweh's wrath against Israel. None of them qualify the message that the kingdom, cult, and the whole form of present national life will come to an end. Three of the exhortations (5.4f., 14f., 24) involve rejections of Israel's cult and so function as words of judgment. In 5.15 the offer of life is highly tentative and extended at best to a remnant of the present Israel. Amos has taken the familiar language of the cult and made it heard against the background of his announcement that the end has come for Israel. Perhaps there is no logical consistency between the two, but the exhortations do testify that Yahweh remains the life of his people even in a situation in which they deserve the sentence of death.

14. MAN'S INJUSTICE BRINGS GOD'S JUSTICE: 5.7, 10-11

5 [7](Woe are)[a] those who change justice into wormwood,
    and discard righteousness;
[10]they hate the advocate of right in the gate
    and despise him who speaks with integrity.
[11]Therefore, because you make tenants[b] out of the weak,
    and take tribute of corn from him,
you have built houses of hewn stone,
    but you shall not dwell in them;
you have planted splendid vineyards,
    but you shall not drink their wine.

The courts are being used to exploit the weak, but the justice of God will frustrate the lives of the exploiter. The saying is an excellent example of Amos' critique of Israel's society, for it shows clearly the interrelation of his normative concepts, justice and righteousness, the perversion of judicial process, and the oppression of the poor. Taken together, vv. 7 and 10f. make up a complete announcement of judgment with indictment (vv. 7, 10) and announcement of punishment (v. 11). In vv. 8f. a fragment of a hymn to Yahweh interrupts the continuity between vv. 7 and 10. The piece was inserted during the editorial development of the book (see the comment on 5.8f. in the following section). Verse 12 appears to continue vv. 7, 10f.; its open-

a 'Woe' (*hōy*) does not appear in MT; the line begins with a definite participle; see the discussion in the comment.
b For this translation of *bšs*, see *KB*, p. 158.

ing word *kī* ('for'?) appears to connect it with v. 11, and it does resume themes similar to those in vv. 7 and 10. But it is another indictment and is best taken as the opening of a saying completed in vv. 16f. (see the comment on 5.12f., 16f.). The audience could well have been the residents of Samaria, particularly the officials of the royal court and their favourites.

[**7**] Verse 7 begins with a definite plural participle that is un-accompanied by any introductory particle, vocative, or subject or predicate. The definite plural participle seems to be an element of the style of a woe-saying (cf. 5.18; 6.1), and used alone may have the effect of a woe-pronouncement.[a] Restoration of a *hōy* before the participle is not necessary; 6.13 begins in the same way. The definite participle as a device for characterizing the group to whom his indict-ments applied is a feature of Amos' style (2.7; 3.10; 4.1; 6.3–6; indefinite in 5.12). Here the cry seeks the attention of all those who turn justice (*mišpāṭ*) into wormwood, and thereby discard righteous-ness (*ṣedāqā*) as something worthless. Wormwood, a Palestinian plant of exceedingly bitter taste (cf. 6.12b), was frequently used in meta-phors to describe the bitterness of calamity (Jer. 9.15; 23.15; Lam. 3.15, 19). The justice administered in the courts had been changed by the alchemy of greed to bitter calamity. The terms righteousness and justice play a central role in Amos prophecy and deserve special comment.

In his indictments of Israel's conduct Amos usually cites specific deeds; when he resorts to concepts, he uses *mišpāṭ* and *ṣedāqā* as comprehensive notions primarily. Good (*ṭōb*) and evil (*raʿ*) occur in 5.14f., but even there *mišpāṭ* is the defining term (5.15a). *Mišpāṭ* and *ṣedāqā* occur three times as pairs in *parallelismus membrorum* and *mišpāṭ* once alone:

5.7:   They who turn *mišpāṭ* into wormwood
      and cast *ṣedāqā* to the earth.
6.12b: For you have turned *mišpāṭ* to poison
      and the fruit of *ṣedāqā* to wormwood.
5.24:   Let *mišpāṭ* roll down like water
      and *ṣedāqā* like an unfailing stream.
5.15a: Hate evil, love good
      and make *mišpāṭ* operative in the gate.

The first two texts are indictments; *mišpāṭ* and *ṣedāqā* have been

[a] On the problem see E. Gerstenberger, 'The Woe Oracles of the Prophets', *JBL* 81, 1962, pp. 252, 254.

completely perverted in Israel. These formulations could stand as summations for all of Amos' complaints against Israel's social order. The last two are exhortations: what Yahweh expects from Israel is *mišpāṭ* and *ṣᵉdāqā*; they express the quintessence of his will. Both exhortations appear in connection with Amos' critique of the cult, so they emphasize the basic problem of worship in Israel.

Mišpāṭ is the primary term. It appears first in the parallelisms, and once by itself as the explication of 'seeking/loving good'. But *mišpāṭ* is called 'the fruit of *ṣᵉdāqā*', and the two are so closely coordinated that Amos' use of *mišpāṭ* is not to be understood out of relation to its source in and orientation to *ṣᵉdāqā*.

The setting for *mišpāṭ* in Amos is the court in the gates (6.12 and the comment on 5.10, 12). *Mišpāṭ* means the judicial process of establishing in a case before the court what the right is (and therefore who is in the right), and rendering that opinion as the judgment of the court. This fundamental function of the court is defined in its essence by Deut. 25.1: When a legal dispute arises between two men, they shall come before the court and the court shall decide between them (*šāpaṭ*); the just/innocent (*ṣaddīq*) shall be vindicated by being declared in the right; the wicked/guilty (*rāšāʿ*) shall be found in the wrong. When the court successfully performs this function, then *mišpāṭ* is done.[a] This duty of the court was not understood in terms of dealing out an impersonal, objective, even-handed justice. Where a dispute arose, both parties were endangered—the accused because he was placed in the position of a foe of the social order; and the accuser because his rights had been allegedly breached and his position was at stake in his accusation. The court's process had a redemptive dimension; to judge meant to help the just party, and to protect the social order by determining where the wrong lay and correcting it. This was particularly important in the case of the weaker members of society who, left without power or influence, could not maintain themselves in the social order apart from the *mišpāṭ* of the court.

Amos coordinates *mišpāṭ* so closely with *ṣᵉdāqā*, because the latter is the source of the former; *mišpāṭ* is the fruit of *ṣᵉdāqā* (6.12). *Ṣᵉdāqā* in the Old Testament is not a righteousness that is oriented to an absolute ethical norm. It is a relational concept whose content and meaning is determined by the particular social context in which it is used. *Ṣᵉdāqā* is the quality of life displayed by those who live up to the

[a] H. J. Boecker, *Redeformen des Rechtslebens im Alten Testament* (WMANT 14), 1963, pp. 122f.

norms inherent in a given relationship and thereby do right by the other person or persons involved. The two most important spheres for righteousness were the relationship between Yahweh and Israel defined in the covenant and expressed in the cult, and the relationship of men in the social order of the folk. In Israel the borders between the two relational systems overlapped, but each had its own significance.[a] In Amos *ṣᵉdāqā* applies to the relational life of the social partners in the people of Israel. Of course Yahweh is regarded as the patron and enforcer of the social order, but what is in view is the righteousness of Israelites in relation to each other. Because the court was the primary instrument for controlling and repairing the integrity of the social fabric, the righteousness of its members was crucial.

[10] The perverters of justice set themselves in opposition to the proper function of the court in the gates. *The gate* was the regular place in which the local courts of Israel's towns and cities was held (Ruth 4.1, 10f.; Amos 5.12, 15).[b] It was a fortified building set in the walls, which protected the entrance to the city and provided a place where the legal assembly convened to regulate the life and property of the citizens according to the accepted ethos. The proceedings were not so formally organized as in the western tradition, nor presided over and directed by professional officers. All the adult male citizens of a town, who were not disqualified in some way, were eligible to sit as assessors. Any of them could testify as witnesses and offer advice as to which norms applied and how in the case before the court. The *advocate of right (mōkîaḥ)* was any who spoke to the purpose of a proper finding of the court, rebuking wrong and calling for the support of right (Isa. 29.21; Job 9.33; 32.12).[c] Precisely because proceedings were conducted in such fashion, the competence of the court depended on the integrity of the assessors in speaking the truth and upholding what was recognized as right in the community. The ninth word in the Decalogue (Ex. 20.13) made the prohibition of false witness a matter of the very policy of Israel's divine suzerain, and a number of the stipulations in the legal traditions of Israel are concerned with the integrity of courts. Therefore to hate the advocate of right and abhor those who speak 'the whole truth' is tantamount to personal opposition to the essence of the system.

[a] Cf. K. H. Fahlgren, *ṣᵉdaka, nahestehende und entgegengesetzte Begriffe im alten Testament*, 1932; G. von Rad, *Theology of the Old Testament* I, 1962, pp. 70ff.

[b] L. Köhler, 'Justice in the Gate', *Hebrew Man*, ET, 1956, pp. 149ff.

[c] Cf. H. J. Boecker, *op. cit.*, pp. 45ff.

[11] 'Therefore' makes the transition to the announcement of judgment. But another description of conduct is inserted after the conjunction, which with its direct address style fastens on the audience in Amos' presence and uncovers the basis of the court's corruption. The old institution of the court in the gate is being undermined to make way for the economic exploitation of the weak (*dal*). Amos speaks to a group who are steadily driving the landed peasantry away from their earlier solid independence into the condition of serfs. The small farmer no longer owns his own land; he is a tenant of an urban class to whom he must pay a rental for the use of the land, a rental that was often a lion's share of the grain which the land produced. The court in the gates was the one social institution which stood in the way of this process. The urban group, probably made up primarily of officials in the royal administration and supported by royal power, were corrupting these courts and shifting the control of social life away from the villages to the royal court.

Yahweh's punishment of these avaricious men will correspond to their crime. They have been greedy for wealth and land. Out of the profits from the suffering of the poor they have built houses of hewn stone such as were possible before only for temple and palace (I Kings 6.36; 7.9, 11; cf. Isa. 9.10). They have planted luxuriant vineyards in the fields that belonged to the small farmer. But it shall all come to nought! They will not live in the houses, or drink the wine of the vineyards. The formulations ('to build houses and not live in them; to plant vineyards and not drink their wine') are actually fixed expressions which belong to the category of futility curses. Outside the Old Testament such curses are found in treaties where the curses are the sanctions which enforce the terms of the treaty; the curses fall on those who violate the terms. These sentences appear in the curse series in Deut. 28 (cf. vv. 30, 38–40) where they are sanctions against covenant disobedience in Israel; they are used as words of judgment in Zeph. 1.13; cf. also Micah 6.14f. Formulated positively, the sentences are used so as to depict the blessings which result from Yahweh's actions in behalf of Israel (Deut. 6.10f.; Josh. 24.13) and also in salvation-oracles (Amos 9.14; Isa. 65.21f.; Jer. 29.5, 28; Ezek. 28.26).[a] When Amos uses these formulations he is saying in effect that Yahweh will invoke the sanctions of his covenant with Israel against these perverters of Israel's social order. The maintenance of

[a] Cf. D. R. Hillers, *Treaty Curses and the Old Testament Prophets* (BO 16), 1964, pp. 28f.; and the comment on Amos 4.6–11.

that order and particularly the expression of justice and righteousness through the courts is a requirement of his covenant. For those
who violate his will, the salvation-history will become a judgment-
history.

15. LORD OF HEAVEN AND HISTORY : 5.8–9

5 8. . . . .
    maker of the Pleiades and Orion;
    who changes deep darkness to morning,
    and darkens day into night;
    who summons the waters of the sea,
    and pours them upon the face of the earth—
    Yahweh is his name!
    9aThe one who sends down[a] destruction upon the stronghold,[b]
    and brings destruction upon the fortress. . .[c]

The use of predicative participles, the refrain ('Yahweh is his
name'), and the exaltation of Yahweh distinguish these verses from
their context. In style and theme they are kin to the hymnic sections
in 4.13 and 9.5f. On their literary relation to the text of Amos, cf.
the comment on 4.13. These verses stand out as a later insertion even
more clearly than the others, for they separate v. 7 from its sequel in
v. 10; cf. the opening comment on 5.7, 10f. In their present position
5.7f. are a puzzle; they are not located so as to lend dramatic emphasis
to an announcement of Yahweh's verdict of judgment on Israel as
are the other two hymnic passages. If they followed v. 6 they would
serve that function and perhaps they stood there at one time. The
appearance of 'change' (hpk) in both vv. 7 and 8 have caused the displacement in an attempt to put 'catchwords' in sequence. If the two
verses were a continuous section from an original hymn, we would
expect the refrain to come at the end, as is the case in the other two
hymnic sections; because of the fragmentary condition of the piece no
certain explanation is possible. Verse 8 praises Yahweh as the
Creator who made the stars, rules over the day and night, and sends

---

  a–a Reading hammappīl; MT's hammablīg means 'become happy, brighten up'.
  b Vocalizing ʿōz for MT's ʿāz.
  c According to G. R. Driver the verse is related to the first measure of v. 8 and
contains the names of three constellations: Taurus (šōr), Capricorn (ʿēz) and
Virgo (mᵉkaṣṣēr); 'Two Astronomical Passages in the OT', JTS 4, 1953, pp. 208ff.

the rain to water the earth. Like the wandering ruminations of Job on the marvels which the Creator wrought (cf. Job 9.9; 38.31 for a similar reference to the Pleiades and Orion) this exaltation of Israel's God as the power behind the existence and processes of the universe attributes an incomparable majesty to Yahweh in whose name the messages of Amos are delivered. Verse 9 turns from the heavens to earth, from creation to history and celebrates Yahweh's exercise of his power as a God of war (Ex. 15.3) in overturning the strength of men and invading the imagined security of their fortresses. Let none imagine himself invulnerable to Yahweh. To live in the universe is to be his dependent. To exist in history is to be subject to his power.

16. YOUR FUTURE IS A FUNERAL: 5.12–13, 16–17

5 ¹²For^a I know how many are your crimes,
    how numerous your sins—
  opposing the innocent, taking bribes,
    and turning away the poor in the gate.
¹³Therefore the prudent will keep quiet in such a time, for it is an
    evil time.
¹⁶Therefore this is what Yahweh, ^bGod of hosts, Lord,^b has said:
  'In every square there shall be wailing,
    and in every street they shall say, "Ah! Ah!"
  The farm workers shall be summoned to mourning,
    to^c wailing the skilled at lament.
¹⁷Among all the vineyard workers^d there shall be wailing,
    for I will pass through the midst of you,'
  has said Yahweh.

5.12, 16f. is a saying whose unity has been lost in the arrangement and redaction of the book. Verse 12 accuses the audience of using the courts to oppress the poor; this accusation hardly belongs to 5.7, 10f., which is a complete announcement of judgment without it. Verses 16f. depict the mourning that will come upon Israel because Yahweh will pass through their midst; an announcement of coming punishment. 'Therefore' at the beginning of v. 16 points back to an accusation which cannot be found in the exhortation in 14f.; in Amos

---

^a *Kī* is an editorial transition, or possibly 'Yea'.
^{b–b} 'Lord' is certainly secondary, as is possibly the entire title.
^c Placing the preposition *'el* before the noun, which it follows in MT.
^d Vocalizing *kōrᵉmīm* with H. Gese, *VT* 12, 1962, pp. 432ff.

'therefore' always binds the two parts of an announcement of judgment together (3.11; 4.12; 5.11; 6.7; 7.17). Taken together vv. 12 and 16f. compose a coherent saying made up of accusation and announcement of punishment. The exhortations in vv. 14f. have been set in the midst of the saying by the collectors. Verse 13 is a comment inserted by an editor who thinks with the vocabulary and viewpoint of later Wisdom. For different reconstructions of the unit, see among others Weiser (5.12, 11a, 16b, 17), and Amsler (5.7, 10–12, 16f.).

[12] Probably the prophet is the subject of 'I know'. The assertion that the numerous crimes of his audience are well known to him has the ring of a response to claims of innocence on their part. Against such protestations he answers that their deeds are crimes (*peša'*) and sins (*haṭṭā't*); they are rebellion against Yahweh and disobedience of his requirements. The three specifications of conduct in 12b all belong to the sphere of judicial practice. The addressees are men who appear in court as the enemies of the innocent (*ṣaddīq*); the term designates the man in a legal case whose status is right, who is in accord with the social norms which the court ought to support (Ex. 23.7; Deut. 25.1). The accused take bribes and decide cases on the basis of profit instead of right (Ex. 23.8; cf. I Sam. 12.3). When the poor come to court seeking protection, they are turned away from their only source of help (Ex. 23.6; cf. Isa. 10.2; 29.21; Mal. 3.5). The list of crimes is similar to the one in 2.6b, 7a. Yahweh's requirements for conduct in court are stipulated in two clusters of commands incorporated in the Book of the Covenant (Ex. 23.1–3, 6–8; cf. Deut. 16.18–20). The same motifs (defence of the just, rights of the poor, bribes) are the subjects of these admonitions. For Amos the court in the gate is the central institution in Israel, and the integrity of the members of the legal assembly the most crucial issue of Yahweh's authority over society. He looks neither to the royal administration nor to the cult as the source and centre of righteousness and justice, but to the legal assembly in the villages (5.7, 10, 15). It is there that Yahweh's will for Israel's social order has been implemented in the days of the tribal league, and during the early monarchy. Its corruption under the growing power of the commercial class, sponsored by the monarchy, is in his eyes the destruction of the instrument by which Yahweh's justice has been administered. Yahweh is a God who protects the right of the weak and poor, the widow and orphan (Pss. 68.5; 82.3f.; 146.9; Deut. 10.18). Where those rights are denied, and his administration through the court frustrated, he intervenes

himself as judge—and the word of that judgment is precisely the commission of Amos.

[13] Verse 13 is a judicious comment of a follower of Wisdom. The line is in prose; the prudent man (*maśkīl*) is a figure beloved in Wisdom sayings (Prov. 10.5, 19; 17.2; 21.11); the sentiment expressed has no natural connection with the message of Amos in the situation in which it was delivered. The style is that of an impersonal observation. In a time when the courts are corrupt and the powerful have their way without restraint, the man of wise judgment will keep quiet, knowing that to raise complaint or plead his case will only lead to trouble for him. The commentator doubtless lives in such a time and, trusting Amos' message that God will judge the wicked as valid in his own day, he believes that wisdom lies in waiting for the justice of God rather than in appealing to the judgment of men.

[16–17a] The punishment of the oppressors is portrayed by a word-picture of a time when the land will be filled with funerals. The description of rites for the dead to be held in the future was one of the prophetic devices for painting the terrible reality of coming judgment (e.g. Jer. 9.17–22; Micah 2.4; cf. Amos 8.2, 10). Note Amos' use of a funeral song in 5.1–3 and his employment of the 'Woe' (5.18; 6.1, 4). The prophet saw in the periodic rites for the dead which belong to the rhythm of regular life the destiny of Israel writ small. The funeral was the future of the oppressor of the poor. A time was coming when everywhere the air would be vibrant with the sound of grief. Wailing and mourning are the loud public lamentations which mark customary funeral rites in Israel. 'Ah' is the grief-cry of those who mourn (here *hō*, usually *hōy*; cf. I Kings 13.30; Jer. 22.18; 34.5). The prediction is a sentence against those indicted in v. 12, the economically powerful who had expropriated the weak and amassed estates. There is therefore a bitter irony in the scene when farm workers and vineyard labourers are recruited to bury them. The labourers on farms and in vineyards were landless serfs, an economic class that did not exist in Israel much before the eighth century and the development of estates by the displacement of small landholders.[a] The oppressed will bury their oppressors in the ground which they coveted! 'The skilled at lament' were persons outside the family who were adept at the traditional rites and elegies (II Chron. 35.25; Eccles. 12.5; Jer. 9.17ff.).

[17b] The prophet does not identify the catastrophe, whether

[a] Cf. Isa. 61.5; II Chron. 26.10; Joel 1.11 and H. Gese, *VT* 12, 1962, pp. 432ff.

pestilence or military defeat, which will work this grim havoc. The reality of the disaster with which Israel must reckon is not so much some natural or historical circumstance as the act of Israel's God. Behind and within the terrible calamity of endless funerals is the greater terror of the divine I; it is he whom Israel must meet in this coming time of woe (4.12). 'I will pass through the midst of you' is the counterpart of the final decree of Yahweh's decision revealed to Amos in his third and fourth visions: 'I will not again pass him (Israel) by' (7.8; 8.2). Yahweh, whose 'passing over' Israel to pass through the land of Egypt as its Nemesis was celebrated at every Passover (Ex. 12.12), will deal with Israel as he did with her ancient foe. The coming of Yahweh will now mean death. Those who will not 'seek Yahweh' that they may live (5.4, 6, 14) will be found by him.

17. NOT EVERY ONE WHO SAYS 'LORD, LORD': 5.14–15

> 5 ¹⁴Seek good, not evil,
>   that you may live;
>   and so Yahweh (God of hosts)ᵃ may be with you,
>   as you have said.
> ¹⁵Hate evil, love good,
>   and put justice into effect in the gate;
>   perhaps Yahweh (God of hosts)ᵃ may show favour
>   to the remnant of Joseph.

Once again Amos offers his audience instructions about the way to life. The opening sentence takes up the form of 5.4b and 6a: 'Seek me (Yahweh) that you may live.' But here 'good' (*ṭōb*) replaces Yahweh as the object of the verb 'seek'. Verses 14 and 15 have a similar structure: exhortation followed by conditional promise. Each could stand alone as an independent saying, but the chiasmus created by the repetition of *good* and *evil* ('Seek good, not evil'/'hate evil, love good'); and the specific illustration of what good means in the second exhortation hold the two together in a rhetorical unit. The exhortation is cast in the style of a priestly *tōrā*; it was the word of the priest which called Israel to turn to the divine presence in the shrines in order to receive the gift of life (cf. the comment on 5.4f.). The themes of the conditional promises (Yahweh's presence with Israel and

---

ᵃ The title overloads the metre and is probably an editorial addition.

favour toward them), which explain what is meant by life, are also concerns of the cult. In 14b Amos quotes his audience; he incorporates the point of view of his hearers in his word as he often does, and so the situation also contributes to the formulation of the saying. Style and motives which occur in Wisdom's instructional forms are also present. The antithetical style of paralleling opposites, the opposing pair love/hate (Prov. 1.22; 9.8; 12.1; 13.24), the concern to show the way of life (Prov. 4.4; 11.19; 12.28; 15.27) are all features of Wisdom sayings.[a] Two Wisdom poems in the Psalter contain very interesting parallels to the style and themes of Amos 5.14f.: Pss. 34.12–14; 37.3, 27f. The nearest prophetic parallel is Isa. 1.16f. See the Deuteronomic formulation: 'Justice you shall follow, that you may live' (Deut. 16.20). Amos has used the speech of the cult and Wisdom of his time to formulate an exhortation specifically for the situation in which his mission placed him; its words have to be interpreted primarily out of the saying's setting in his prophecy.

'Seek good, not evil': Seek means 'be concerned about, devote yourselves to' (cf. *dāraš* in Isa. 1.17; 16.5; and the comment on Amos 5.4). The imperatives, hate and love, in v. 15 intensify the exhortation and emphasize the personal involvement that is called for. For the Hebrew 'hate' and 'love' are not only powerful emotions, but also actions in which a person sets himself for or against; yet the verbs lose nothing thereby in the passion they connote. Loving and hating mean bringing into force all the resources and powers of feeling, will, and thought in devotion to or rejection of a person or value. The cogency of the connection between good and life and evil and death is not some impersonal moral mechanism built into the structure of existence, but Yahweh himself. The decision about good and evil is a decision for or against Yahweh and therefore an invocation of his blessing or his judgment.

In Amos' theological vocabulary 'good' is the middle term between Yahweh and justice (*mišpāṭ*) and must be understood within this structure. 5.4a: 'Seek me and live'; 5.14a: 'seek good that you may live'; 5.15a: 'love good and put justice into effect in the (court in the) gate.' The gradient in the sequence runs from *Yahweh* through *good* to *justice*; for Amos the order and interrelation of the terms is indissoluble. One cannot speak here in terms of morality versus religion or ethics versus faith as though they were alternatives. Such distinc-

---

[a] Cf. H. W. Wolff, *Amos' Geistige Heimat* (WMANT 18), 1964, pp. 30ff.

tions miss the thrust of Amos' summons (cf. Micah 6.6–8). The consummate response to Yahweh is the practice of good. According to Amos one turns to Yahweh, not in cult, but in the social sphere of relations between one Israelite and another. On *mišpāṭ* and the court in the gates see the comment on 5.7, 10f. The normative values which make up the structure of good are those belonging to righteousness in the social order, those protected and maintained by the *mišpāṭ* of the court. The court is the place where the poor are protected, the widow and orphan receive help, right is advocated—and so righteousness bears its fruit. Amos' concentration of good on the justice of the court is not a reduction of ethical meaning to a judicial legalism; one has to remember how crucial the court in the gates was as an expression and creator of the total structure of human relations in Israel. Moreover, Amos uses the general categories of good and righteousness precisely to show that his interest in the court and its norms is essentially concerned about the good and righteous will of Yahweh. The individual laws that furnish a background to his indictment of Israel are simply particular articulations of good and righteousness through which Israel's devotion to Yahweh ought to be expressed.

Each of the exhortations is followed by a promise (14b, 15b). But these promises are not announcements of unconditioned hope and certain salvation. They are subordinate to the exhortations; their fulfilment depends on obedience to the exhortations. Amos sets the salvation that Israel took for granted under the condition of reform in Israel's life. Moreover, the promises are formulated in the light of the judgment which Amos proclaims. In 14b Israel's central religious belief, the affirmation repeated again and again in the shrines, is wrenched out of the present and thrust into a very uncertain future. The sentence 'Yahweh is with us' is a formulation of the election faith, an affirmation of trust and confidence that belonged to the history of Yahwism from the beginning. Spoken in the first person as a divine saying, it was a salvation-word conveying the blessing of Yahweh (Gen. 26.3, 24; 28.15; 31.8). It referred particularly to Yahweh's role as the powerful God who fought for and protected his people (Judg. 6.12f.; Num. 14.43; 23.21; Deut. 31.8). Because Yahweh was with them, they were safe within a mighty fortress (Ps. 46.7, 11); disaster would not touch them (Micah 3.11); the individual Israelite need not fear for 'you are with me' (Ps. 23.4). Israel still said 'Yahweh is with us' at Bethel and found in the dogma the source of their confidence that no disaster would strike them (6.3; 9.10).

Amos subsumes the confession under the prior principle that life belongs to those who seek Yahweh by loving good. The cultic dogma is with one stroke ethicized and personalized. It is no longer an objective independent fact on which Israel can base an autonomous self-confident existence. The presence of Yahweh as life-bestowing power is actualized and appropriated only in righteousness, the living that is responsible to the relational context of Israelite living with Israelite. When Israel says 'Yahweh is with us' they must say something about themselves—else the grand old confession is empty and meaningless.

In the second promise (15b) there is a sharp reservation in favour of Yahweh's sovereign freedom in his relation to Israel. 'Perhaps' characterizes the prospect of Yahweh's gracious help as a matter beyond human control and guarantee. The Lord is no national god of Israel; he will be gracious toward whomever he wills to be gracious (Ex. 33.19). He is not bound to Israel by any kind of cultic or legal guarantee; rather, Israel is completely in the hands of his sovereignty. The verb 'to be gracious' means the bestowal of favour and help which the recipient has no grounds to expect. Amos uses 'Joseph' as the name for the northern kingdom (6.6); the 'remnant of Joseph' refers to those who will be left after the destroying decimation of Yahweh's judgment (1.8; 5.3). 'Remnant' is not so much a theme of hope for the future, like the 'remnant' of Isaiah (Isa. 1.24–26; 10.20f.), as a dire recognition that punishment for Israel has been decreed— that the possibility of favour can be held out only to a handful of survivors. The exhortation of Amos does not constitute an alternative to judgment; rather, his summons to Yahweh and the good interprets the crisis that is upon Israel. And yet in his imperatives the prophet expresses the faith that even in the penultimate time between the decree of punishment and its execution, Yahweh's will to be Israel's God still exists—and could offer a foundation of hope, for a few.

18. THE DAY OF YAHWEH: 5.18–20

5 ¹⁸Woe are those who desire the day of Yahweh!
    What indeed will the day of Yahweh be for you?
    It is darkness, not light.
    ¹⁹(You are) like the man who flees from a lion—
    and a bear pounces upon him;

> or the one who goes home, leans his hand on the wall—
> and a snake bites him.
> ²⁰Is not the day of Yahweh darkness, not light—
> gloomy, without brightness?

Amos' famous saying on the Day of Yahweh is one of the speeches in which he takes up a central theme of Israel's faith and turns it against his audience (cf. 3.2; 9.7). The prophet, knowing the decision of Yahweh, contests the piety of his hearers, warning against the disastrous outcome of their piety. He begins with a woe-cry (18a), composed of the interjection *hōy* followed by a definite participle describing the conduct which is lamented (cf. 6.1; the definite participles without an introductory *hōy* in 5.7; 6.3, 13). The interjection *hōy* was used as a wail of grief over the dead (I Kings 13.30; Jer. 22.18; 34.5). The woe-cry pronounced over a living audience is found only in prophetic sayings; the prophet, knowing in advance the punishment decreed by Yahweh, would lament the death of his audience as a dramatic way of disclosing the dire consequences of their conduct.[a] Here the woe-cry simply introduces the saying to identify its addressees and to characterize their desperate plight; after 18a Amos shifts to the style of the discussion-saying, questioning and arguing against the faith of his hearers. The questions in 18b and 20 challenge the interpretation of the Day of Yahweh. Set between the questions are two comparisons, sentence-parables which disclose the real situation of the audience (v. 19). There is no final announcement of punishment or exhortation; the saying's purpose is fulfilled in disclosure, in bringing to light the folly and fate of these men who yearn for Yahweh's day.

[18] Verse 18 furnishes the earliest datable reference to the 'Day of Yahweh'. The term appears only in prophetic texts: Isa. 2.12; 13.6, 9; 22.5; 34.8; Jer. 46.10; Ezek. 7.19; 13.5; 30.3; Joel 1.15; 2.1, 11; 2.31; 3.14; Obad. 15; Zeph. 1.7, 14–18; Zech. 14.1; Mal. 4.5; with an exception in Lam. 2.22. The notion is not the creation of Amos; he clearly attacks the hope of those who already anticipate its coming. The problem of the origin of the idea and its meaning to Amos' contemporaries has been the subject of a long discussion. Among the more important hypotheses are these: (1) that the notion

[a] See G. Wanke, "*ōy* und *hōy*', *ZAW* 78, 1966, pp. 215ff. E. Gerstenberger concludes that the woe-cry is formally a Wisdom-saying (*JBL* 81, 1962, pp. 249–263), and C. Westermann sees it as a development of the curse-form (*Basic Forms of Prophetic Speech*, 1967, pp. 190ff.).

COMMENTARY

belongs to popular Israelite eschatological piety which had been
developed out of eschatological mythical material borrowed from
other religions;[a] (2) that 'Day of Yahweh' referred originally to a
New Year's festival in which Israel celebrated Yahweh's victory over
his cosmic and historical adversaries and his renewal of prosperity for
his devotees; the prophets reverse the expectations connected with
the day and proclaim the time as one of doom;[b] (3) that the notion
was a unique creation of Israel in which the old traditions of Yahweh's
theophanies were used to formulate an expectation of how their God
would decisively shape the life of the nation in the future.[c] The most
probable hypothesis is that the idea emerged from the traditions of
Holy War in Israel's earliest history.[d] The texts which include a
description of what happens on the Day portray an event of primarily
military character, depicted with a more or less fixed set of motifs.
Yahweh rises against his enemies, goes into battle, and defeats his foes
in a setting of cosmic and historical gloom and commotion. The
expectation that Yahweh would act in this fashion against their
national enemies was alive in Amos' audience and was a primary tenet
of their religious and political faith. The prophet does not have to
define the notion. The piety of his audience gives him his theme. Probably he addresses crowds assembled at Bethel for the annual autumn
festival, 'the day of the festival of Yahweh' as it was called in the
northern kingdom (Hos. 9.5). Stimulated by the celebration with its
many sacrifices, songs, rituals, and feasting (4.4f.; 5.21ff.), the religious fervour of the crowd was raised to fever pitch. 'Yahweh is with
us,' they cried (5.14b) and longed with lusty, confident anticipation for
the victory of Yahweh over the nations, which they may have celebrated
in the ritual of the festival, to become fact so that the field of history
would be left to them and their national aspirations. In the prophet's
eyes, knowing as he does the verdict which Yahweh has issued upon
this people, Israel is invoking its own doom (Jeremiah will later
disavow any longing for 'the day of disaster'—Jer. 17.16). So his only
reaction to this fervent faith can be to cry 'Woe!', to lament over them
as if they were already dead. In the assertion (18bβ) and question
(20) about the darkness of the Day of Yahweh, Amos selects one of the
recurring motifs used to picture its occurrence (Ezek. 30.3; Isa. 13.10;

[a] H. Gressmann, Der Ursprung der israelitisch-jüdischen Eschatologie, 1905, pp. 141ff.
[b] S. Mowinckel, He That Cometh, ET, 1956, pp. 125ff.
[c] L. Černy, The Day of Yahweh and Some Relevant Problems, 1948.
[d] G. von Rad, 'The Origin of the Concept of the Day of Yahweh', JSS 4, 1959,
pp. 97–108; Theology of the Old Testament II, 1965, pp. 119–25.

Joel 2.1f., 10f.; Zeph. 1.15f.; cf. Amos 8.9). When Yahweh fights his
foes, the heavenly luminaries will fail, thick clouds gather, gloom and
thick darkness will shroud the scene. In these descriptions the darkness is phenomenological. When Amos pairs darkness with light, the
opposites take on symbolic character and stand for calamity (*ra'*) and
salvation (*šālōm*) (cf. Isa. 45.7; 9.2; 59.9; Jer. 13.16). Apparently the
audience already knows of this feature, but they see their enemies in
the darkness. They understand the theology of the Day of Yahweh;
what they do not understand is Yahweh and themselves.

[19] Amos portrays their predicament with two proverbial comparisons. Using metaphors drawn from life in the country and villages
as a device for illuminating a situation is a feature of his style (3.3–6;
2.13; 3.12; 6.12; 9.9). A man escapes from a lion, only to fall prey to
a bear! A man comes home, to his place of security, and is bitten by a
snake! Both metaphors portray a situation in which a man escapes to
his death. So is it with Israel. This people yearns for Yahweh's
intervention against their foes as their way to security, and thereby
invoke their doom. They flee into danger; the salvation they desire
is in fact their death, for they are enemies of Yahweh.

In this saying Amos once more takes up a fundamental theme of
Israel's faith, and turns it against the community of believers. His
theological strategy here is similar to his treatment of the election
(3.2), the Exodus (9.7), and the salvation-history (2.9–11). He does
not reject or significantly modify the faith in the Day of Yahweh. But
out of his personal encounter with Yahweh in the visions (7.1–9;
8.1–3) he has been given as an absolute and unshakable foundation
for interpreting the articles of Israel's faith. He knows Yahweh himself,
and he knows the decision of Yahweh. From the perspective of that
absolute certainty he can see what Yahweh's Day means for his
contemporaries, and the expectation of that Day becomes a dominant
feature of his announcement of judgment.

19. THE HATED WORSHIP: 5.21–24

21'I hate, I despise your festivals;
   I take no pleasure in your assemblies.
22For, though you present burnt offerings to me . . .ᵃ

ᵃ 'For, though' (*kī 'im*) introduces a protasis whose apodosis is missing; it is
possible to find it in the next line (see RSV), though the regular bi-cola of the saying
resist this solution.

Your offerings I will not accept;
   your communion meals of fatted calves I will not notice.
²³Spare me the noise of your hymns;
   the music of your harps I will not hear.
²⁴But let justice roll on like waters,
   righteousness like an unfailing stream!'

The hatred of Yahweh against the worship of his people—that is the shock of this word. Righteousness in the courts and markets instead of liturgies and offerings in the shrines—that is the revelation in this word. It is formulated as a divine saying, composed of four bi-cola. 22a is an extra colon, a protasis without an apodosis. Supposing the apodosis has been lost from the text, one might conjecture that it read originally something like: 'Even though you present burnt offerings to me, (I will not receive them).' Or it is possible that the half-verse is an editorial addition to make the list of sacrifices more complete. The structure is easily discernible: Yahweh's evaluation of Israel's worship (vv. 21–23), and a concluding call for righteousness and justice (v. 24). Whether the saying continues to include all or part of vv. 25–27 is disputed; see the comment on those verses below. Verses 21–24 correspond to the structure of Isa. 1.10–17, its companion piece in the prophetic collections. It has been suggested that the saying has been formulated on the pattern of a cultic-decision-word, a divine saying spoken in the cult by a cultic prophet for the purpose of announcing whether or not an offering of the community pleased the deity and was acceptable.[a] Isaiah called his similar saying 'instruction' (tōrā, Isa. 1.10) and the alternation in both between negative and positive, between rejection or prohibition and command, support the appropriateness of the term.[b] Other prophetic sayings formulated similarly are Hos. 6.6; 8.13; Jer. 6.19–21; 14.11f.; Mal. 1.10; 2.13.

[21–23] In vv. 21–23 the essential elements of Israel's worship are taken up one after another: festivals (v. 21), sacrifice (v. 22), and praise (v. 23). Yahweh's announcement proceeds category by category so as to make it unmistakably clear that all of Israel's worship is totally rejected. Festival (ḥag) is the term used in the old festival lists as the common name for Unleavened Bread (maṣṣoth), Weeks, and Harvest, the three annual pilgrimage festivals (Ex. 23.15–18; 34.22,

[a] So E. Würthwein, 'Kultpolemik oder Kultbescheid' in *Tradition und Situation*, Festschrift für A. Weiser, ed. E. Würthwein and O. Kaiser, 1963, pp. 115–31.
[b] H. Gunkel and J. Begrich, *Einleitung in die Psalmen*, 1933, pp. 327f.

25; Deut. 16.10–16). Feast-day (*'aṣārā*) is a term for festive times (Isa. 1.13; Joel 1.14; II Kings 10.20) when the people took a holiday from work to celebrate (Lev. 23.36; Deut. 16.8; Num. 29.35). The burnt offering (*'ōlā*) is the sacrifice in which the entire animal is consumed on the altar and 'sent up' to the deity in smoke (Lev. 1.3–7). The communion sacrifice (*šelem*, elsewhere in the OT *zibḥē šelāmīm*; cf. Lev. 3) is a sacrifice in which only part of the specially prepared animal is burnt on the altar; the rest is eaten by the devotee and so deity and people share a meal which re-establishes the wholeness and vitality of their relationship. Offering (*minḥā*) is here a comprehensive term for any sacrifice brought as a gift, presented as the tribute of an inferior to a superior; the name was later specialized as a designation for vegetable offerings (Lev. 2).ᵃ Hymn (*šīr*) is the cultic song, the praise of exaltation and joy sung to God (cf. the use of *šīr* as a title in the Psalter). At Bethel the hymns were sung to the music of the *nebel*, a harp with its sounding box at the top after the Assyrian fashion.ᵇ All these items, which hardly exhaust the concerned categories, add up to a picture of the richness and vigorous enthusiasm of the cult of Bethel in the eighth century. The prophet did not address secular or indifferent people, but a folk who went about public religion with zeal and extravagance. The festivals which they celebrated and the ritual they followed were ancient and well established in Yahwism in their day. There is no hint that the ritual was regarded as irregular or pagan; the sacrifices were for Yahweh.

Yet the first person verbs in which Yahweh discloses his reaction to their worship of him reiterate nauseated disgust and vehement rejection. The first verb is the strongest; 'hate' expresses the total resources of a person set against someone or something (cf. 'hate' and 'love' in 5.14f.); Yahweh typically hates the cult of Canaan (Deut. 12.31; 16.22) Israel's cult is on the level with that of Canaan before him. The negated verbs (take pleasure in, accept, notice, hear) are those which normally describe Yahweh's positive reaction to Israel's worship in Israel's own cultic vocabulary. 'Take pleasure in' (literally 'smell, savour'): Gen. 8.27; I Sam. 26.19; 'accept': Ps. 51.18, and in the priestly declaratory formula by which a sacrifice is denominated as efficacious, Lev. 7.18; 19.7; 22.27; 'regard': Pss. 13.4; 80.15; 142.5;

ᵃ On the types of sacrifice in Israel and their significance see W. Eichrodt, *Theology of the Old Testament* I, 1961, pp. 141–72; G. von Rad, *Theology of the Old Testament* I, 1962, pp. 250–61.

ᵇ O. Sellers, *BA* IV 3, 1941, pp. 33ff.

108   COMMENTARY

'hear': generally in the Psalter as Yahweh's response to lament and
prayer. These denials of the expected response undermine the fundamental purpose of the cult. They run in contradiction to precisely what
Israel understood their ritual to be. Cult for them was 'the socially
established and regulated holy acts and words in which the encounter
and communion of the Deity is established, developed, and brought
to its ultimate goal'.[a] The divine word cancels the cult as a way of
communication and contact from God's side. In the central matter of
relation to their God Israel is left with the divine word's 'no' to what
they are doing and its demand for something else. The oracle throws
them into the crisis of having nothing to do but listen to the divine
word while God himself takes over and defines the nature of their
relationship to him.

[24] The basis of Yahweh's 'no' is first explicitly implied in the
instruction at the end of the saying: the demand for justice (*mišpāṭ*)
and righteousness (*ṣedāqā*). Verse 24 has been interpreted as an announcement of judgment, instead of an instruction: the judgment of
Yahweh and his righteous punishment will roll down on Israel like a
mighty river.[b] But Amos consistently uses righteousness and justice as
terms for the qualities which ought to be present in the social order
(6.12; 5.7, 15), and this movement from rejection of sacrifice to a call
for a kind of life described in these or similar terms is found in Isa.
1.10–17; Micah 6.6–8; Hos. 6.6. In Amos *mišpāṭ* is specifically
associated with the court in the gates and means the judicial process and
its decisions by which right order is maintained in social relations, and
especially the protection of weak and poor through the help of the
court. *Ṣedāqā* is the rightness that belongs to those who fulfil the responsibilities which their relationships to others involve. Yahweh is of
course included in the dimension of these terms because they are
comprehensive concepts which summarize the content of his will for
Israel, but their execution belongs to the horizontal sphere of society.
See the discussion of *mišpāṭ* and *ṣedāqā* in Amos in the comment on 5.7.
In effect Amos is saying that the worship of the cultic community is
unacceptable because Israel does not live as the community of
Yahweh (Matt. 7.21). They are to desert the sanctuaries, renew righteousness by recognizing and fulfilling their responsibilities to their
neighbours, and see that that rightness bears fruit in the justice of the

[a] S. Mowinckel, *The Psalms in Israel's Worship* I, ET, 1962, p. 15.
[b] Cf. the commentaries of A. Weiser, E. Sellin, *ad loc.*; and the somewhat
different proposal of J. P. Hyatt, *ZAW* 68, 1956, pp. 17ff.

THE HATED WORSHIP: 5.21-24

courts. To describe what that renewal must be like, Amos uses another of the metaphors drawn from his familiarity with the open country. Justice and righteousness must roll down like the floods after the winter rains, *and* persist like those few wadis whose streams do not fail in the summer drought (Deut. 21.4; Ps. 74.15). That is, the response should swell with sudden force, and continue unabated.

The absence of justice and righteousness is the issue. That Amos condemned Israel's worship because it was cultic is not implied by the text. Amos does not speak to any general and theoretical question such as: Should Israel's religion be cultic or non-cultic? His attacks are directed against the specific worship carried on by these Israelites in their shrines. The rejection of *that* cult is total and unqualified. He does not propose any reform of the cult or a different type of cult that would be appropriate for Yahweh. He simply calls the one that exists sinful (4.4), useless (5.21–23), and doomed (5.4f.). And the basic cause is that the people of Israel are at odds with their God. Amos works this conflict between persons into the very formulation of vv. 21–23 by setting second person plural pronouns (Israel) over against the first person verbs (Yahweh). '*I* hate *your* festivals'—the opposing pronouns carry the weight of meaning in the rejection. Possessive pronouns qualify every item in the cult and so identify them as expressions of Israel's personal piety. Yahweh delivers through Amos a pronouncement on the acceptability of Israel's cult; the evaluation is negative and the message is 'no'.

Behind this viewpoint of Amos must lie a tradition that runs back to the days of the tribal league in the pre-monarchical period when the celebration of Israel's relation to Yahweh emphasized the proclamation of Yahweh's will as the central concern in the relationship.[a] The conviction that the validity of worship offered to Yahweh depended upon the qualification of the worshipper is most clearly expressed in the liturgies for admission to the sanctuary found in Pss. 15; 24.3–5, and Micah 6.6–8; the form and content of the liturgy appear also in Isa. 33.14b–16 and Ezek. 18.5–9.[b] In Israel's shrines the priests were no longer proclaiming the requirements of the covenant and teaching that the congregation gathered in the sanctuary must be composed of those who were loyal to Yahweh's will. Amos takes up the post deserted by the priests at the gates of the sanctuary

[a] Cf. M. Noth, *The Laws in the Pentateuch and Other Essays*, ET, 1966, pp. 28–51.
[b] K. Koch, 'Tempeleinlassliturgien und Dekaloge' in *Studien zur Theologie der alttestamentlichen Überlieferung*, Festschrift für G. von Rad, 1961, pp. 45ff.

and declares that, because the requirements of appearing before
Yahweh are ignored, the cult is sinful and useless, and is not the source
of life; and he revives the teaching of righteousness as the way to the
life which Yahweh offers.[a]

20. SACRIFICE WILL NOT SAVE YOU: 5.25–27

5 25'Was it sacrifices and offering you brought to me
    in the wilderness (forty years), O house of Israel?
26You shall take up Sakkut[b] your king,
    and Kaiwan[c] (your images) your (star-) god(s) (which you
                             made for yourselves),
27And I will send you in exile
    beyond Damascus,'
has said Yahweh (God of hosts is his name).

In this divine saying Yahweh points back to the wilderness period
as an epoch in which Israel did not respond to him by cultic sacrifice
(v. 25), and then announces that he will exile the nation somewhere
in the distant east (v. 27). So much seems clear from the text. But v.
26 contains formidable problems which complicate the interpretation of the whole. Both versions and modern commentators have
struggled uncertainly with its difficulties; see the material and proposals collected by W. R. Harper[d] of which subsequent proposals are
repetitions and variations. These three verses have often been treated
as a continuation of 5.21–24; the divine first-person style continues,
and 'sacrifices and offering' repeats a theme of v. 22. However, these
connections could be the reason for separate sayings having been
placed sequentially in the arrangement of the book. 5.21–24 is
formally a complete saying without these verses. The question in v. 25
appears to be an opening rejoinder of Amos to some reference to their
sacrifices to Yahweh on the part of his audience (cf. Amos' use of
questions in disputation-sayings in 3.3ff.; 9.7). The understanding of
the saying proposed in the translation suggests that Amos denies the

    [a] On the general problem of prophetic sayings on the cult see H. H. Rowley,
'The Prophets and Sacrifice', *ExpT* 58, 1946/7, pp. 305–7; H. W. Hertzberg,
'Die prophetische Kritik am Kultus', *TLZ* 75, 1950, cols. 219–26; R. Hentschke,
Die Stellung der vorexilischen Schriftpropheten zum Kultus (BZAW 75), 1957.
    [b] MT *sikkūt*; see the comment.
    [c] MT *kiyūn*; see the comment.
    [d] ICC, pp. 129f., 136ff.

efficacy of sacrifice as a means to satisfy Yahweh (v. 25), and announces that his audience will fall into the power of foreign gods
(v. 26), and be taken into exile in their territory (v. 27).

[25] The opening question is a denial that sacrifice and offering
were the mode of Israel's relation to Yahweh during the wilderness
years. Seen in connection with v. 24 it implies that in those normative
original years Israel responded to Yahweh with obedience, and produced justice and righteousness instead of presenting sacrifice. The
pre-exilic prophets frequently announce Yahweh's preference for
right conduct to cultic sacrifice (Amos 5.21–24; Hos. 6.6; Micah
6.6–8; Jer. 6.20). The view that sacrifice was not indigenous to the
relation established between Israel and Yahweh at the beginning is a
tradition explicitly stated by Jeremiah (7.21–22). There is no way to
reconcile this view with the extant Pentateuchal tradition which
knows nothing of a period in Israel's beginnings when sacrifice was
not offered; the Passover with its sacrifice certainly belonged to
earliest times. But, for Jeremiah and Amos at least, sacrifice had no
authorized place in the constitution of Israel as the people of Yahweh.
Jeremiah thinks in terms of a covenant which requires obedience in
manner of life. Amos sets justice and righteousness over against the
entire cult (5.21–24) in abrupt contrast. 'Forty years' is probably an
addition to the text (cf. 2.10). This precise reckoning of the length of
the wilderness period began with Deuteronomic circles (Deut. 2.7;
8.2, 4; 29.5; Josh. 5.6) and became a feature of later references to the
wilderness (P: Ex. 16.35; Num. 14.33; 32.13; also Ps. 95.10; Neh.
9.21). But 'in the wilderness' is certainly authentic; it involves a
radical claim which later glossators would have found in contradiction to their own tradition. 'In the wilderness' is one of the themes
of the salvation-history which Amos recites in 2.9–11; it refers to the
time when Yahweh's action defined Israel's way and life. This ideal
notion of the wilderness period is held by other prophets, and in their
view what pertained to the wilderness era rises to the level of the
canonical for Israel (e.g., Hos. 2.14f.; Jer. 2.1–3). For the tradition in
which Amos stands, the acts of God in the Exodus, Wilderness and
Conquest, and the requirements of the covenant are so central that all
else is displaced in considering the relation between Yahweh and
Israel; this theological conviction is given historical formulation in
the circles which hold it. In the crisis of Israel's disobedience and cultic
extravagance, the relatively true is raised to absolute fact in order to
set the folly of Israel in starkest relief. The emergence and use of such

a tradition must be seen in the context of Israel's combination of disobedience to the covenant and rich development of her cult. Those who hold to the old amphictyonic tradition with its emphasis on the will of Yahweh in the cult were forced to choose between sacrifice and covenant, and ultimately set one against the other.

[26] The MT of v. 26 reads: 'You shall take up (or the verb could be frequentative: 'you take up') *Sikkūt* your king and *Kiyūn* your images the star of your gods which you have made for yourselves.' The major difficulties centre on the words *sikkūt* and *kiyūn* and on the length of the line. The form of *sikkūt* and *kiyūn* is a result of pronouncing their consonants with the vowels of 'abomination' (*siqqūs*), a scribal device for derogating names of false gods. The gods referred to were probably *Sakkūt and Kaiwan*, both known from Babylonian sources as names of the astral deity Saturn.[a] G reads the first word as 'tabernacle' (sukkat); following this clue some have found the Hebrew word 'pedestal' in the second, and seen here only references to cultic objects used in the worship of Yahweh. But the entire development of the text, and G itself, took the words as names of deities. The line is much too long to scan as poetry and its syntax is awkward. 'Star' is a comment added to explain the astral character of the deities named. It is possible that 'your images . . . which you have made for yourself' was also added by a tradent who understood that Amos was accusing the Israelites of having made images to use in the veneration of these gods. The reconstruction proposed here takes the original to be the first element in Amos' announcement of the coming punishment. The Israelites who sought to discharge their obligations to Yahweh through sacrifices will be forced to venerate the gods of a conqueror from the east. They have refused to obey Yahweh as King and God, so they shall be delivered up to enemies who force other deities upon them. Every reconstruction of v. 26 is precarious, because there is no way to be sure that Amos could have known the names of these deities, or whether they might have in fact been worshipped in Israel in his time. Amos makes no explicit issue of the worship of foreign gods (see the comment on 8.12), as does his successor Hosea, who concentrates on Israel's affinity for Canaanite deities and cultic practices. It is possible that v. 26 reflects the situation in Israel's territory after the Assyrian conquest and the introduction of a variety of cults into the north (cf. II Kings 17.29–31). The reference in v. 27 to exile 'beyond Damascus' might depend on

[a] J. Gray, 'Sakkuth and Kaiwan', *IDB* IV, p. 165.

the awareness that it was to this specific region that Assyria deported
the Israelites. Verses 26f. would then be an addition after the fact to
explain the exile in terms of the Deuteronomic passion against foreign
gods and to make the prediction of punishment precise. If this were
correct, then v. 25 would belong to 5.21–24.

[27] Yahweh himself will exile the nation; the God who delivered
them from Egyptian captivity will bring them into a new bondage.
The verb of which Yahweh is subject in this announcement means the
absolute reversal of the salvation-history. No historical agent is
mentioned; this calamity belongs to the history which Yahweh creates.
Amos speaks of a coming exile in 5.5; 6.7; 7.11, 17. 'Beyond Damascus'
is the only designation of the region to which the exiles will go. The
phrase points to the territory of Assyria and that nation may be con-
cretely in mind here. 'Exile' is a word with implications of horror which
outrun the ruin and pain of defeat and capture by an enemy. For
Israel it meant being removed from the land promised to the fathers,
displacement from the geographical locus of the unfolding history of
election, and so was in effect a kind of excommunication.

21. THE AFFLUENT SOCIETY: 6.1–7

6 ¹Woe to the carefree in Zion
   and the confident in mount Samaria,
the pre-eminent men of the first of nations
   to whom the house of Israel comes.
²'Cross to Calneh and look;
   go from there to great Hamath;
then go down to Gath of the Philistines.
Are they better than these kingdoms,
   or their territory greater than yours?'
³They who dismiss the day of disaster,
   but you bring near the seat of violence.
⁴They who lie on ivory beds,
   and sprawl upon their couches;
who eat lambs from the flock,
   and calves from the stall.
⁵Who improvise to the sound of the harp,
   (like David)ᵃ compose for themselves melodies.
⁶Who drink with great wine bowls,
   and with the best oil anoint themselves—
but they feel no pain at the ruin of Joseph.

ᵃ 'like David' is a gloss derived from a tradition like the one in II Chron. 7.6.

⁷Therefore, now they shall go into exile at the head of the
exiles,
and the revelry of the sprawlers shall vanish.

In eighth-century Israel the rich got richer and the poor got
poorer. In this Woe-saying Amos sketches the well-being enjoyed by
the upper classes in the capital cities, the splendid society that was
built upon the misery of the weak and poor. The style is predominantly
that of the woe-cry: an introductory *hōy* followed by definite plural
participles which depict and identify those whose conduct prepares
their downfall. On the woe-style, see the comment on 5.18. The
description is intensified by a quotation (v. 2) which dramatizes the
attitude of those portrayed. Only in 3b is the impersonal style interrupted by a second-person verb, betraying the fact that those for
whom the woe is meant are Amos' audience. The sequence focuses
first on the proud self-confidence of the ruling class (vv. 1–3) and then
on their elegant luxury (vv. 4–6a). The portrayal closes with a
lamenting cry over such callous unconcern (6b); the announcement
of punishment introduced by 'therefore' follows in v. 7. The 'woe-
saying' is the basis for the punishment. The announcement picks up
both the primary themes of vv. 1–6 (the pride in being first and the
sprawling indolence) and so confirms the rhetorical unity of the
stylistically somewhat uneven sequence.

[**1**] Both Samaria and Zion (Jerusalem) were royal cities whose
history was directly linked with the monarchy in Israel and Judah.
Neither had an old tradition of identity with the people and their
past. Omri had purchased property and developed Samaria to be the
seat of his government; it was a crown possession (I Kings 16.24), the
residence for his court, the home town for the expanding officialdom
whose insatiable hunger for the good life had steadily undercut the
old society based on the life of the clans in the villages. The political
and economic history of Israel was moving in their favour and they
were obsessed with an optimism about their future which still per-
sisted in the days of Isaiah, who reported that it was said in Samaria:
'The bricks have fallen, but we will build with dressed stones; the
sycamores have been cut down, but we will plant cedars in their
place' (Isa. 9.9f.). Doubtless the upper class in Samaria knew the
worries and troubles that belonged to all leading groups; but to Amos,
who knew Yahweh's decision about Israel's future, its optimism was
an incredible folly. In the light of what lay ahead he could only cry
'Woe' over the carefree and confident society; see Isaiah's similar

description of the women in Jerusalem, Isa. 32.9, 11. Under Jeroboam II Israel had moved into a relatively dominant position in relation to the surrounding states. Syria was immobilized by past defeats; Assyria had withdrawn from Syria-Palestine for the time being; the other neighbouring nations offered no threat. For a while it was possible for the ranking persons in government to dream of themselves as the top men in the top nation. The entire 'house of Israel' must come to them in all affairs of importance—and who else counted but Israel? Amos gives these leaders a title that mirrors their pride, the first of the first, but confers it with an irony that is fully revealed only at the end of the saying. The inclusion of Zion in the opening line is surprising for a prophet who elsewhere appears to speak only to the northern kingdom. But the shoe fits people in Jerusalem as well as in Samaria; in the general impersonal style of the woe-saying Amos has simply begun in an inclusive fashion. Though his mission was to Israel, he had no different word for similar folk in the south. Isaiah (9.8ff.) and Micah (1.5) both spoke oracles against both kingdoms.

[2] Verse 2 is best understood as a quotation which Amos puts in the mouth of the leading class.[a] This command to see how well Israel comes off in comparison with other nations is simply a case of unmitigated bragging. The technique of using a quotation to typify the attitude of his audience is employed by Amos in 8.5; 9.10; 5.14; 6.13. 'Let our countrymen travel to Calneh, Hamath and Gath, and observe that none of these countries is so large as Israel and Judah!' Hamath (cf. 6.14) and Calneh (= Calno in Isa. 10.9) were city-states to the north of Israel, the former in upper Syria on the Orontes River and the latter still farther north in the vicinity of Carchemish. Gath was a city in the Philistine Pentapolis to the west of Jerusalem. In Isa. 10.9 Hamath and Calno are ranged together with Samaria. The allusion to Gath is puzzling since it appears that in the time of Amos' ministry the city was held by Judah.[b] Another interpretation takes v. 2 as the warning of Amos to Israel to go see nations which were greater than they and yet had met their doom. This interpretation requires the emendation of the text ('*your* borders than *their* borders'; cf. BH), and is embarrassed by the uncertainty whether Hamath and Calneh had been captured by the Assyrians in the mid-eighth century; we cannot be sure that Hamath was put under Assyrian

[a] With E. Sellin, KAT, p. 242.
[b] J. Bright, *A History of Israel*, p. 236.

tribute before 738.[a] The MT conveys a vivid sense as a quotation. The boast articulates a pride that is nurtured by the success of Jeroboam's reign (6.13) and a belief in their manifest destiny as the people of Yahweh (5.14).

Living in such complacent confidence, the leaders are in no mood to hear dire predictions of a 'day of disaster', no patience with a country Cassandra. 'Day of disaster' is an alternative term for the day of Yahweh (cf. 5.18, 20; 8.10). They take their own accomplishments as the sign of God's favour and presence with them and boast that misfortune will never be their lot (9.10). They reject the judgment day warning of Amos, and busy themselves with plundering the poor. 'Seat' is used in its technical sense of throne or judicial seat (Pss. 122.5; 74.20). Violence (3.10) reigns where they sit to govern; these men are doing too well at creating misfortune for others even to consider the possibility that they may be digging their own graves.

[4–6] Verses 4, 5 and 6ab sketch a scene of opulent feasting. Expensive furniture, indolent ease, succulent food, the sound of music, and extravagant indulgence—so the affluent in Samaria live. Every item represents a luxurious sophistication that had been possible in earlier times only for royalty, and remained a world apart from the life in the villages. The hollowness of it all only becomes apparent in 6c where this heedless hedonism is thrown into relief against the 'ruin of Joseph' from which it is completely insulated. 'Ivory beds' are couches whose frames are inlaid with ivory designs.[b] Lambs and stalled calves are choice animals fed and finished as delicacies in a culture where eating any meat at all was exceptional (I Sam. 28.24; Luke 15.23). The custom in Israel had been to sit on rugs or seats when eating; the practice of reclining for meals is mentioned here for the first time, a foreign innovation of *Hochkultur*. The specific meaning of v. 5 is not certain. 'Improvise' (*prṭ*) occurs only here and may mean something like 'sing extemporaneously'. When feasting they sing to the harp, making up all kinds of songs to enliven their revelry. The great bowl (*mizrāq*) is mentioned elsewhere in the Old Testament only in connection with ritual procedures (e.g. Ex. 27.3; 38.3; Num. 4.14; I. Kings 7.40, 45; Jer. 52.18f.). Only the finest oil will do for their anointing. The Hebrew word for 'anoint' (*mšḥ*) in this verse is generally used for the cultic act, while other verbs (*sūk*, *dšn*) generally stand for the personal cosmetic use of olive oil.

[a] *Ibid.*, p. 253.
[b] *IDB* II, pp. 773ff.

The whole sequence pictures an upper class so self-centred and intent on its own pleasure as to find Amos' prediction of catastrophe incredible. Some interpreters (Gressmann, Sellin, Maag) have found in vv. 3–6 the description of a private cultic ritual like those mentioned in Isa. 65.11 and Jer. 44.17, whose function was to exorcise by magic any coming evil time. They point to the practice of cursing the evil day in Job 18.18; render 'dismiss' as 'adjure, swear away'; point to the cultic character of 'basin' and 'anoint'; take 'revelry' in v. 7 as a technical word for 'cultic banquet' (*marzēaḥ*, elsewhere only in Jer. 16.5). It is credible that people who desired the day of Yahweh against their enemies might also resort to unofficial cultic procedures to ensure their well-being. But the opening lines (vv. 1f.) emphasize their self-confidence, not their insecurity; it is more likely that the revelry is simply that of privileged powerful people who enjoy the indulgences which they can afford. The guilt in this indolence comes to focus in 3b and 6c! The economic base of such luxury is violence (*ḥāmās*; cf. 3.10) against the poor. In all their luxury they have not the slightest concern for the breakdown of Joseph (= Israel). The sufferings of the oppressed and wronged in the nation do not touch them. They neither see nor hear their covenant brother. Surely the God who made himself known to Israel in Egypt as one who heard their cry and knew their sufferings there (Ex. 3.7) cannot bear this revelry. Just as he rejects the sound of their worship (5.21–24), he is nauseated by the noise of their amusement.

[7] 'Therefore'—it shall all come to an end. The leaders of today shall tomorrow lead the pitiful column of captives who go into exile! (5.27, 5). With tragic irony Amos lets them be first to the bitter end. Where revelry filled the air, there shall remain only the vacancy of ominous silence. No historical foe is mentioned. The announcement of judgment simply predicts a tomorrow in which the pride and mirth of the present are swallowed up and disappear.

22. THE WRATH OF GOD: 6.8–11

6 ⁸Lord Yahweh has sworn on his own person, (a saying of Yahweh,
God of hosts)ª
'I abhorᵇ the pride of Jacob;

ª The oracle formula seems superfluous at this place, and is missing in G.
ᵇ MT 'longs for' (*mᵉtāʾēb*); read *mᵉtāʿēb*.

I hate his strongholds;
I will deliver up the city with its inhabitants.'
⁹It will come to pass that if ten men be left in one house, they shall die. ¹⁰When a man's kinsmanª lifts him to bring the corpse from the house, he will say to the one in the back part of the house, 'Is there yet anyone with you?' He will say, 'None.' He will say, 'Hush, for we must not invoke the name of Yahweh.'
¹¹For behold, Yahweh is the one who commands!
He shall smash the great house in pieces,
and the small house in bits.

The common theme of 6.8–11 is Yahweh's wrath against city and house. The variety in formal and literary character indicates that the sequence is composed of fragments and summaries of original sayings which have been brought together because of similar subjects. Verse 8 is a divine oracle in the first person introduced by an oath formula and stating Yahweh's decree of judgment against Israel's urban magnificence. In vv. 9 and 10 there is a miniature prose narrative describing a scene of death and religious dread. Verse 11 has its own formula introducing the announcement that great and small houses alike are marked for shattering destruction. The character of the disasters foretold seems to be in turn military conquest, disease, and earthquake, which the collectors may have regarded as a comprehensive summary of the total doom predicted by Amos. The subject matter of this material makes it follow appropriately the condemnation of urban pride and affluence in 6.1–7.

[8] 'Yahweh has sworn . . .' is used three times by Amos (4.2; 8.7) to introduce a divine decree of punishment. That Yahweh takes oath on his own person (as in Jer. 22.5; 49.13; 51.14) makes the decree the more final, because the total force of Yahweh's personal integrity is invested in this solemn oath, the ancient Near East's most binding form of personal commitment. The 'pride of Jacob' (8.7) speaks of Israel's preening national self-confidence which had become the real centre and concern of the nation's upper classes. Yahweh loathes this pride as one abhors an unclean thing because they regarded their national destiny as the work of their own hands (6.1, 13) and because it was expressed in an indulgent luxury which ignored the unfortunate. Pride in Israel meant the displacement of Yahweh as the foundation of their national existence and led to a casual disobedience of his lordship over them. 'The city' must refer to Samaria

ª 'Kinsman' translates two Hebrew words; see the comment.

(6.1) which as Israel's capital was the focus of her national optimism. The 'strongholds' there were filled with the gain of robbery and violence against the poor (cf. the commentary on 3.10). 'The city and its strongholds', repeatedly the target of Amos' messages, enshrines the worst of Israel's guilt. The powerful rich may think themselves invulnerable against any foe, but when Yahweh is against them their strength is useless and their defences already breached.

[9] Verse 9 presupposes some foregoing description of disaster leaving only a remnant of the city's population. But its narrative, prosaic, style in contrast to the oracular form of v.8 makes an original connection between the two unlikely. And why ten men in one house? That would seem an inflated number of male occupants even under normal conditions, unless 'house' here means 'palace'. Lacking the original context, we can say of the verse only that it is one more of those awfully final kinds of sentences by which Amos declares how total and comprehensive will be the coming judgment. Whoever is left (after the rest have been deported?) will only face death.

[10] The relation of v. 10 to what goes before is equally uncertain, though it also plunges *in medias res* and assumes some foregoing description of disaster. That the dead man's corpse is in his house indicates that the cause of death must be something like contagious pestilence. Perhaps a plague is in view in v. 9, and v. 10 supplies a vignette depicting a typical scene during its course. 'Kinsman' is an interpretation of two words in the text (*dōd* and *mᵉsārēp*). *Dōd* is a kinsman on the father's side, uncle or cousin. *Mᵉsārēp* is usually translated 'he who burns him' (so RSV, on the assumption that *srp* = *śrp*). But cremation was not an accepted funeral practice among the Israelites. T. H. Robinson[a] thinks that it means kinsman on the mother's side and is a synonym of *dōd*. The 'kinsmen' have the responsibility for the rites of burial and they have come to do their duty. The terse, conversational exchange is reported in such spare fashion as to allow for only a conjectural reconstruction of the scene. One of the kinsmen calls to another who has gone to the back of the house to see if any other member of the family is left. The latter responds that none is left, but, before he can say more, is interrupted by the first, lest he add some pious expression of grief or invocation using the name of Yahweh. The command to silence, 'Hush' (*hās*), in its other appearances in the prophets (Zeph. 1.7; Zech. 2.13) is used in ritual-like fashion as a cry in the face of Yahweh's theophany

[a] HAT, p. 94, following a suggestion of G. R. Driver.

against his enemies. This may furnish some clue to its use here. The first speaker, realizing in the terror of the destruction which has come upon the city, that the day of Yahweh has come, fears lest another mention of the divine personal name renew the terrible curse which the Lord's appearing has brought. Once again Amos portrays a time of judgment so fraught with the reality of Yahweh's personal presence as to leave Israel no possibility but to acknowledge that the Lord of Hosts is the power in whose hands they are.

[11] In its present position v. 11 reinforces this sense of dread that it is Yahweh himself who brings the disaster upon the city: 'For behold! Yahweh is the commander. . . .' 'Great house' and 'small house' are hardly symbolic terms for Judah and Israel (Wellhausen, Harper). The two terms are rather a comprehensive way of saying that the destruction will be total (cf. 3.15); when Yahweh's decree is carried out nothing but debris will remain. By such oracles and stories Amos reinforces the inexorability and terror of Yahweh's revelation that 'the end has come for my people Israel'. City, buildings, and their builders are doomed to show that Israel is allowed no pride except a pride in their God.

23. THE ABSURD HAPPENS IN ISRAEL: 6.12

6 ¹²Do horses run on a crag
        or does one plough ªthe sea with an ox,ª
    that you have changed justice into a poison weed
        and the fruit of righteousness into wormwood?

The saying is composed of a question (12a) and an observation (12b) which together are meant to uncover the incredible character of what is happening in Israel's public life. 12a asks if the absurd could happen; 12b asserts that it is happening. The double question creates the feeling of astonishment at the impossible; the observation turns the mood on the actuality. The style is characteristic of the technique of folk wisdom which makes its point through leading questions and comparisons.ᵇ 12b is quite similar to 5.7.

ᵃ⁻ᵃ Dividing MT's consonants *bbqr ym*; MT's vocalization ('with oxen') obscures the riddle. One does plough with oxen!
    ᵇ See the questions in 3.3–6 and the discussion in R. B. Y. Scott, 'Folk Proverbs of the Ancient East', in *Transactions of the Royal Society of Canada* 55, 1961, pp. 52f.

Horses do not run on perpendicular cliffs nor is the sea ploughed with an ox—both are ridiculous ideas! The question poses what all would recognize as impossible, as does Jeremiah's question about the Ethiopian and the leopard (Jer. 13.23). Yet in Israel the absurd is fact! Justice is transformed into poison weed and the fruit of righteousness into wormwood. Righteousness (*sedāqā*) is rightness of life according to the authoritative norms. Justice (*mišpāṭ*) is the judicial process whose integrity ought to be maintained by righteousness, and therefore is the fruit of righteousness. Cf. the discussion of *mišpāṭ* and *sedāqā* in the comment on 5.7. When the poor and afflicted come to the courts of Israel expecting their rights to be protected and vindicated, instead of justice they are dealt out the very same injustice from which they sought relief. To Amos, who will allow Israel no other identity and way of life than that given her in the election of Yahweh, such a reversal of things staggers the mind, and he can only compare it to some incredible perversion of the normal order of things. And with this argumentative saying he seeks to make the leaders of the nation see their deeds as Yahweh sees them.

24. THEY WHO LIVE BY THE SWORD: 6.13–14

6 ¹³Those who rejoice about *Lō'-dābār*,
   those who say, 'Was it not by our strength
      that we took Karnaim for ourselves?'
   ¹⁴For behold, I am raising against you,
      O house of Israel (a saying of Yahweh, God of hosts),ᵃ a
                                                              nation.
   They will oppress you from the entrance of Hamath
      to the brook of the Arabah.

The oracle juxtaposes the boasting of Israel in its own strength and the plan of Yahweh for Israel's downfall. Pride goes before the fall. The prophet cites the self-congratulation of the nation as complaint against them (v. 13) and then speaks Yahweh's announcement of judgment in first-person style (v. 14). The complaint is formulated by using definite participles to characterize the culpable activity and identify the addressees, a frequent stylistic device of Amos (cf. 5.7;

ᵃ The oracle formula lengthens the line unduly and comes in the midst of the sentence; its presence here is due either to the editors or to disarrangement of the text.

6.3–6; and on the relation of the style to the woe-saying the comment on 5.18; 6.1). In the second line of v. 13 Amos uses another of his favourite techniques, the quotation (2.12; 5.14; 6.2; 8.5, 14; 9.10); the addressees are dramatized in the complaint and their own words are cited in testimony against them.

[13] The background of Israel's self-congratulation lay in the remarkable resurgence of national power which Israel had experienced under Jeroboam II. With her constant adversary, Damascus, crippled by Assyrian campaigning, Jeroboam had been able to recoup Israel's previous losses east of the Jordan; II Kings 14.25 implies that Jeroboam had recovered all of the territory in that quarter which Israel had ever held.[a] *Lō'-dābār* means 'no-thing'; the name as Amos pronounced it was a pun on the name of the town variously called *Lō-debār* in II Sam. 9.4f. and *Lō'-debār* in II Sam. 17.27. It is probably the Gadite city *Debīr* (Josh. 13.26, text?) located in the eastern part of Gilead. Karnaim was farther to the north-east on the upper reaches of the Wadi Yarmuk, the sister city of Ashtaroth (Gen. 14.5). Apparently both had been the sites of successful campaigning against the Arameans. The names furnish Amos an opportunity for biting sarcasm. He changes the first to a pun by mispronouncing it; the second, Karnaim ('horns'), is a metaphor for strength. Israel's leaders celebrate what is really nothing and think to have captured strength by their own strength! The reiterated emphasis on 'our . . . we . . . ourselves' in the second line mocks the boasting assessment which the people make of Jeroboam's success. An Israel which saw its own strength as the foundation of military victory was flying in the face of the old theology of Holy War. Yahweh was a God of war (Ex. 15.3) and had revealed himself in Israel's battles; when she won it was because Yahweh himself had given the enemy into her hand. For Israel to think that she had prevailed on the field of battle was a perversion of the ancient faith and a usurpation of Yahweh's role in the nation's existence.

[14] The punishment corresponds to the sin, for in Yahweh's judgment they would learn again at terrible cost who presides over the nations and holds the outcome of war in his hand. Yahweh, Lord of history, is even now raising a nation to defeat and oppress them throughout the length of their land. The 'entrance (?) of Hamath' is the name for a location used to mark the northernmost limits of

---

[a] See the discussion in J. Bright, *A History of Israel*, 1959, p. 239; and M. Noth, *The History of Israel*, 1960[2], p. 250.

Solomon's and Jeroboam's kingdom (I Kings 8.65; II Kings 14.25). The precise meaning and exact location of the name and site are disputed.[a] The Brook of the Arabah may be the Brook Zered at the south end of the Dead Sea; it is meant to indicate the southern limit of Jeroboam's territory. Israel will be harried from north to south; no corner of the kingdom will be spared the foe's harassment. The clear candidate for the threatening nation is Assyria, but the eyes of the prophet are focused not so much upon international history as upon the sovereignty of the Lord and the conduct of his erring subjects. In their defeat, they will come to know again whose strength it is that leads all nations and determines their destiny (9.7).

25. VISION AND REALITY: 7.1–8.3

The block of material in 7.1—8.3 is made up of five narratives. Sayings do appear within the block; there is an oracle against the priest Amaziah in 7.16f., and two fragmentary announcements of punishment in 7.9 and 8.3. But these sayings are embedded in the narrative reports. Four of the narratives are vision-reports, composed in autobiographical style (7.1–3, 4–6, 7–9; 8.1–3). The other (7.10–17) stands between the third and fourth vision-reports; its subject is a confrontation between Amos and the priest of Bethel; it is told in biographical style. This difference in style indicates that the block is not an original oral or literary unit. The biographical narrative has been set in its present place because of the connection between 7.9 and 11; the third vision report ends with the announcement that Yahweh will rise against the dynasty of Jeroboam with the sword (v. 9), and the biographical narrative relates that Amaziah reported to his king this word of Amos: 'Jeroboam shall die by the sword.' For other cases of the juxtaposition of first- and third-person reports in prophetic books, compare Hosea 1 and 3 and Isa. 6.1–7.17. A fifth vision-report appears in 9.1–4. Its distinctiveness in form sets it apart from the sequence of 7.1–9; 8.1–3.

The four vision-reports are formulated on the same basic pattern:
(a) the introductory formula—'Thus Lord Yahweh showed me . . .';

[a] See H. G. May, *IDB* II, pp. 516f.

(*b*) the vision-content—'Behold . . .' (followed by a report of what was seen);

(*c*) a dialogue between Amos and Yahweh.

The four fall into two pairs which are distinct in the nature of what is seen, the order of the dialogue, and the outcome of the experience. In the first two (7.1–3 and 4–6) Amos sees an event; as he watches in the supranormal experience of charismatic perception, it moves toward completion. The meaning of the event goes without overt interpretation, for its significance is transparent in the fact of what happens and in the nature of the event in relation to the tradition about Yahweh's action. In the second pair (7.7–9 and 8.1–3) Amos is shown mundane objects whose meaning is not obvious, a plumb line and a basket of summer fruit. The interpretation of what is seen is given in the dialogue. The objects serve as symbols and correspond to a keyword in a divine decree. The difference in the order of the dialogues corresponds to the distinction in what is seen. In the first pair, Amos initiates the exchange; knowing the meaning of what Yahweh is about to do, he intercedes and pleads for a change of divine policy. In the second pair the Lord begins the conversation, and by interpreting the symbolic object announces his decree concerning Israel. The outcome in turn follows the other contrasts. At first Yahweh hears the intercession, changes his mind, and revokes his decision. In the last two the decree is final; Amos makes no rejoinder.

The second pair of vision-reports contains an element which stands outside the common structure. Both conclude with a description of the action which Yahweh will take against Israel (7.9 and 8.3). In content they are typical of Amos' portrayal of the work of Yahweh's wrath; there is no reason to doubt that they derive from him. As concerns their form, these verses are announcements of punishment in divine first-person style; in function they belong to the public oracle rather than to the dialogue. Their present location could be explained in three ways. (1) They represent a nugatory formulation of the message given by Yahweh to Amos in the visions. (2) They were used by Amos in the formulation of the vision reports to make clear the consequences of Yahweh's withdrawal of forbearance. (3) They were added by the first collectors of Amos' sayings for the same reason. The verses had to be present in the reports at an early stage because the biographical narrative, which represents contemporary tradition, is attached to 7.9.

The phenomenon of vision was a constitutive element in the prophetic experience.[a] Prophets received their call and were told the plans of Yahweh through visions. To name only some of the best-known examples, see I Kings 22.17, 19; Isa. 6; Jer. 1.11–14; 24.1ff.; Ezek. 1; 8–9; Zech. 1–8. When Amaziah called Amos a 'seer' (*ḥōzeh*, 7.12) he may have done so because he had heard of Amos' visions. The experiences of Amos in seeing and hearing under divine constraint were a fundamental source of his message and were formulated themselves as word.

The vision-reports have been prepared with conscious art. The experiences are not recounted in shapeless or discursive narrative, but reduced to essentials and ordered according to a clear pattern. In style and content the reports show similarities to vision-reports from other prophets.[b] The first pair of Amos' visions belong to the type called 'event-vision', the second pair to 'wordplay-visions'. The opening formula, though variously stated, is a regular part of the pattern; for Amos' expression 'he showed me' cf. Num. 23.3; II Kings 8.13; Jer. 24.1; 38.21; Ezek. 11.25; Zech. 1.20; 3.1. Almost exact parallels to the reports in Amos appear in Jeremiah (1.11f., 13f.; 24.1ff.) and Zechariah (5.1–4; cf. 4.1–7). This parallel in form and content is hardly due to literary dependence. The pattern belongs to the prophetic succession itself and appears to have developed before Amos and lasted long after as an element of prophetic speech.

The formal character of these narratives requires that a distinction be made between the reports and the experiences behind them. The visions themselves belong to one moment in Amos' career; their formulation and use as part of his prophetic activity belongs to another. More can be said about the latter with confidence than the former. The autobiographical style of the narratives indicates that they were composed by Amos himself. They were hardly prepared for private use or for circulation to a small, intimate group. In their consistent, concentrated style these reports are a type of proclamation. They testify to the revelations of Yahweh, to his decisions concerning Amos' audience, and so serve the same function as oracles, albeit with a different form. The purpose of this special proclamation is the vindication of the proclamation itself. From time to time Amos'

[a] On vision and prophecy see J. Lindblom, *Prophecy in Ancient Israel*, 1962, pp. 122ff., and the literature cited there.

[b] See the article by F. Horst, 'Die Visionsschilderungen der alttestamentlichen Propheten', *EvTh* 20, 1960, pp. 183–205, where all the reports are surveyed and classified according to form and content.

oracles reflect the stubborn protesting dissent which met his announcement of judgment for the entire people (cf. 3.3–8; 5.14; 7.13; 9.10).
The reports are an answer to these objections. By their severe concentration on the decisions of Yahweh set in juxtaposition to the
prayer of Amos they make clear that the final radicality of Amos'
sayings is grounded exclusively in Yahweh. Each pair of reports
drives at a corresponding argument; the prophet says in effect: the
judgment of Israel is not my will, for I have twice turned away the
wrath of Yahweh by my intercession; it is Yahweh's final decree, and
even intercession is now forbidden me. My direct predictions are in
obedience to the decree of your God: 'The end has come for my
people, Israel.' To serve this purpose the reports would have to have
been delivered all together. The twofold vindication is incomplete
without both pairs. The repetition of form has been used as a device
to create a rhetorical series similar to those in 1.3–2.16 and 4.6–12.
The series must have been spoken as the objections intensified, probably at Bethel. When Amaziah called Amos a 'seer', he could have
been provoked to use the title because he knew of the vision-reports
(7.12).

The narratives offer almost no clues about the time and place of
the experiences themselves. Amos figures in them only as participating
in the conversation with Yahweh; details of his personal life play no
role in their purposes. The chronological and biographical evidence
to be deduced from what he saw is quite ambiguous. This is all the
more the case if the visual element of the experience belonged to the
visionary. And if the events and objects were actual, one has no more
than an unidentified locust swarm, drought, plummet, and basket of
fruit. The fifth vision (9.1) is located at a sanctuary; Bethel is the
likeliest candidate. No overt element of a call appears. In the one
reference to his call (7.15), Amos tells nothing of the experience
involved. It is not certain that call-visions always included a specific
commissioning, though those in Isa. 6; Jer. 1.4–10; Ezek. 1–2 do.
If the visions were not inaugural, they must have come at the latest
before the beginning of his proclamation in Israel. The bulk of the
oracles assume the final decree of the third and fourth visions. The
shift from the first to the second pair has been seen as evidence of two
phases in Amos' career, and it has been argued that the successful
intercessions indicate that Amos worked at first as a salvation-prophet.[a]
The intercessions do effect a respite from judgment for Israel. But the

[a] So E. Würthwein, 'Amos-Studien', ZAW 62, 1950, pp. 10ff.

real burden of the visions themselves is not blessing and salvation, but the revelation of Yahweh's burning wrath against his people. The wrath is reserved, but the situation remains ominous, threatening, and unresolved.

Uncertainty about the biographical locus of the visions does not obscure their crucial significance for the mission and message of Amos. Their role in changing a rural Judean into a prophet was undoubtedly great. These personal encounters with Yahweh created a reservoir of confidence and insight, and set his existence in living contact with a reality beside which the authority of men and the truth of theologies paled in contrast. Amos saw and spoke with Yahweh. Out of this seeing and hearing came a doing and speaking which set him apart from his fellows. The shepherd became a spokesman who yielded no ground to the priest of Bethel. He left his own country and presumed to announce the fall of the king into whose land he came. He maintained his 'Thus says Yahweh' against the stubborn and scornful rejection of his audience. He took up the tenets of national piety, the articles of faith in Yahweh, and reinterpreted them so drastically that their proclamation became the judgment of those who believed in Yahweh. He knew the God with whom the theology and piety dealt, and so knew how to let that God speak through the theology. Yahweh's word of the end reverberated in all his oracles. His proclamation was the sound of a new era in the history of Yahweh and Israel.

(a) THE LOCUST SWARM: 7.1–3

7 ¹This is what Lord Yahweh showed me: Behold, he was creating a locust-swarm just as the late planting began to come up. And behold, it was the late planting after the king's mowing. ²ᵃWhen it was about to finishᵃ devouring the crops of the land, I said, 'Lord Yahweh, forgive! How shall Jacob survive? for he is small.' ³ Yahweh repented concerning this. 'It shall not take place,' said Yahweh.

In the first vision Amos is shown a locust swarm being created and made ready just when the 'late planting' (*leqeš*) had begun to spring up.ᵇ The threat looms when the last growth of pasture and field before the summer's dry season is beginning; if it were lost the people

---

ᵃ⁻ᵃ Regrouping MT's consonants and vocalizing: *wayhī hū' mᵉkalleh*, with C. C. Torrey (*JBL* 13, 1894, p. 63).
ᵇ See *leqeš* in the Gezer Calendar, *ANET*, p. 320a.

would have nothing to carry them over until the next harvest. The
reference to the royal mowing (2b) suggests that the king had the
prerogative to claim the first cutting of hay for the use of his military
establishment (I Kings 18.5). But a second sentence introduced by
'Behold' is unexpected in the structure of the vision reports; 2b may
well be a gloss added to make the time of the appearance of locust
more precise. The recurrent appearance of locust swarms was one of
the most dreadful plagues that afflicted the population of the ancient
East.[a] When the swarm made their ravenous way across the land, the
face of the earth was stripped of every green plant. Nothing was left
but the suffering and death of famine and the despair of men in the
face of menace against which they were helpless. The horror was the
greater in Israel because the locust was regarded as the plague of
Yahweh, the instrument of his curse upon Israel (Ex. 10.12ff.; Deut.
28.38, 42; Joel 1; Amos 4.9). When Amos was made to see the locust
swarm being made ready by Yahweh, the event carried its own
portentous message; Yahweh's wrath had broken out against his
people; punishment had been decreed for Israel. In the elevated
consciousness of the vision, time is telescoped and Amos watches the
progress of the plague until the crops and pasture of the land are
almost gone. The event belongs completely to the realm of vision, is
not yet actual event. It is the dramatic portrayal of the divine purpose
shaped into revealing experience for the sake of the prophet that he
may know the decision of Yahweh before it is executed (cf. the vision
of Micaiah ben Imlah, I Kings 22.17). It is none the less real because
it is a preview; what Yahweh prepares in heaven will inexorably
unfold on earth. The timing of his appeal indicates that, were the
event to be completed in the vision, its re-enactment on earth would
be an accomplished fact, a decree that could not be turned back. At
this crucial juncture Amos addresses Yahweh. The fact that Yahweh
bestows vision upon him puts him in the divine presence. The event
concerns Israel, but its visionary presentation is for him. By the vision
Amos has been selected as the one person on earth to whom the
heavenly king discloses his counsel. He is the intermediary between
the divine sovereign and his subjects, the figure by whom the decree
of the heavenly court is to be proclaimed. Now, like Moses (Num.
14.11ff.), he is constituted the mediator between Yahweh and Israel
precisely by this revelation and is alone in a position to step into the
breach and appeal from earth against the divine decision.

[a] See 'Locust' in *IDB* III, pp. 144ff.

Amos' intercessory appeals (vv. 2 and 5) are terse prayers constructed of the petition itself in an imperative and of a reason why it ought to be heard. The petition implores Yahweh to forgive (slḥ), a verb of which Yahweh alone is subject in the Old Testament. The nature of the locust plague as punishment for sin is recognized and accepted. What Yahweh is about to do is a response to the guilt of Israel in their relation to him as their Lord. The only appeal that can be made against this just decree is to Yahweh himself, to a capacity within the sovereign freedom of the divine person who can, if he will, take upon himself the rebellion of his subjects and deal with them in mercy. To forgive means here for God to bear with the sin of Israel without repentance or atonement from the side of Israel. Amos throws himself on the divine sovereignty and prays simply that Yahweh desist (ḥdl, the synonym used in the similar prayer in v. 5). The basis upon which Amos rests his appeal is the fact that Israel will cease to exist if the divine decree is carried out. The rhetorical question, 'How can Jacob survive, for he is small?' states the danger. 'Jacob' is Amos' favourite personal name for the northern kingdom (3.13; 6.8; 8.7; 9.8). Amos has a quite different estimate of Jeroboam's nation from that held by the people. They lived in pride and thought themselves invulnerable (6.1ff., 8, 13). But Amos sees them before the awesome majesty and might of Yahweh's wrath in their true helpless, hopeless littleness. Amos does not base his appeal upon Israel's election, or upon any guarantee of salvation in Yahweh's deeds in the past. In his view the special relation between Yahweh and Israel and the events of the salvation-history established Yahweh's sovereignty over Israel instead of Israel's rights before their God (see the exegesis of 3.2 and 2.9–12). In Amos' theology the election was not a ground for indulgence; it was a basis for judgment. When Amos in his intercession represents Israel as vulnerable and small, he appeals to a personal characteristic of Yahweh. The Yahweh whom Amos knows is a God who is passionately concerned for the weak, the poor, the helpless. (See the comment on 2.6–8.) Therefore the only hope for their survival before Yahweh lay in the very contradiction of religious confidence and national pride.

The appeal is heard; Yahweh revokes his plan by a countervening decree: 'It shall not be.' The divine reaction to Amos' prayer is a response within the personal nature of Yahweh which occurs without any cultic manipulation or legalistic calculation. The verb 'repent' (niḥam) when used with Yahweh as subject does not include any sense

of regret or remorse about a course of action seen as wrong.[a] It is one
of the Old Testament's anthropomorphic expressions which insist on
the reality of Yahweh's personal involvement in his action toward
man, the emotional awareness of the responsibility and consequences
of his acts. He does not coldly calculate, but 'feels' his way into the
change in his policy and displays a sensitivity to his creatures which
prevents his rule over Israel from being rigidified into an abstract
mechanical sovereignty. The outcome of the first vision leaves a sense
of unbearable tension. Israel has been spared the cataclysmic outbreak of the divine wrath only because of Yahweh's willingness to
hear the intercession of one man. But the circumstances which
provoked the decree of punishment continue unchanged.

When Amos averts the wrath of God from Israel by his intercessions,
he performs a function which is characteristic of the prophet. This
capacity to intercede on behalf of others was regarded as a prophetic
speciality (Gen. 20.7; I Kings 13.5f.; 17.20ff.; II Kings 4.33; Isa.
37.4; Jer. 7.16; Ezek. 13.4f.; etc.).[b] To claim that prayer for another
or for the whole nation was exclusively a prophetic function would
outrun the evidence. Intercession was made by kings: David (II
Sam. 21.1; 24.17), Solomon (I Kings 2.22ff.), Hezekiah (II Kings
19.14ff.).[c] However, in every case where intercession to turn the
wrath of God away from the people is reported, the intercessor was a
person who had an established status in the scheme of Yahweh's
relation to the people. The only possible classification for Amos'
function is prophet.

(b) THE DIVINE FIRE: 7.4–6

7 [4]This is what Lord Yahweh showed me: Behold he[d] was summoning [e]a rain of fire.[e] It consumed the great Deep, and was consuming
the land. [5] I said, 'Lord Yahweh, desist! How shall Jacob survive? for

[a] W. Eichrodt, *Theology of the Old Testament* I, 1961, pp. 216f.
[b] On the intercessory function of prophets, see G. von Rad, 'Die falschen
Propheten', *ZAW* 51, 1933, pp. 109ff.; N. Johansson, *Parakletoi*, 1940; J. Lindblom, *Prophecy in Ancient Israel*, 1962, pp. 54, 204–206.
[c] For reservations about intercession as a prophetic function, cf. H. W. Hertzberg, 'Sind die Propheten Fürbitter?', in *Tradition und Situation*, Festschrift für A.
Weiser, 1963, pp. 63–74.
[d] MT has 'Lord Yahweh' at the end of the sentence.
[e-e] Redistributing the consonants and vocalizing *lerābīb 'ēš* with D. R. Hillers,
'Amos 7.4 and Ancient Parallels', *CBQ* 26, 1964, pp. 221ff. MT reads 'a trial
(*rīb*) by fire'.

he is small!' Yahweh repented concerning this. 'Neither shall this take place,' said Lord Yahweh.

A second time the experience of vision comes upon Amos and he is conscious of the power of Yahweh giving him a preview of what is about to occur. He beholds the Lord calling for the divine fire, the instrument of his wrath upon those who rebel against his sovereignty (cf. 'I will send fire upon . . .' in the structure of the oracles against the nations. 1.4, 7, 10, 12, etc.; and Num. 11.1ff.; 26.10; Lev. 10.2; I Kings 18.24). Like the locust plague, the onslaught of the fire is an event which requires no interpretative words; the preparatory enactment of Yahweh's decision is seen by the prophet as a decree of punishment for Israel (cf. Deut. 32.22). He watches what is to happen later on earth unfold in the world of vision. In its terrible, inexorable progress the fire dries up the 'Great Deep' (*tehōm rabbāh*), the cosmic sea, which in the mythic cosmology of the ancient East lies under the earth as the source of springs and rivers (Gen. 7.11; Ps. 36.6; Isa. 51.10). Then the searing flames begin to consume 'the apportioned land' (*ḥēleq*) which means either the territory of Israel (Micah 2.4), or Israel as the portion of Yahweh (cf. Deut. 32.9). Confronted with this revelation of Yahweh's planned course of action, the prophet again intercedes, this time with the bare plea that Yahweh desist (*ḥdl*). A second time the prayer is heard, and Yahweh countermands the plan. See the comment on 7.1–3 whose form, except for the vision-object, is virtually identical.

(c) THE PLUMB LINE: 7.7–9

7 ⁷This is what ᵃLord Yahwehᵃ showed me: Behold heᵃ was standing beside a wall built with a plumb line, and in his hand was a plumb line. ⁸Yahweh said to me, 'What do you see, Amos?', and I said 'A plumb line.' Then the Lord said, 'Behold I am setting a plumb line in the midst of my people Israel. No more shall I pass him by.'
⁹'The high places of Isaac shall be destroyed;
    the sanctuaries of Israel shall be devastated;
    and I will rise against the house of Jeroboam with the sword.'

[7] The third and fourth visions change in content, form, and outcome. The introductory vision-formula remains the same. But instead of seeing a punitive event unfold, the vision of Amos is focused

ᵃ⁻ᵃ MT: 'This is what he showed me: Behold the Lord . . .' Cf. the opening formula in 7.1, 3; 8.1.

on an object whose function is symbolic of what Yahweh has decided to do. Amos sees his Lord stationed beside a wall with a plumb line in his hand (cf. 9.1; Isa. 6.1). In the terse form of the vision-report nothing is made of the divine figure by way of description. The one concern of the report and the experience behind it is the disclosure of the divine counsel and decision. The reality of Yahweh in his relation to the prophet is concentrated on what is communicated.

[8] The object upon which Amos' seeing is focused is something from everyday life; a plumb line (*'anāk*), a cord and weight used by builders to be sure that walls were erected on the vertical. The etymology of the word, found only here in OT, indicates that *'anāk* means the lead weight itself.[a] The scene in the vision suggests the testing of a wall built with the use of a plumb line, a parable for Israel which had been built correctly, but was now out of line. But in the dialogue the plumb line alone is symbolic; its significance is not inferred by Amos, but disclosed by Yahweh! In contrast to the first two visions, what Amos sees is not an unfolding event whose theological significance can be read immediately. The plumb line acquires meaning as a catchword for the divine plan only when it is interpreted by Yahweh. The object is mute and mysterious. Amos recognizes what he sees, and can identify it when he is asked. But what does it signify? Why is he grasped by inspiration to see a plumb line? The disclosure of Yahweh's counsel is withheld and there is no chance to intervene with intercession. Amos is led in the dialogue to speak the name of the object, now pregnant with potential meaning. When he answers, 'A plumb line', he has thereby taken upon his own lips the key-word to Yahweh's decree. He has pronounced it on earth, not yet knowing what its being spoken will bring. Then, and only then, he is given the decree which interprets the clue: 'I am going to set a plumb line in the midst of my people Israel.' Amos is shown a symbol which he must translate into word before he knows its meaning. He is displaced as intercessor and allowed only to name the symbolic object whose significance lies wholly in Yahweh's intention. The theological name, 'my people', makes it clear that Israel is to be judged precisely in her identity as the covenant people. The covenant slogan, 'Yahweh is our God and we are his people,' is no security, but a threat and the ultimate source of their guilt. The emphasis on the theological title for Israel stands in tension with the basis of Amos' intercession in the first two visions. There he pled that Jacob could not survive the

[a] O. R. Sellers, 'Plumb Line', *IDB*, III, p. 828.

prepared punishment; here the decree reveals that Yahweh has decided that 'my people' should not survive. 'Only you have I known from all the families of earth, therefore I will punish you for all your iniquities'—that is the radical interpretation of the election theology which comes to Amos in the third and fourth visions (3.2). The second line of the divine decree hammers home its finality, slams the door on any intercession, and precludes any 'repentance' on Yahweh's part (vv. 3, 6). In 4.6–12 Amos reports a long history of punishments sent by Yahweh, which were aimed at turning the people to him in repentance. That epoch of God's dealing with Israel is now closed. The vision sequence discloses a radical and drastic change in Yahweh's policy. In the time ahead, no more passing over Israel's defection, no more desisting for the sake of the election. The covenant system has failed to hold Israel in real encounter with her Lord. He will no longer 'pass over'; he will 'pass through' (5.17).

[9] The vision-report is rounded off and completed with the interpretation of the symbol by the decree of Yahweh. In v. 9 there is a further divine word which in style and content is an announcement of punishment. The announcement contains an eloquent correspondence to the symbol of the plumb line; devastation will fall upon the principal structures of the Israelite state, its religion and its dynasty. Yahweh has measured the shrines and the 'house' of Jeroboam and found them of no use. 'Your highest and holiest shall perish' (Wellhausen). Isaac is used as a name for the northern kingdom (cf. 7.16) High places and sanctuaries are inclusive of all the religious sites in the nation. The high place (bāmā) was a shrine on a hill in open country; usually they were equipped with altar, sacred grove and trees, pillars, etc. Many had been in continuous use by the residents in local areas since Canaanite times. The sanctuary (miqdāš) was a holy place, usually a temple. The sanctuaries are the official religious centres of the northern kingdom, Bethel (7.13) and Dan, established by Jeroboam I. The instrument of devastation and death will be 'the sword' (cf. 9.1, 4). Amos names no historical protagonist, only the divine one. The fall of Israel's national existence will be Yahweh's act; Israel's God has become his executioner.

(d) PROPHET, PRIEST, AND KING: 7.10–17

7 10Amaziah, the priest of Bethel, sent to Jeroboam, the king of Israel, saying: 'Amos has conspired against you in the midst of the

house of Israel; the land cannot endure all his words. [11] For this is
what Amos has said: "By the sword shall Jeroboam die, and Israel
shall surely go away from its land into exile." ' [12]Then Amaziah said to
Amos, 'Seer, go; flee to the land of Judah, and there eat bread and
there prophesy. [13]But at Bethel you shall not prophesy any more, for it
is the sanctuary of the king and it is the temple of the kingdom.'
[14]Amos answered and said to Amaziah, 'No prophet was[a] I, nor a son
of a prophet, but I was[a] a herdsman and a dresser of sycamores.
[15]Yet Yahweh took me from following the flock, and Yahweh said to
me, "Go, prophesy to my people Israel."
  [16]Now hear the word of Yahweh:
    You say "You shall not prophesy against Israel,
      nor shall you preach against the house of Isaac."
  [17]Therefore this is what Yahweh has said:
    "Your wife shall become a harlot in the city;
      your sons and daughters shall fall by the sword;
      your land shall be portioned out by the measuring line.
    You shall die on unclean land,
      and Israel shall surely go into exile away from its land." ' '

  This story of the encounter between Amos and Amaziah, the priest
of Bethel, the only piece of prophetic biography in the book, falls
into three parts: the priest's report to the king (vv. 10f.); the priest's
command to Amos (vv. 12f.); Amos' answer to the priest (vv. 14–17).
This answer contains an oracle against the priest, the only example
in Amos of an oracle of judgment against an individual. The oracle
may have occasioned the composition of the narrative; it supplies the
introduction of characters and the setting which the oracle presupposes. The occasion must have been a crisis in Amos' career, and
may have marked the end of his activity, at least at Bethel. But what
happened as a sequel to the encounter is unknown. The composer
of the story must have been a contemporary, either an eyewitness or
an associate to whom it was told. The quotations from Amaziah and
Amos are direct and the report is well informed. Amos is placed at
Bethel. The exasperated remark of Amaziah that the land could not
bear all Amos' sayings implies that the prophet's activity had already
extended over a period longer than a few days. The priest is acquainted with Amos and knows he is a Judean. This encounter between
prophet and priest has its successor in the violent confrontation of
Jeremiah and Pashhur (Jer. 20.1–6), and belongs to the long history
of tension between charisma and institution in Israel's religious life.

  [a] Both 'was' and 'am' are possible. The Hebrew sentence is a nominal clause
which has no verb; see the discussion of the problem in the commentary.

[10] When Jeroboam I was organizing and consolidating the national life of Israel after the northern tribes had separated from Judah and from the rule of Rehoboam, one of his most significant projects was the founding of state sanctuaries at Bethel and Dan to compete with the established religious centre in Jerusalem (I Kings 12.26–33). He erected golden calves as cultic symbols, rejected the old levitical priesthood connected with the traditions of the sacral covenant league and ordained priests from the laity, set a different time for the autumn festival, and offered sacrifices himself in Bethel. All these moves were steps in a calculated policy to break the relation of the northern tribes to the central sanctuary in Jerusalem by creating a religious structure identified with his own dynasty. The state religion of Israel was an expression of its monarchy and an instrument of its politics. The shrine at Bethel was the sanctuary of the *king* and the temple of the *kingdom* (v. 13); Amaziah's justification of his explusion of Amos unabashedly states the official view held in Israel's ruling circles. Amaziah was certainly a successor of the state priesthood ordained by the first Jeroboam. When he reports to his king he is doing no more than was expected of him, but his action discloses whose creature he is and whose power is the real defining concern of the cult at Bethel. What counted was the reign of Jeroboam. In this context the priest judges Amos' messages to be the first stratagem in a political conspiracy to overthrow the government. He had historical reason for his estimate; in past times a prophet's predictions of the fall of a king had been followed by internal revolt (I Kings 11.29ff.; 19.15ff.; II Kings 8.7ff.; 9.1ff.). Condemnation of the national life and forecasts of the kingdom's fall would sooner or later stir some dissident rebel to turn such words to deeds. The land could not bear those reiterated messages of catastrophe; it was not good for the state of the nation. Amaziah's reference to all Amos' speeches (literally 'his words') was not a charge that he was verbose; 'word' (*dābār*) is used in the sense of prophetic saying, message. Amos was not verbose; but he was persistent.

[11] Amaziah documents his intelligence by reporting what Amos had said. In the extant speeches of Amos there is no saying precisely equivalent to Amaziah's summary, but the priest can be credited with accurate reporting. The fall of the royal dynasty (v. 9) is enough of a threat to the royal person. Amos spoke also of an exile of Israel (5.5, 27; 6.7), and the prediction of coming devastation by military conquest which he intoned repeatedly implied as much. The priest,

however, does make a fundamental change in the quality of Amos'
prophecy; it is described in quite neutral terms and de-theologized.
'This is what *Amos* said . . .' Not the divine word 'I will rise against
. . .', but the simple horizontal fact, 'Jeroboam will die.' There is no
hint of any reckoning with Amos' presentation of his message as the
word of Yahweh and therefore a message from the God of Israel.
Amaziah's readiness to reduce the whole crisis to an incident of mere
political proportions is one more measure of the true state of official
religion in Israel.

[12–13] The narrative does not tell of Jeroboam's response to the
intelligence of his royal chaplain. It may well have been that Amaziah
did not wait for action on the government's part, but undertook to
resolve the problem himself. As priest he had authority over Bethel's
cult and jurisdiction over the personnel who functioned there.
Behind his instruction to Amos is the presumption that the problem
could be worked out at this level of jurisdiction. He does not deny the
legitimacy of Amos' office, but hails him forthrightly as 'seer'. The
title *ḥōzeh* was an alternate term for prophet (*nābī'*) in the eighth
century and testified to the experience of visions among the prophets
and to one of the roots of the office in the ancient profession of the
seer of earlier times. *Ḥōzeh* was not in itself a derogatory name (II
Sam. 24.11; II Kings 17.13); when Amos shifts to 'prophet' in his
answer he shows that the two were synonymous for him. Since Amos
used the vision reports in 7.1–9; 8.1–3 as a vindication of his message,
the title was certainly justified in Amaziah's mouth. Amaziah's
instruction need not have been scornful. Indeed, because of the
status which a prophet enjoyed in the religious history of Israel and
with the people, he probably was acting with considerable circumspec-
tion. He wanted no trouble from Amos, nor did he want a martyr
on his hands. So he gives Amos a way out. He commands Amos to
prophesy no more at Bethel; this he could do because he had official
authority based on royal appointment. But he also recommends that
Amos flee to Judah, doubtless to escape the anticipated anger of
Jeroboam. If Amos would only leave the sphere of his responsibility,
Amaziah's problem would be resolved. Obviously he was not
concerned with the truth of what Amos was proclaiming, but only
with the decency and order of the cult at Bethel. The expression 'eat
bread' could mean 'get bread, earn a living' (Gen. 3.19?), and the
phrase may imply that Amos ought to earn his bread by practising
prophecy in his own country. Prophets, like priests, in Israel

received gifts and fees from individuals or courts for whom they functioned (I Sam. 9.6ff.; Micah 3.5, 11; etc.). But the clear emphasis of the line is on the repeated *there*. The issue is spatial and jurisdictional: 'prophesy in Judah if you will, but I forbid you to do it at Bethel.'

[14] The interpretation of v. 14 is the most controverted problem in the Book of Amos. When Amos answers Amaziah, does he deny that he is a prophet (*nābī'*), or does he say that he had not been a prophet until Yahweh called him (v. 15)? Are the sentences in v. 14 to be translated in the present tense or in the past tense? The problem lies in the ambiguity of Hebrew syntax; the sentences are nominal sentences which could be translated in either tense.[a] Tense, however, has not been the only issue. Amos 7.14 is a crucial proof text in the discussion about the meaning of the term *nābī'* and the relation of the so-called classical prophets to the older *nᵉbī'īm*. Whatever tense Amos may have intended to use, the implication of his statement depends also upon what kind of function or office *nābī'* designates. Opinions about this problem, which cannot be settled by this one text, inevitably play a role in understanding the passage.[b] The problem of tense is not soluble by resort to grammatical analysis. Nominal sentences tend to follow the time reference of verbs and adverbs in the immediate context. If this were an infallible rule then 'he took me' at the beginning of v. 15 would be an argument for the past tense. But it is hypothetically possible for the nominal sentences to refer to the present in contrast to following inflected verbs. If objective indications in the text itself could settle the matter, the question would have had a convincing answer long ago.

One can speak, then, only in terms of probabilities which are indicated by over-all considerations and what makes plausible sense in the context. There are two other references to *nābī'* in Amos. Both view the *nābī'* favourably. One (3.7) is probably a later addition to the text. In 2.11 prophet and Nazirite are regarded as Yahweh's creation. If this verse is authentic, then it shows that Amos knew of

---

[a] See the discussions and the literature cited in: H. H. Rowley, 'Was Amos a Nabi?', *Festschrift O. Eissfeldt*, 1947, pp. 194ff.; E. Würthwein, 'Amos-Studien', *ZAW* 62, 1950, pp. 10–40; S. Lehming, 'Erwägungen zu Amos', *ZTK* 55, 1958, pp. 145–169; H. Reventlow, *Das Amt des Propheten bei Amos* (FRLANT 80), 1962, pp. 14–24.

[b] For recent discussion citing the important literature see R. Rendtorff, 'Reflections on the Early History of Prophecy in Israel,' *JTC* 4, 1967, pp. 14–34; G. von Rad, *Theology of the Old Testament* II, 1965, pp. 6–32.

prophets with whom he would not deny identification. Many proponents of the present-tense hypothesis reject the verse (Lehming, Weiser, T. H. Robinson, et al.), so its value in the question at hand is conditioned. What is known of Amos from the undoubtedly authentic material in the book adds up, however, to a total picture which is connected with other men who were called nābī'. Amos received visions and reported these experiences in terms and patterns typical of other prophets. His intercessions (7.2, 5), are a characteristically prophetic function. He was called and sent by Yahweh to Israel (7.15). In his mission he used predominantly the formulae and forms of the messenger and the judgment word, which represent the basic style of earlier prophets. Amaziah took him for a 'seer', an alternate name for nābī' (7.12). The verb 'to prophesy' (hinnābē') was used by Amaziah and by Amos to designate his speaking (7.12, 15, 16). What is such a man to be called? If he were not a prophet, he was functioning as a prophet. In the exchange between Amos and Amaziah the past-tense interpretation makes good sense. Amos would not have evaded the priest's authority by claiming to be a layman. The emphasis of his answer lies on the command of Yahweh with which he counters Amaziah's command.

It is that issue to which Amos speaks in his famous rejoinder to Amaziah. 'The authority is not yours, but Yahweh's; the place is not there in Judah, but here in Israel!' Amos deals with the issue of authority by a brief account of his call to prophesy. 'I was no prophet, nor a son of a prophet.' 'Son of a prophet' is the term for a member of a prophetic guild or order such as the one assembled around Elisha (cf. I Kings 20.35; II Kings 2.3ff.; 4.1, 38; etc.). Instead, the immediate background of Amos' life lay in a normal secular life among the people as a herdsman and a dresser of sycamores. The precise meaning of both terms lacks certainty because they appear only here in the Old Testament. The first (bōqēr), if its cognates are any guide, means 'a keeper of cattle', the word is emended by many (cf. BH) to the nōqēd of 1.1, 'a shepherd'; after all, Amos says in v. 15 that he was following the flock (sheep) at the time of his call. The 'sycamore' is a tree of the mulberry family which produces a fig-like fruit; the species was abundant in the land at altitudes below the frostline, especially in the Shephelah. 'Dresser' (bōlēs) means some kind of work as a husbandman of the tree, probably puncturing the forming fruit to make it sweeten and become more edible. His prophetic activity is the result solely of Yahweh's initiative. 'To take from following the sheep' is used of Yahweh's selection of David for kingship (II Sam. 7.8; Ps. 78.70); and the verb is used of the divine appointment of the Levites to their cultic function (Num. 18.6). Once Amos was a shepherd; now he is a prophet of Yahweh; between then and now as the single cause of this radical change of vocation lay the event represented by the unadorned, terse statement: 'Yahweh took me.' This is Amos' one direct reference to his own call, and it is given in such bare, laconic fashion that nothing is disclosed of its setting in Amos' own experience. None of the five vision-reports can be attached to the call with any confidence, because none of them contains the slightest hint of a commission or commencement. The brevity of the report is a result of its place in the story of Amos' reply to Amaziah's command. Amos is prophesying on the authority of Yahweh. He himself could not resist the overwhelming compulsion of Yahweh's word pressed upon him (3.8), and Amaziah cannot outbid Yahweh in the matter of authority. Implicit in this way of describing his call as a being taken by Yahweh from his own life and compelled to prophesy is a claim to be a different kind of prophet from the ones with whom Amaziah is acquainted. Amaziah was accustomed to the corps of cultic prophets who were attached to shrine and court, and who served a recognized function by prophesying disaster for the nation's enemies and prosperity (*šālōm*) for its king and people. Amos rejects the assumption that he has anything to do with such a group. He stands rather in the succession of Micaiah ben Imlah (I Kings 22) and Elijah as a messenger of the heavenly King whose exclusive role is to declare what has been revealed to him. His office has its place in the structure of Yahweh's rule over Israel, and not within the framework of Jeroboam's kingdom in which Amaziah and the state prophets function. Amos' report of his commission carries the point further and answers the question of jurisdiction. In the divine commission the covenantal designation for Israel is used; the northern kingdom is 'my people' (*'ammī*). This theological identity of Israel takes precedence over any royal or cultic definition of the nation. Amos refuses to acknowledge any other authority in Israel than Yahweh and any other understanding of the people except their definition by the election. In the name of that theology he rejects the advice and command of Amaziah and proceeds to put the priest himself under its jurisdiction.

[16–17] The oracle against Amaziah is in the standard form of an oracle of judgment. It opens with a summons to hear (16a), states the indictment against its addressee (16bc), then uses the messenger formula (17a) to introduce the verdict of punishment (17b–e). Amaziah is guilty of having contradicted the command of Yahweh to Amos. The messenger of a king who came bearing the king's own word was an extension of the royal person; Amaziah has pitted his order against the very will of Yahweh in presuming to exercise authority over his messenger. In doing so the priest stands in a company of others who have opposed prophets raised up by Yahweh and so added to the guilt of Israel (2.11f.). His punishment will be to suffer the judgment which will fall upon the nation as a whole, and therein lies its poignant appropriateness. When the divine sentence of exile for Israel is carried out Amaziah will go too. His wife will be publicly shamed, used as a harlot for the soldiers of the victorious enemy (Isa. 13.16; Zech. 14.2). His heirs will be slain. His own property will be divided up and parcelled out by the victors (II Kings 17.24; Micah 2.4; Jer. 6.12). He himself, the priest whose office it was to protect the cult and people against all uncleanness (Lev. 10.10), will be carried away to die in a land that is unclean because it is the dominion of foreign deities (I Sam. 26.19; Hos. 9.3f.; Ezek. 4.13). All this will happen to others, but it has a terrible particularity for Amaziah. The desecration of his wife, the end of his house, the loss of his inheritance in Israel, and his contamination—all, in effect, constitute a fearful divesting of office. His priesthood will be brought to a terrible and final end.

(e) The Basket of Late Fruit: 8.1–3

8 ¹This is what Lord Yahweh showed me: Behold, a basket of summer fruit. ²He said, 'What do you see, Amos?' I said, 'A basket of summer fruit.' Then Yahweh said to me, 'The end has come for my people, Israel. No more will I pass him by.'
³'They shall wail the hymns of the temple
   in that day,'
a saying of Lord Yahweh.
'Many are the corpses;
   in every place they are cast out.'ᵃ

[1] The fourth vision-report is similar to the third; only the symbolic object changes. In the possession of divinely bestowed seeing, Amos beholds a basket of summer fruit. No figure, divine or

ᵃ Reading *hišlīkām*, an impersonal passive; the text is corrupt.

human, is connected with the object. It is simply there as the focus of a charismatic concentration, mysterious and pregnant with a meaning not yet disclosed. If the basket of fruit were actual, then the time would have been at the end of the fruit harvest just as the hot, dry summer closed. Possibly the basket was an offering brought to Bethel on the occasion of Israel's autumn festival, when the worshippers who came to the sanctuary celebrated the coming of a new year and hoped by their ritual to secure blessing and prosperity in it.[a] If these suppositions are correct, the time was fraught with anticipation of divine renewal coming in harmony with the change of seasons (cf. Jer. 8.20).

[2] But the meaning of the vision contradicts the hope. The message is 'end', not beginning; ruin, not renewal. The significance of the symbol is related to the message by a sound-play on the key-words: 'summer fruit' (*qayiṣ*) and 'end' (*qēṣ*). The use of assonance to connect an ordinary object with a divine word is a feature of Jeremiah's vision of the almond rod (Jer. 1.11–12). The decree which interprets the symbolic word announces a decision of Yahweh concerning his covenant people that is severe and unrelieved in its finality. *Bā' haqqēṣ*: 'the end has come!' The key-word 'end' includes a temporal and a qualitative dimension. The time of punishing to correct and of passing over sin is at an end. The next event of Yahweh's dealing with Israel will bring them to an end of death and destruction. The fifth vision (9.1–4) furnishes a description of the totality of this approaching end with its inexorable exclusion of every possibility of escape. See Ezekiel's prophecy of the Day of Yahweh built around the theme-sentence: *qēṣ bā'* (Ezek. 7); and the use of *qēṣ* in Lam. 4.18; Jer. 51.13.

[3] The word of judgment in v. 3 evokes in two taunt lines the horrible reality of the 'end' decreed for Israel: wailing fills the air, corpses everywhere. 'In that day' is a temporal formula pointing to the Day of Yahweh, the time of his judgment (2.16; 8.9, 13). The location of the scene of judgment in the temple continues the concentration of 7.9 on the religious sites of Israel and perhaps the two verses were originally part of the same oracle. The hymns of the temple were songs of exultant joy and hope in Yahweh, but under the lash of Yahweh's wrath the sound of wailing, the howling chants of lamentation, would replace them (cf. 8.10). The second line of v. 3 could be taken as a quotation of the lament; this would explain the tense of its

[a] Cf. the suggestions of E. Sellin, KAT; and J. D. W. Watts, *Vision and Prophecy in Amos*, 1958, pp. 36ff.

verb. 'Place' (*māqōm*) is often used to refer to shrines and, if that is its
sense here, then the line continues the picture of the destruction of the
religious centres. The choirs who used to shout the praises of Yahweh
will intone a lament over omnipresent death. Judgment begins at the
house of the Lord! By the instruction of death Yahweh will teach that
those who look to him only to bless and prosper the life they already
have shall have no life at all.

26. NEVER ON SUNDAY: 8.4-8

8 ⁴Hear this, all who trample the poor,
    and would do away with the land's afflicted,ᵃ
⁵(saying:)
'When will New Moon pass that we may sell grain,
    Sabbath that we may put wheat on sale;
That we may measure with a small ephah, weigh with a heavy
                                                            shekel,
    and cheat with rigged scales;
⁶That we may buy the needy for silver,
    the poor for a pair of sandals
    and sell the refuse of the wheat?'
⁷Yahweh has sworn by Jacob's pride,
    'If ever I forget all their deeds . . .'
⁸Shall not the land quake on account of this,
    and all who dwell in it mourn,
    all of it rise like the Nileᵇ (and be tossed)ᶜ
    and sinkᵈ like the Nile of Egypt?

The markets of Jeroboam's kingdom traded in human misery. It
was not only in the court in the gates that the officials of the government had found an opportunity for profit. The change in Israel's
social structure had created a need for commerce and the upper
classes exploited the opportunity with ruthlessness. The saying opens
with a herald's summons to his audience (cf. 3.1; 4.1; 5.1). The
addressees of the message which he has been sent to deliver are
identified in the initial summons (v. 4), and then portrayed by an
ironic quotation which discloses their deeds and motives (vv. 5f.).

ᵃ Following the Qᵉre.
ᵇ Reading *kayᵉ'ōr* with some MSS and most versions; see 9.5. MT has 'like the
light'.
ᶜ The verb is missing in 9.5 and G.
ᵈ Following the Qᵉre: *wᵉnišqᵉ'ā*.

The quotation is a favourite tactic of Amos for bringing to light the deeds of his audience (2.12; 4.1; 5.14; 6.2, 13; 8.14; 9.10); it is a self-incriminating testimony to the crime which has provoked Yahweh's terrible oath. The oath itself (v. 7) is the message which Amos has to announce; the foregoing characterization serves as commentary to 'all their deeds'. The rhetorical question in v. 8 rounds out the saying with a prophecy of what will befall the land because of these deeds; the question of its relationship to the original saying is discussed in the comment below. Samaria's market place is the most likely setting for the oracle.

[4] This saying is essentially another of Amos' indictments of those who oppress the poor (see 2.6ff.; 4.1; 5.12). The normative presupposition of the indictment is not so much any single instance or list of commandments in Israel's legal tradition, as the total tendency and intention of the covenant law to protect and maintain the disadvantaged members of society. The weak and unfortunate were not to be exploited; they should be treated with the respect and concern due to kinsmen and neighbours. (See the discussion in the comment on 2.6–8; 5.7, 10f.) Amos speaks to a group who are steadily pressing the weaker citizenry to the limits of existence.

[5] The scene which Amos sketches in the extended quotation portrays an economic situation that was relatively new in Israel. In the older peasant society, which largely continued the practices of clan life, every man owned his own land and was economically relatively autonomous. Buying and selling played a minor role, and exchange for money was not a major factor in the system. The rise of urban culture under the monarchy led to the development of commerce and an economic upper class. As more and more small farmers were pressed off their land and forced to shift to service and labour, their dependence upon the market became acute. The urban merchants appear to have monopolized the market; they were able to sell to landless peasants at a high price. They had the resources for stockpiling grain, and in a time of poor crops were in a position to control the economy completely. This is the group whose avarice is dramatized in the quotation. Amos applies to this new situation the old norms of the covenant. What appeared to be progress and good business to the merchants was in his eyes disobedience to Yahweh. No so-called progress excused an Israelite from dealing with his fellows as neighbours and brothers. Clearly the merchants saw nothing wrong with what they did. The quotation paints them as

respectful of religion. They observed the holy days but underneath their piety was a restless impatience. 'Ah, we can hardly bear the interruption of holy days, so impatient we are to get on with our business, our wheeling and dealing that brings the property and person of every man into our hands!' New Moon, the first day of the lunar month, was observed in ancient Israel as a festival occasion and is often paired with Sabbath in lists of holy times (e.g. II Kings 4.23; Isa. 1.13f.; Hos. 2.11). It seems to have been of wide provenance in the ancient Near East, was adopted as a family festival by Israel, and later regularized in the temple cult. The observance of the Sabbath was required in the earliest strata of Israel's law (Ex. 23.12; 34.21; 20.8). Both days were times for cessation from normal work. Those whom Amos quotes observe the days and show how devout they are in matters of public religion. But what matters this keeping of holy days, this proper piety in the sight of God and man, if all the while they are straining toward the 'unholy days' when their true dedication to greed fills the time? Once again the prophet shows the failure of faith which accompanies the success of religion, for the business they were so eager to continue was the enterprise of betraying their Lord. The *ephah* was a unit of dry measure, here the vessel in which a standard portion of grain was measured. The *shekel* was Israel's basic unit of weight, here the weight itself which was used in the weighing scales to establish by balance the amount of silver or kind owed by a purchaser.[a] In selling grain to the poor these cunning merchants used a small 'peck' to measure what they gave, and a heavy weight to determine what they got. The practice was prohibited by commandments forbidding Israelites to own weights and measures of different kinds (Deut. 25.13–16; cf. also Lev. 19.35f. and Prov. 20.10). At root the practice was a breach of the commandment against stealing (Ex. 20.15). In the excavations at Tirzah shops were found dating to the eighth century which had two sets of weights, one for buying and one for selling.

[6] Man and property represented wealth in those days as well as marketable goods, and these crafty minions of the market place did not boggle at the profit to be made in acquiring a man as a slave or taking over his property for his debts. 8.6a is quite similar to 2.6b (cf. the commentary there). The 'refuse of the wheat' is the mixture of chaff and trash left after winnowing; it may have been re-mixed with

---

[a] Cf. O. Sellers, 'Weights and Measures', *IDB* IV, 828ff.; R. B. Y. Scott, 'Weights and Measures of the Bible', *BA* XXII 2, May 1959, pp. 22–39.

the clean grain or sold as such to the desperate poor in hard times. Amos speaks of men who miss no trick of trade; they sell refuse for profit. The quotation as a whole sketches a portrait of men who can see only profit and are blind to the reality of the man whom they exploit. They love the Lord less, mammon more, and their fellows not at all. Their character is in utter contradiction to the person of Yahweh who redeemed them from slavery, raises up the poor and weak, and wills righteousness among all under his rule.

[7] Yahweh binds himself by oath to act against these merchants. The oath is a particularly intense form of the announcement of judgment. An oath sworn by men was the most solemn form of obligation; how much more certain was punishment when Yahweh himself swore. In 4.2 and 6.8 Yahweh swears 'by himself', but in this text 'by the pride of Jacob'. In 6.8 'the pride of Jacob' refers to the self-confidence of the nation, but an oath sworn by the very sin condemned is strange. 'Pride of Jacob' could well be a divine title similar to the one in I Sam. 15.29.[a] The conditional sentence ('If I ever forget all their deeds . . .') is only the first half of the oath-form; the following clause would contain the invocation of a curse invoked on the swearer in case he broke the oath.[b] The use of this form shows with what vehemence Yahweh reacts to the market of Samaria.

[8] In the present arrangement of the text, the rhetorical question in v. 8 announces the dire consequences which will befall Israel and so supplies the element of Yahweh's concrete action missing in Amos' report of the divine oath. The very land will quake, bringing grief upon all its residents with its shattering ruin. Earthquake as the anticipated expression of Yahweh's wrath seems to be in view at other places in Amos (2.13, 3.14f.; 9.1). No disaster was more likely to make ancient man feel himself completely in the power of the divine and grip him with dread. The comparison of an earthquake's tremors with the seasonal rising and falling of the Nile is hardly apt and betrays an awareness only that the river did go up and down without any knowledge of how it occurred. Verse 8 corresponds largely to 9.5, one of three hymnic fragments which have been inserted in the text. See the discussion of the hymnic insertions in the commentary on 4.13. Did Amos himself quote from a current hymn which portrayed the earth-shaking effects of a theophany of Yahweh?

[a] Emendation with BH; cf. F. Horst, 'Der Eid im Alten Testament', in *Gottes Recht: Gesammelte Studien zum Recht im Alten Testament* (Th. Büch. 12), 1961, p. 306.
[b] Cf. the texts listed under *'im*, para. 5, in *KB*, p. 58.

Certainty is impossible, but Amos' use of one line from such a hymn would explain the attraction of the other hymnic portions for the collector(s) and arranger(s) of his book.

27. GLOOM AND GRIEF: 8.9–10

8 ⁹'It will come to pass in that day,'
       a saying of Lord Yahweh,
   'that I will make the sun set at noon,
       and darken the earth during daylight.
¹⁰I will change your festivals to mourning,
       and all your hymns to a dirge.
   I will put sackcloth on the loins of all,
       and baldness upon every head.
   I will make it like mourning an only son,
       and its outcome like a day of bitterness.'

Using the motifs of gloom and grief, Yahweh foretells the future which he will create for Israel. The oracle is a divine saying whose first-person verbs establish the dominant theme of Yahweh's action, telling of a time whose events will manifest the 'I' of Israel's God. After the introductory line (9a) with its temporal and oracle formulae, the saying unfolds in two movements constructed around the motifs of darkness (9b) and mourning (v. 10). The saying is an announcement of doom, a counterpart of the announcements of salvation which Israel was accustomed to hear from the usual prophet of the time.

[9] In general usage the temporal phrase 'in that day' would point to a time identified in the context (I Sam. 3.2). Here the context offers only the coming deeds of Yahweh as a specification of the time in question. 'That day' is more a matter of what than when. The phrase appears in Amos' sayings consistently in connection with descriptions of events which will occur in the time of Yahweh's punishment of Israel (2.16; 8.3, 13; in 9.11 as introduction of an oracle of salvation). In Amos' usage and in the understanding of his audience the phrase may have belonged to the vocabulary of the Day of Yahweh, the time wholly defined by the action of Yahweh (see 5.18–20). The notion of the sun's disappearance during daylight hours is no doubt dependent phenomenologically upon experience of eclipses. But its primary significance here comes from its association with the complex of features belonging to the Day of Yahweh; see the

comment on darkness and the Day of Yahweh in 5.18, 20 and Isa. 13.10; Joel 2.10; 3.15. The failure of light from the luminaries of heaven was a sign that a time of woe had arrived.

[10] The general description of mourning rites does not disclose whether they are a ceremony of lamentation at the sun's disappearance or the rites which follow other unnamed disasters to the people. The intention of the stylized description is not so much to present a programme of what occurs as to characterize the personal situation of those caught in the toils of 'that day' (cf. Isa. 3.24ff.; 15.2ff.; 22.12; Jer. 47.5). Israel's religious festivals (*ḥag*, cf. 5.21), which were meant to be times of rejoicing at Yahweh's blessing upon his people, will become rituals of lamentation (5.16f.). Israel will know only the divine curse and her hymns of exultation will be replaced with dirges for the dead (*qīnā*, cf. 5.1). Sackcloth was a hair garment worn about the loins as part of the customary mourning practices at a time of personal grief or national calamity; at such times the head was also shaved as a sign of sorrow. The bitterness of the experience could be compared only to the extreme grief felt at the death of an only child whose funeral dashed every hope for the future (Jer. 6.26; Zech. 12.10). But dread of darkness and intensity of grief is not what determines the experience so much as the repeated first-personal verbs which beat through the whole passage in throbbing announcement that Yahweh is the author of it all. The only worship that will be left to Israel will be lament, the only life one of mourning, the only feeling hopelessness.

28. NOT BY BREAD ALONE: 8.11–14

8 11'Behold, days are coming,'
        a saying of Lord Yahweh,
    'when I will send a famine in the land.
    Not a famine for bread,
        nor a thirst for water,
        but for hearing the words[a] of Yahweh.
    12They shall stagger from sea to sea,
        wander from north to east
        seeking Yahweh's word—and not find it.
    13(In that day) fair virgins and young men
        shall faint with thirst.

a The plural may be a result of dittography.

148
COMMENTARY

¹⁴(They who swear by the guilt of Samaria.)
They shall say, "As your god lives, O Dan . . .,"
and "As the way^a of Beersheba lives . . ."
but they shall fall and arise no more.'

In another oracle of doom Amos adds to the description of the time of Yahweh's judgment. 8.9f. portrayed the time in terms of the effects of divine wrath; here the experience of the absence of God's mercy and help is depicted. Yahweh will send a famine and drought such as Israel has never known, a famine of Yahweh's word. In their need Israel will seek Yahweh's answer in every corner of the land, swear oaths from Dan to Beersheba, but the famine will continue until the strongest faint and the fall of the nation is final. The divine saying opens with one of the eschatological formulae which points to the coming days when Yahweh will intervene decisively (4.2; 9.13). Verses 13f. are set off from 11f. by the formula 'in that day', but they continue the description of the famine of Yahweh's words. 'The thirst' (v. 13) is the absence of any divine response to their desperate appeals (v. 11). The assertions of fealty taken in Dan and Beersheba continue the motif of the search for Yahweh to the limits of Israel's religious space. The continuity of vv. 13f. with the foregoing has been obscured by the redactor, who applied v. 14 to the idolatry in Samaria after 621 BC; the presence of 'in that day' is probably his work. See the comment below.

[11] Famine was one of the catastrophes which Yahweh used against Israel as a manifestation of his anger; it belonged to the standard list of punishments used by Israel's God as sanctions against the nation's unfaithfulness. In 4.6ff. Amos speaks of the famine and drought which Yahweh had brought on Israel in chastisement, but the nation had not returned to their God (see the comment on 4.6ff.). Now Yahweh announces the coming of a different type of famine—the absence of his word(s). 'Word of Yahweh' refers specifically to the oracle of a prophet which persons in need of information and help received when they inquired after ('sought') Yahweh through the prophet (I Sam. 3.1; 28.6; I Kings 22.5; II Sam. 21.1). The divine answer would bring assurance that their God was paying attention to their need, and it would often come as an oracle of salvation promising help. In times of national crisis the people would come to the shrines to seek Yahweh's response through the cult (cf.

^a Or 'power of . . .'; see the comment.

Hos. 5.6). The failure of prophetic vision and word would mean that Yahweh had turned away from them and abandoned them to their troubles (Ps. 74.9; Lam. 2.9; Jer. 37.17; Ezek. 7.26). Amos called upon Israel to seek Yahweh and his will that they might live (5.4–6, 14), but the time when Yahweh's help was available was almost gone (cf. the same notion and imagery in Isa. 55.1–7). The time of the famine of Yahweh's word approached, and it meant the absence of God for Israel (cf. Hos. 5.15).

[12] In wandering from sea (Dead Sea) to sea (Mediterranean) and from north to east, the Israelites would make a complete circuit of Israel's territory in search of someone to answer their laments with a word from Yahweh. The picture is that of people fluttering against the limits of their spatial cage in vain hope of transcending the prison of their situation by finding the opening to the divine. They ignore the word of the Lord in their prosperity and security, but when they suffer under the wrath of God they will learn anew that what they spurned was the only source of life and they will seek it with the desperation of men with empty stomachs and parched tongues. Then they will learn that man does not live by bread alone (Deut. 8.3; Matt. 4.4). Their knowledge of Yahweh will be the anguish of his absence, the void that mocks their clutching for help.

[13] Virgins and young men are the element of the population just coming to maturity, the ones with the greatest physical vigour and endurance; when they swoon from exhaustion, the rigours of the time will have overcome all (cf. Isa. 40.30). The thirst by which they will be overcome is the need and lack of any response from Yahweh in their plight (v. 11).

[14] 'They who swear by the guilt of Samaria' is the addition of a later interpreter who understands the divine titles in the rest of the line to be the names of foreign gods and wants to apply Amos' prophecy to the situation in Samaria after its resettlement by Assyrian deportees who established their own cults there (II Kings 17.29ff.; cf. the comment on Amos 5.26). 'Guilt' (*'ašmā*) is a word otherwise confined to Chronicles, Ezra, Leviticus, and the late Psalm 69 (v. 5); in II Chron. 24.18; 33.23 it refers specifically to idolatry. Other proposals interpret 'guilt of Samaria' as the revocalization of the name of a deity which stood in the text originally: (1) Ashimah (*'ašīmā*), the goddess of the men of Hamath whose cult was introduced in Samaria after its fall; (2) Ashera (*'ašērā*), the Canaanite goddess (e.g. I Kings 18.19); (3) Eshem-bethel (*'ešem-bēt'ēl*), a divine name

appearing in the Elephantine Papyri.[a] Amos does not refer to any shrine or public cult in Samaria nor is there any mention in other sources of one after the destruction of the shrine to Baal by Jehu (II Kings 10.18–27). There were famous shrines at Dan and Beersheba. Dan was the sister sanctuary to Bethel established in the northern part of his kingdom by Jeroboam I for the worship of Yahweh; Amos refers to pilgrimages by Israelites to Beersheba in the south of Judah which continued after the schism (5.5). He mentions these two shrines in the far north and south to encompass the sacral territory of Israel. The Israelites may roam from Dan to Beersheba seeking a word from Yahweh, but their farthest pilgrimages will be in vain. The expression 'as [name] lives' is an oath formula. It is part of an oath-sentence which would run something like: 'As surely as [deity] lives, I will [will not] do. . . .' In the ancient Near East men swore oaths by the deity to whom they were devoted; the expression involves an assertion of allegiance. The divine titles in these oath formulae contain no specific name; the redactor who added 'the guilt of Samaria' certainly took them for references to strange gods. But they were both probably current appellations of Yahweh. 'Your god, O Dan' is formulated so as to emphasize the relation between deity and shrine, which may reflect the Canaanite tendency to individualize Baal according to the shrine at which he was worshipped. The appellation 'the way (derek) of Beersheba' is obscure, though some think it possible that an oath could be taken on the manner of cult or pilgrimage as closely connected with the deity.[b] The occurrence of the Ugaritic cognate drkt with the meaning 'dominion, power' suggests that derek may be an epithet for the deity: 'the power of Beersheba'.[c] Others support the emendation dōdkā ('your beloved') as a possible appellation. Though the Israelites may appeal to Yahweh by the appellation favoured in shrines from Dan to Beersheba, their asseverations of loyalty will be too late. They will fall, and in Yahweh's absence there will be none to raise them up (5.2). God's wrath has two expressions, his absence and his action; both are equally terrible manifestations of his judgment.

[a] But see the discussion of W. F. Albright, who doubts that the cult of the god was flourishing until after the middle of the seventh century: *Archaeology and the Religion of Israel*, 1956, pp. 168ff.

[b] W. R. Harper, ICC, p. 184.

[c] See the notes and literature cited in M. Dahood, *Psalms* I (1–50), 1966, p. 2.

29. NO HIDING PLACE: 9.1-6

9 ¹I saw the Lord
    standing by the altar;
  ªand he said, 'Smite the capital
    so that the thresholds shake.
  Shatterᵇ them on the head of them all,ª
  and those who are left I will slay with the sword.
  Those who try to escape shall not escape;
    their fugitives shall not flee.
  ²If they dig into Sheol,
    my hand will take them from there.
  If they climb into heaven,
    I will bring them down from there.
  ³If they hide on Carmel's peak,
    I will find them and take them from there.
  If they conceal themselves from my eyes at the sea's floor,
    I will order the serpent to bite them there.
  ⁴If they go into captivity before their enemies,
    I will order the sword to slay them there.
  I have set my eye upon them
    for woe and not for weal.'
  ⁵The Lord, Yahweh of Hosts,
    who touches the earth and it totters,
    and all its inhabitants mourn;
    like the Nile all of it rises,
    and then sinks like Egypt's Nile;
  ⁶who builds in the heavens his upper chamber,ᶜ
    and founds his reservoir upon the earth;
  who calls to the waters of the sea
    and pours them upon the face of the earth—
  Yahweh is his name!

9.1-4 is the fifth of the vision-reports in the book of Amos. In the first four (7.1-9; 8.1-3) Amos tells about Yahweh's revelations of his decision to bring judgment upon the kingdom of Jeroboam. In this report Amos speaks of a revelation which confirms the others and

ᵃ⁻ᵃ According to MT the visual element of the report ends with the word 'altar'; the following divine saying is somewhat unclear. To whom are the imperatives addressed? What is the antecedent of 'them' in 'shatter them'? BH, incorporating emendations and rearrangements often adopted, reads: '. . . smiting (*makkēh*) the capital, and the thresholds shook (*wayyir⁽ᵃ⁾šū*), [and he said] "I will cut them (i.e. the people) off (*'ebṣā⁽ᵉⁿ⁾ēm*) by an earthquake (*ra⁽ᵃ⁾aš*) . . ."'
ᵇ Piel instead of Qal.
ᶜ MT's *ma⁽ᵃ⁾lōtāyw* (Qᵉre) has arisen by dittography; read *⁽ᵃ⁾līyātō* as in Ps. 104.13.

portrays how inexorable the judgment will be. In the experience about which the report tells, Amos saw and heard (see the discussion of 'the vision' in the comment on 7.1ff.); both auditory and visual perception are usual features of prophetic visions. In MT the visual element is restricted to the sentence in which Amos reports that he saw Yahweh and where (1aα). 'And he said' introduces the divine saying which Amos heard (1aβ–4). Yahweh's word begins with imperatives calling for the temple (?) to be brought down around the ears of those present (1aβγ); any who remain will fall to the sword (1aδ). Verse 1b then states the theme: none shall escape, which is elaborated in 2–4a by similarly formed sentences. The saying concludes with an announcement of Yahweh's curse (4b). In most proposed reconstructions of the text (cf. the text notes above) the visual element is enlarged to include a report of Yahweh's action so that it is Yahweh himself who smites the capitals and shakes the sanctuary. Verses 5f. contain one of the hymnic fragments which have been inserted into the text of Amos.

In structure and theme this report is different from the other four; its present location in the book suggests that the vision was not received nor the report formulated in direct connection with them. The opening sentence is similar to Isa. 6.1, but the visual element is not elaborated, nor is there dialogue between God and prophet. What is seen simply sets the stage for the divine word, the real content of the vision. The vision comes to Amos in a sanctuary; he sees the Lord standing beside 'the altar'. The sanctuary in question must be the one at Bethel. It is the only holy place at which tradition locates Amos during his ministry (7.10ff.); in 3.14 he speaks of 'the altar' which is to be smitten in judgment. Jerusalem is an unlikely setting because it is the congregation assembled in the shrine who are the object of Yahweh's wrath. The pronoun 'them', which occurs repeatedly without specific identification, can only refer to the congregation assembled at the sanctuary, perhaps for the autumn festival.

The other four visions supply the background of Amos' message and belong at the beginning of his career; this one probably came in the midst of his activity. Its purpose is to establish once and for all the fact that there is no way to evade the judgment which Amos announces. Repeatedly Amos was confronted by his audience with the confident assurance that no harm would befall them (9.10; 6.3). 'Yahweh is with us,' they said (5.14). In the vision Yahweh reconfirms the basic message which Amos had been sent to deliver. Amos in turn reports the vision to the congregation as an answer to their rebuttals. Yes, Yahweh is present in the sanctuary as they believe. Amos himself has seen him. But Yahweh's word for them is the cancellation of every possibility of escaping his wrath. There is no hiding place from his anger.

[1] 'I have seen the Lord (*'ᵃdōnāy*)' establishes the irrefutable authority of the following report. Yahweh lets himself be seen by those through whom he deals with his people. To see him is to be in the most intimate contact possible for a man. Those upon whom vision comes are set aside from the rest of the people as the chosen instruments of Yahweh's communication. '. . . standing beside the altar' locates the revelation in a sanctuary. This the audience would have expected. The shrine was the place of the *deus praesens*; within the court of the shrine one stood in the presence of Yahweh. The altar was the point in the sanctuary upon which communication with the deity focused. Through the sacrifices offered upon it the worshipper reached the deity, established community with him, and opened the way for the divine ministry of blessing. That a prophet should announce that Yahweh was present by the altar was an auspicious revelation. The congregation would have anticipated next some divine word that Yahweh accepted their offerings and regarded them with favour. But the announced word contradicts their assumption. The attitude of the deity is hostile (4b); altar and sanctuary are to be destroyed, a way of saying that from his side Yahweh breaks off the intercourse through the cult. Yahweh has commanded that the sanctuary be shaken to its foundations. To whom the imperatives are addressed is not said. Probably they are simply rhetorical, a way of saying with emphatic authority: 'Let the capitals be smitten . . . be shattered. . .' (cf. the imperative in 3.9; Isa. 13.2; Jer. 5.10). Other proposals are: that Yahweh speaks to the supernatural beings who surround him in his court (Isa. 6.2); that the command is addressed to Amos who is summoned to strike the capital with his fist in an act of prophetic symbolism, dramatizing what will soon occur; that the original text contained no imperatives and described Yahweh as the one who smote the capital (cf. the textual notes). The essential meaning of the text is clear enough. That 'capital' (*kaptōr*) can refer to an architectural feature of a building, probably the head of the central pillar upon which the roof rested, is confirmed by Zeph. 2.14. 'Threshold' (*sap*) is the great stone slab on which the door posts were fixed (Isa. 6.4). The entire structure from roof to foundations was to

be shaken until it collapsed. It is as though the sacral status of Bethel's shrine were being cancelled, and the sanctuary of salvation transformed into a scene of death (7.9; 8.3). Disaster at the sanctuary will be only the beginning of a pursuit that will lead to the ends of the earth. Any who are left will fall to the relentless sword of Yahweh. On the divine sword see the comment on 9.10. The thematic statement that none shall escape recalls 2.14f., and prepares the way for the following description of the futility of flight before Yahweh.

[2–4a] With five lines of similar structure, the theme of the judgment's inexorable certainty is hammered home. The farthest reaches of the universe, the limits of the world, and the events of history are surveyed as possible hiding places. Neither depths nor heights can separate them from the wrath of God. Sheol and the heavens encompass the universe; the top of Carmel and the bottom of the sea mark off the limits of the nearer world. This survey of the world's limits for the sake of proclaiming that man can go nowhere beyond the oversight of God has a remarkable parallel in the hymn, Psalm 139, especially vv. 7–12. In the Psalm the survey is an affirmation of faith in God's unlimited benevolence. This expression of trusting praise seems to have been rooted in a widespread hymnic tradition of the ancient Near East.[a] In one of the Amarna letters (tablet 264) Pharaoh is addressed as follows:

> Whether we climb up to the heavens
> or descend to the earth,
> Yet is our head in thy hands.[b]

In the vision of Amos the hymnic theme is reversed. The omnipresent sovereignty of Yahweh becomes an ominous and terrible reality which lends to his decree of punishment an absolute finality. Here the inexorable quality of the Day of Yahweh (5.19) is raised to universal proportions. The theological intensity of the survey is keenest in the assertion that not even captivity for the nation will end God's relentless pursuit. The shame of exile ought to be punishment enough. But what Yahweh decrees for Israel outruns suffering and humiliation. In and through their historical calamity they are face to face and feel the very personal act of Yahweh upon them and know the dereliction of sentence and judgment under his covenant with them.

[a] Cf. the 'Lamentation to Ishtar' and the 'Hymn to the Moon-God' in *ANET*, pp. 384–386.
[b] Cited by H.J. Kraus in *Psalms* (BK), p. 919.

NO HIDING PLACE: 9.1-6   155

[4b] In the final line Yahweh discloses his sovereign decision upon which the order of execution is based. Usually the locution 'to set one's eyes upon. . .' is used of favourable oversight (Gen. 44.21; Jer. 24.6; 39.12; 40.4). But Yahweh's purpose is the opposite; he will bring woe ($rā‘ā$) instead of weal ($ṭōbā$) upon Israel. In the ancient ritual of the covenant, the alternative of blessing and curse was set before Israel to make clear the consequence of loyalty and disobedience (cf. Deut. 27f.). The woe which Yahweh brings is sentence under covenant; this exclusion of good and announcement of evil fortune would have been heard as Yahweh's legal verdict upon his people.

[5-6] The sonorous proclamation of the identity of the Lord by the title 'Yahweh of Hosts', breaks with the style of the preceding divine word to introduce a hymnic section. The predicative participles, the glorification of Yahweh's majestic works, and the concluding refrain are typical of hymnic poetry. In style and theme this section is of a piece with the other hymn fragments (4.13; 5.9f.) which have been inserted in Amos' book. On their relationship to the book and Amos' theology, see the commentary on 4.13. In 8.8 Amos quoted the last three measures of 9.5, and the comment there should be consulted. The opening title, 'the Lord, Yahweh of hosts', is unusual; the regular form in Amos is 'Yahweh, God of Hosts' (seven times). The change may be the work of the redactor who added the hymnic section and wanted to identify the Lord ($’^a dōnāy$), which is the only title used by Amos in the vision-report (9.1). Verse 5 belongs to the theophany tradition of such pieces as Psalms 46.6; 104.32; 144.5; 29; Micah 1.3f.; Nahum 1.5; it rehearses the effect upon earth when Yahweh descends from heaven to touch its surface. The land reels and rocks, people are gripped with terror, and the earth's surface heaves up and down like turbulent water. The phenomenon behind the poetic hyperbole is undoubtedly an earthquake, but the comparison with the Nile's annual states is hardly appropriate. The theme of v. 6 is Yahweh as creator. The blue vault which arches across the earth is his handiwork. Above it in the heaven he has built his 'upper chamber', perhaps the heavenly residence; in Ps. 104.3, 13 a similar use of the term is connected with the heavenly sea and the pouring out of rain, as is the case here. In heaven Yahweh calls for water from the heavenly sea and pours it as rain upon the earth. Such is the majesty and power of Israel's God, Yahweh! The effect of the hymnic section as a conclusion of the vision-report is to exalt the unqualified power

of the God who passes judgment on Israel. His role as covenant Lord
does not so exhaust his nature that Israel can find in her election
some security from his anger. The whole world is in his hands!

30. THE FREEDOM OF YAHWEH: 9.7–8

9 ⁷'Are you not like Cushites to me,
   O Israelites?' A saying of Yahweh.
   'Did I not bring up Israel
   from the land of Egypt,
   and the Philistines from Caphtor,
   and Aram from Kir?
   ⁸Behold, the eyes of Lord Yahweh
   are upon the sinful kingdom;
   and I will destroy it from upon
   the face of the earth.
   However I will surely not destroy
   the house of Jacob.' A saying of Yahweh.

No other saying in the book of Amos shows how far the prophet
went in bringing together Yahweh's revelation to him that Israel's
end was at hand and Israel's traditional faith in Yahweh as the God
of salvation-history. There is no other text quite like it in the entire
Old Testament; compared to the usual statements about Israel's
relation to Yahweh it is radical and perplexing. Israel is like the
Cushites to Yahweh, and the Exodus is ranged along with migrations
of other peoples!

Whether vv. 7 and 8 compose one rhetorical unit or are separate
sayings is not certain. The style throughout is the first-person speech
of the divine saying; the reference to Israel in 7b and the phrase 'the
eyes of Lord Yahweh' in 8a are not really interruptions of the style.
The name, Israel, is used as a parallel to the following names (Philistines, Aram); 'Lord Yahweh' is the third person of direct speech by
the sovereign. The interrogatory form of v. 7 marks it as a disputation-
saying, a frequent feature of Amos' speech when the attitude or
arguments of his audience provoke a rejoinder (cf. 3.3–8; 5.18–20;
6.2). Usually the disputation-saying is the prophet's own word,
defending his vocation and message; but here Yahweh himself, as it
were, takes up the debate and makes the rebuttal to some argument
against the word of his messenger (cf. 2.11; 5.25). Verse 8 is an

announcement of punishment introduced by the exclamation
'Behold' (cf. 2.13; 4.2; 8.11), and could have followed the disputation-
saying directly. It asserts Yahweh's surveillance over 'the sinful
kingdom' and proclaims his decision to annihilate it. After the disputation-saying has undercut the theological position of Israelites
laying claim to secure status with Yahweh, the announcement re-
affirms Amos' basic message of judgment. The God whose true
position in history is clarified by v. 7 will certainly not overlook the
sin of any kingdom under his jurisdiction. The last line (8b), with its
reservation in favour of the 'house of Jacob', flatly contradicts the
point of the whole. It is a later addition to the text; see the comment
below.

[7] The opening questions are rhetorical; they are in fact assertions
made by Yahweh in an assault upon the theology of the addressees.
Both questions take up the theme of 'Israel and Yahweh', but their
intention is to bring to light a dimension of that relationship with
which Israel does not reckon. Precisely why Amos chose the Cushites
for comparison with Israel must unfortunately remain somewhat
obscure. Cush was the Old Testament name for the territory of
Ethiopia and Nubia, but Cushites are seldom mentioned. An isolated
tradition in Num. 12.1 reports that Moses' Egyptian wife was a
Cushite, and that Aaron and Miriam opposed him because of her.
Cushites appear as servants and eunuchs in Israel occasionally (II
Sam. 18.21; Jer. 38.7). Jeremiah's proverb about the Cushites' colour
is at least a play on their strangeness (Jer. 13.23). On the evidence
one can say no more than that the Cushites were a distant, different
folk whom Israelites knew mostly as slaves. 'You are to me,' says
Yahweh, 'as these Cushites are to you.' What the comparison does is
to humiliate Israel completely with respect to Yahweh, to reduce
them to the role in Yahweh's order of things which the Cushites
played in their own society. The relation of Israel to Yahweh creates
no privileges, no special status which qualifies his sovereignty; it is
rather one which manifests that sovereignty in radical fashion.

In the second question the Exodus from Egypt is listed along with
the migration of the Philistines and Arameans, and therefore put on
the same footing. The reference is a clue to Amos' surprisingly full
knowledge of the general historical traditions of the region, even more
striking than the material used in the oracles against the nations
(1.3—2.3). The migrations of the Philistines from the Aegean area
(Caphtor = Crete) and of the Arameans from Kir (a Mesopotamian

locale; cf. 1.5) had occurred early in the twelfth century, not long after Israel was settled in the hill country of Palestine. The Philistines and Arameans had been the classic foes of Israel; and yet their history, says Yahweh, was none the less his work than the Israelites' move from Egypt. Putting the matter in this way brings into focus the pivotal utterance in the text: 'Did I not bring Israel up from the land of Egypt. . .?' This basic datum of Yahweh's historical relationship with Israel is neither denied or robbed of emphasis by its expansion to include the Philistines and Aram. What is denied and shattered is a theology based on that datum—that Yahweh's act in the Exodus established Israel in a special status *vis-à-vis* the other nations. The Exodus is set in the context of international history and becomes in this context a manifestation of Yahweh's unconditional sovereignty. It cannot be understood as a point of departure for an automatic history of salvation which runs comfortably and inevitably from it, a kind of history which holds Yahweh the captive of Israel's own existence, a feature of the history which the people make for themselves. Instead it is the act of the world-God who thereby in no way qualifies or limits his sovereign freedom. The effect of this formulation of the Exodus announcement is the same as the question about the Cushites. Yahweh is exalted over against Israel, exalted in such a way that their existence as the people of Yahweh is stripped of all self-assertion and self-security that protects and hides them from the reality of Yahweh.

In a number of texts the thought-world which Amos confronted in the execution of his mission is reflected. There was first of all a theological security expressed in the dogma 'Yahweh is with us' (5.14) and in the lusty hope in the Day of Yahweh (5.18–20). And there seems to have been abroad in the land a more secular self-confidence emerging from the success and prosperity of the kingdom under Jeroboam (6.1, 13). In the immediate context (9.10) Amos quotes what some Israelites say: 'Disaster shall not overtake or confront us.' In his eyes this feeling of invulnerability was in effect a way of not being subject to the God who had revealed himself in the Exodus. Amos' handling of Israel's primary theological tradition here is quite similar to his procedure in 2.9–11 and 3.2. Under the liberating charismatic experience of his call and in the context of the awesome word of Israel's doom which he had been commissioned to deliver, he brings to total expression a concentration on Yahweh himself as the one alone whose act and will are significant. In the verbal sentence 'I brought Israel up' he focuses so intensely on subject and verb that the object is completely subsumed and has no independent place of its own. Of course the understanding that Israel's election was the action of a world God, not a national god, is no invention of Amos. It is fundamental to the structure of the Yahwist's portrayal of Israel's history from Creation to Conquest; it comes to clear expression in sentences like Ex. 19.5 ('You shall be my own possession among all the peoples; for all the earth is mine'). But never before had this sovereignty of Yahweh been read in such radical fashion, its fearful potential cast into immediate reality. Amos had to announce the end of Israel; and, for the sake of the message, Yahweh's complete freedom from Israel and over Israel emerges as the word of the Exodus. There is an analogy between the extension of the verb of the Exodus to other nations in 9.7 and the incorporation of foreign nations within the formal pattern of oracles announcing Yahweh's judgment upon transgressions (chs. 1–2). Amos thinks the rubrics of Yahweh's dealing with Israel out into the sphere of international history because of his fascination by the dimension of divine sovereignty in Israel's theological tradition. In doing so he is both heir and creator, bound and free. He stands within the theological tradition of Israel but understands it in such a way as to leave no place for the way his audience understood it.

[8] The announcement of Yahweh's judgment is founded on the viewpoint developed in the questions. As sovereign over history Yahweh oversees the nations of earth; the sinful kingdom is under his surveillance and it is his policy to destroy it. It is possible that '*the sinful kingdom*' refers to Israel, the definite article having a demonstrative function, i.e., 'this kingdom', the one under discussion, that of Jeroboam (7.13). But the article probably designates class, i.e., 'every sinful kingdom', so that the announcement declares a general policy of Yahweh's government. That would follow the argument of v. 7 better and corresponds more precisely to the indefinite impersonal 'it' of 8a. In fact, the prophet's assault on the theology of his audience continues; Yahweh's dealing with a political entity is not determined by their election but by the norm of *sin*. Note the same pattern of thought in ch. 1—2 and 3.2. The theme of sin, rebellion, iniquity, is the second of the two primary concepts in Amos' theology of history. Yahweh's absolute sovereignty, the first, is worked out in relation to all the nations in accord with his unqualified will for justice and righteousness and his hostility to evil. The relation of Israel and

Yahweh is ruthlessly and consistently interpreted according to its rubrics. It is in its light that Amos can say that the election of Israel means precisely that Israel will be punished for all its guilty acts (3.2). The 'I will destroy' (*hišmadtī*) is taken from the recitation of the classic Yahweh history in 2.9. What Yahweh did of old to the Amorites becomes a feature of his world judgment, just as 'I brought up' in 7b becomes a feature of his world role. The classical Yahweh history continues inexorably into the future, not as a history of salvation for Israel, but as a manifestation of Yahweh's righteous government.

In its present form the text of 8b simply contradicts the rest of the oracle, and makes the foregoing pointless. The opinion expressed in 8b is doubtless that of a Judean redactor who notes in the light of Judah's experience in the sixth century that Yahweh did not intend to obliterate all of Israel in spite of its sin. Amos used 'house of Jacob' as a name for the kingdom of Jeroboam (3.13; Jacob 6.8; 7.2, 5; 8.7); the redactor understood it as a reference to all the descendants of Jacob/Israel, and he could observe in his time that Judah had survived. But is the entire line a gloss? Except for the qualifying conjunction at the beginning, the line fits precisely as the conclusion of the saying. Perhaps the original resumed the questions in v. 7 and began with *hⁿlō'*: 'Shall I indeed not destroy the house of Jacob?' Such questions at the end of a saying of a major part of the saying are an element of Amos' style (5.20; 6.2b; 2.11b) and the metre (3+2) is that of the rest of the saying.

31. GOD'S SIEVE IS HIS SWORD: 9.9–10

9 9'Forᵃ behold! I will give the command
and I will shake the house of Israel ᵇwith all the nations,ᵇ
just as one shakes with a sieve
so that no stone falls to the earth.
¹⁰By the sword shall die
all the sinners of my people—
Those who say, "The disaster shall neither ᶜovertake
nor confront us.ᶜ" '

ᵃ The opening *kī* is editorial, connecting this saying with v. 8.
ᵇ⁻ᵇ The phrase lengthens the line unduly; it is probably a gloss to interpret the judgment as one of worldwide dimensions.
ᶜ⁻ᶜ MT makes no reasonable sense. Read *tiggaš ūtᵉqaddēm ʿādēnū*; cf. G.

Verses 9–10 are an announcement of punishment in the style of the divine saying. Against the protests of the pious that no harm will befall them, Yahweh answers through the prophet to assert that the command for judgment comes from him. He will sieve out every protesting sinner with the sword! The announcement is not accompanied by a preceding indictment of the audience, probably because it was uttered as a rejoinder in dispute with them. But in v. 10 the addressees are classified as sinners and further identified by a quotation of their protest. Since the turn of the century most critical commentaries have connected vv. 9f. with 8b and reckoned the saying to Judean editors, who, in applying the message of Amos to Judah, revised its finality to allow for the preservation of a remnant. Judgment will be selective; only sinners will be taken and a remnant in Judah will be left. But that is not the meaning of the metaphor of the sieve. Moreover, the saying bears characteristic features of Amos' style. 'Behold I (Yahweh) command' appears in 6.11. The metaphor of the sieve is one of the comparisons drawn from rural agricultural life, the primary source of Amos' pictorial language (2.13; 3.3–5, 12; 6.12). 'The sword' is Yahweh's instrument of punishment in 4.10; 7.9, 17; 9.1, 4. The quotation (10b) as a device for uncovering the attitude of his audience and bringing them under indictment is a favourite tactic (2.12; 4.1; 5.14; 6.13; 7.16; 8.5, 14). The saying in style and content has every mark of authenticity.

[9] Yahweh speaks as absolute sovereign over the nations of history (see the comment on 9.7). His command and its fulfilment are inseparably united; what he orders and what happens are one and the same, and no contingency lies between command and event. The command which he gives is for the execution of the sinners among his people. The command is formulated with a metaphor: Israel will be shaken as one shakes with a sieve. Here again it is evident how the nugatory divine word is clothed in imagery drawn from experience of the prophet. The sieve[a] (*kebārā*, mentioned only here in the OT) is one of a large mesh used to separate trash from the grain. In threshing, wheat was first beaten or shredded on the threshing floor to separate the grains from stalk and husk, then winnowed to allow the light chaff to blow to one side. The remaining grain would contain trash and small stones. The large mesh sieve was used to catch the larger debris and let the smaller grains fall through. The primary point of the metaphor is catching the undesirable. The stones represent the

[a] See K. Galling, 'Sieb' in *Biblisches Reallexikon*, 1937, pp. 480f.

sinners (10a). The focus of the metaphor is upon their inexorable elimination, and not so much on the grain. When one lets attention linger on the image itself, the question about what is implied for those who are not sinners very naturally arises. Amos mentions repeatedly a group within Israel who appear in his sayings, not as sinners, but as those sinned against. They are the innocent, the weak and afflicted, the oppressed whose exploitation he constantly cites (2.6f.; 4.1; 5.11f.; 8.4). What of their future? Amos' descriptions of Yahweh's judgment are consistently corporate in nature; punishment falls on the historical nation. He conceives of the future wholly in terms of reality within history, and never suggests the notion of a discriminating judgment. His message was the declaration of the end of the historical Israel, with no provision for a remnant like that hoped for by Isaiah. The logical implication which the metaphor could suggest, the separation of the bad and good, is simply not pursued; the metaphor is completely subject to the following declaration in v. 10. If this be inconsistent or inconsequent, then one must allow the prophet that shortcoming for the sake of the other consistency for which he had to struggle: that Yahweh *did* and *would* punish his own people for sin.

[10] Verse 10a applies and interprets the metaphor as a sentence of judgment. The accused are 'all the sinners of my people'. The sentence is death. The instrument of execution is the sword. All Amos' references to the sword are formulated so as to make it clear that this sword which plays such a significant role in his portrayal of Israel's fall is indeed the sword of Yahweh. He wields the sword himself (4.10; 7.9; 9.1) or he commands the sword as if it were a servant (9.4). The historical work of Yahweh's sword is of course to occur through the attack of an enemy, but Amos uses this stylized language so as to talk of history as divine drama (one notices in Ezek. 21 how the sword of Yahweh [v. 4] and the sword of the king of Babylon [v. 19] are merged). Amos never identifies a specific nation as executioner. It could be that 'the sword of Yahweh' is a motif of the Holy War tradition; in that tradition the historical manifestation would have been Israel's sword (see in Judg. 7.20 the cry of Gideon's army: 'The sword for Yahweh and for Gideon'). Since Amos turns the threat of Yahweh's holy war against Israel, he speaks of the sword exclusively as Yahweh's. Even though the sinners belong to 'my people', they shall die. Israel's relation to Yahweh is not a licence for sinners unlimited; indeed Yahweh's punishment of guilty acts is a corollary of his choice of Israel (3.2).

The sinners among the people of Yahweh are characterized by a quotation (10b) which dramatizes their thinking. The sinners are those who say: 'The disaster shall neither overtake us nor meet us.' The definite noun, '*the* disaster', must refer first of all to the imminent catastrophe foretold by Amos. Those who are quoted flatly reject his basic message. Their conception of the future and of Yahweh's relation to them excludes the possibility which he proclaims (6.3). More generally, '*the* disaster' could refer to the devastation which Yahweh was believed to work against his foes. Amos' audience knew of this dark side of Yahweh's action (5.18–20), the terrors which he brought on his day. But the 'Day of Yahweh' was a hard and fast scheme for them—always catastrophe for the enemies of the nation, a dogma therefore of their invulnerability. This characterization of his audience is a significant extension of Amos' definition of 'sinful'. When Amos speaks of Israel's guilt, he usually cites specific deeds. But here he speaks of a sin of belief, the sin of excepting oneself from Yahweh's judgment and therefore from his sovereignty. Israel's dogmatic security is a real declaration of independence from Yahweh which lies behind all their other transgressions.

32. THE RESURRECTION OF THE KINGDOM: 9.11–12

9 11'In that day I will raise up
　　the fallen booth of David.
　I will wall up their[a] breaches,
　　and his[a] ruins I will raise up,
　　and I will build her[a] as in the olden days—
　12in order that they may possess the remnant of Edom and all the
　nations over whom my name has been called.'
　A saying of Yahweh who does this.

This oracle of salvation announces a future work of Yahweh that is quite different from the other oracles in the book dated by the formula 'in that day' (2.16; 8.3, 9, 13). Where before there have been only proclamations of judgment and oracles of doom, Yahweh now speaks of restoration. He will restore the Davidic kingdom and re-

---

[a] The pronouns in 11b presumably all refer to 'booth' (fem.) as an antecedent, but 'their' is fem. pl. and 'his' masc. sing. G has regularized the sequence by using only fem. sing. pronouns.

establish through it his claim to all the nations that once had belonged to him.

[11] The first sentence establishes the theme with the announcement of an unconditional promise: 'I will raise up the fallen booth of David.' A booth was a rude structure usually made by setting up a simple frame and spreading branches over it. Booths were used to shelter troops in the field, watchers in vanguards, and for pilgrims at the festival of booths or tabernacles (II Sam. 11.11; Isa. 1.8; Lev. 23.42). Here it is a metaphor for the kingdom of David and the point of the image is shelter. The promise looks back to the remembered security of national life under the umbrella of David's rule and announces that freedom from fear of foes will be established again by the revival of the Davidic kingdom. Yahweh will free the nation from the enemies round about, working as he once did through the political instrumentality of Davidic rule. The oracle is spoken in a time when the kingdom has fallen. It is like a city whose walls are breached and whose buildings are ruins. Indeed, the halcyon period of David belongs to the 'days of old', a past distant in time and different in conditions. The expression is redolent with nostalgia and yearning for a time that memory has idealized, and appears in laments, prayers, and prophecies that hearken back to days thought of as the time of salvation (Isa. 51.9; 63.9, 11; Micah 7.14, 20; Mal. 3.4; Pss. 77.5; 143.5; Lam. 1.7; 5.21). Perhaps the verb 'build' reflects the influence of Yahweh's promise to David (II Sam. 7.5, 7, 13, 27). In any case the promise is a poignant formulation of Judean hopes nourished by the theology which regarded the political achievements of David as the acts of Yahweh.

[12] Verse 12 has been added to make it clear that in the restoration all the territory which belonged originally to David's kingdom will be recovered, particularly Edom. The poetic measures of v. 11 are replaced by a prose style; the dominant first-person verbs which gave structure to v. 11 are dropped. The specific reference to Edom and the text's presupposition that Edom is only a remnant fit best into a time after the fall of Jerusalem in 586, when Judean resentment against Edom rose to a shrieking crescendo, and Edom was subject to severe pressure from the south and east (cf. Obad. 10–14; Lam. 4.21f.; Ps. 137.7). It is difficult otherwise to explain the singling out of Edom for particular emphasis; and in the mid-eighth century that nation was independent and intact. 'To call one's name over' means to associate one's name with and in fact to own. It can

refer to the fame and right of a conqueror who takes a nation or city in war (II Sam. 12.28). The background of the idea is once again the Davidic empire; those nations conquered and ruled by David are regarded as Yahweh's possession and will be included in the restored kingdom. What the oracle expects in the future is not a universal world-wide kingdom, but a revival whose contours conform to what had already occurred in Israel's history under Yahweh. Cf. the list of nations in the oracle in Ps. 60. The phrase 'the one doing this' added to the usual concluding formula is hymnic in style.

This promise of salvation is hardly a saying of Amos. Verse 12 clearly belongs to the period after the fall of Jerusalem. If v. 12 is an addition to v. 11, then the latter could have been spoken in the pre-exilic period after the schism during any of the later periods of trouble in the southern kingdom. But Amos seems to have been untouched by the hopes of Jerusalemite Davidic theology. And there remains the difficulty of conceiving a situation and audience in Amos' ministry as we know it for the use of such a prophecy. His commission was as a messenger to the northern kingdom, and the oracle is an unlikely message to them in the context of his announcement that Israel as a kingdom had no future but judgment. It has been placed at the end of the collection of Amos' sayings as a witness that, though Israel finds its end in judgment, Yahweh will yet provide a future for his people. What Yahweh did through David has not lost its meaning; it is a promise of renewal to come. By the renewal Yahweh will bless his people with peace and show that his own rule over the nations still holds good.

33. PROSPERITY AND PEACE: 9.13–15

9 ¹³'Behold, days are coming,'
      a saying of Yahweh,
   'when the ploughman shall overtake the reaper,
      and the one who treads grapes him who sows seed.
   The mountains shall drip with sweet wine,
      and all the hills shall flow.
   ¹⁴I will reverse the fortunes
      of my people Israel.
   They shall rebuild ruined cities
      and dwell (in them).[a]

[a] The phrase does not appear in MT, but without it the line is metrically and syntactically incomplete.

> They shall plant vineyards
>   and drink their wine.
> They shall plant gardens
>   and eat their fruit.
> 15I will plant them upon their land,
>   and they shall not again be uprooted from their land
>   which I have given them,'
> said Yahweh, your God.

The concluding word in the book of Amos promises a time of the richest fertility and unbroken peace. Whereas 9.11f. is concerned with a political renewal and draws on the theology of the Davidic kingdom, this saying deals with the restoration of divine blessing to Israel and is based on the old theology of the land as Yahweh's gift to his people. The opening temporal formula points to a future that will be qualitatively different from the time of the oracle (cf. 8.11). The life that Israel will enjoy in that coming time is portrayed by the use of two motifs: the fertility of the land during each year (v. 13) and the security and stability of life throughout the years (vv. 14f.). The basic theme of the whole is stated between the two motifs in the promise: 'I will reverse the fortunes of my people Israel' (14a).

The setting presupposed by this oracle of salvation is not the period of Amos' mission. Normal life in the land has been disrupted, cities lie in ruins, and the people have been uprooted from their land. Such conditions did not prevail in the kingdom of Jeroboam II. Though the oracle might reflect the troubled final years of the northern kingdom later in the eighth century, it was probably composed in Judah during the exilic period, since it follows 9.11–12, which almost certainly comes from that period.[a] It was Amos' vocation to announce the enforcement of that very divine curse which this oracle promises will be changed to blessing (cf. 5.11 and 9.14b). His period was neither historically nor theologically the appropriate time for this word from Yahweh.

[13] The oracle lifts the eyes of a people, doubtless poor and hungry, to behold the vision of a land 'flowing with milk and honey'. The land shall again become 'the promised land', so productive that

___

[a] For contrary opinions, which assign the oracle to Amos, see J. N. D. Watts, *Vision and Prophecy in Amos*, 1958, pp. 25f.; H. Reventlow, *Das Amt des Propheten bei Amos* (FRLANT 80), 1962, pp. 90ff. Watts postulates a continuation of Amos' mission in Judah as the setting; Reventlow defines the prophetic office as a ministry of the covenant cult which always involves the proclamation of both judgment and salvation.

the year's rhythm hardly allows time to finish the work of each season. In the Palestinian agricultural cycle barley and wheat ripen for harvest in April-May, grapes are gathered for vintage in August-September, ploughing is done after the rains come in October, and sowing follows. In the promised days the crops will be so abundant that the harvester cannot finish before time for ploughing, and pressing out the grapes to make wine will not be finished when sowing-time arrives. The grapes will hang so heavy in the mountain vineyards that the slopes will seem literally to drip and flow with fresh wine (cf. Joel 3.18). The vision is not simply the yearning of physical hunger. Such fertility is the manifestation of Yahweh's benediction, the sacrament that the people live within the sphere of the covenant and enjoy the light of their God's favour (cf. Lev. 26.5).

[14] The descriptions of the future in the entire oracle are details to fill out the comprehensive promise: 'I will reverse the fortunes (šūb šeḇūt) of my people.' The locution šūb šeḇūt is an expression frequently used in the OT as a formula for Yahweh's act of changing the circumstances of the life of the people and even an individual (Job 42.10). Older English versions translated the locution 'bring/turn again the captivity'; the analysis of the idiom and its derivation remains uncertain,[a] but its sense is clear. It refers to the action of Yahweh when he shifts from the wrath to mercy in dealing with his chosen people (e.g. Deut. 30.3; Hos. 6.11; Jer. 29.14; Ezek. 16.53; Pss. 14.7; 85.1; 126.1, 4), and here specifically has the change from curse to blessing under the covenant in view. All the marvellous things listed in the impersonal language of vv. 13f. are manifestations of the personal change in Yahweh. Israel's times are in his hands and the content of the times is the revelation of his way with them. The remaining three lines of v. 14 develop the description of restoration with promises of the successful fulfilment of work. To be allowed to enjoy the fruit of one's labours is also to experience the benediction of God and know his favour (Ezek. 12.20; 36.10, 33; Zeph. 1.13; Isa. 65.21f.).

[15] Verse 15 with its metaphor of planting and uprooting (Jer. 24.6) gathers up all that has gone before and makes it final. Yahweh's change will be permanent, and blessing will never depart. Possession of the land was the goal and consummation of the old salvation history.

---

[a] Cf. E. L. Dietrich, *Die endzeitliche Wiederherstellung bei den Propheten* (BZAW 40), 1925; E. Baumann, *ZAW* 47 (1929), pp. 17–44; R. Borger, *ZAW* 66 (1954), pp. 315f.

Yahweh's judgment does not obliterate that goal, for a new planting of the chosen people becomes the consummation toward which the purpose of the covenant God is working.

The themes and formulations of the oracle appear in significant concentration in Lev. 26 and Deut. 28, the two collections of blessings and curses in the Pentateuch. The curses are sanctions against Israel's breach of their covenant with Yahweh and the blessings are the benefits which come when Israel remains true to the covenant.[a] The theme of unending fertility (13a) appears in Lev. 26.5. The assurances of enjoying the fruit of their labours (v. 14) are blessings which reverse specific curses; see the series of futility curses in Deut. 28.30f., 38–40, especially vv. 30, 39, and cf. Lev. 26.16, 33.[b] The background of the motifs and ideas of the oracle lies in the same covenant ritual out of which the basic material in the pentateuchal collections came. The oracle promises the end of punishment for disloyalty to Yahweh and the restoration of covenant blessings. However, there is no reference to repentance and renewal on the part of Israel; the oracle is an unconditional promise of blessing which detaches its themes from their covenant context. The return of blessing is Yahweh's act and rests alone on his will to restore the fortune of his elect people.

[a] See the discussions in D. R. Hillers, *Treaty Curses and the Old Testament Prophets* (BO 16), 1964, pp. 30–42; H. Reventlow, *op. cit.*, pp. 90–110.
[b] D. R. Hillers, *op. cit.*, pp. 28ff.